SAN FRANCISCO
BAY AREA MURALS

San Francisco Bay Area Murals

COMMUNITIES CREATE THEIR MUSES
1904–1997

Timothy W. Drescher

For Jo and Sarah and Meagan, with love

ISBN 1-880654-13-X

Library of Congress Catalog Card No. 97-76508

Cover Mural: Haight-Ashbury Muralists. OUR HISTORY IS NO MYS-TERY, 1977. Detail from a destroyed mural. #151.

Printed and bound in Hong Kong by Everbest Printing Company, Ltd.

Contents

OFFICE OF THE MAYOR
SAN FRANCISCO

WILLIE LEWIS BROWN, JR.

Since the turn of the 20th century, when the earliest murals we know of celebrated shipping and imperial expansion, through the New Deal period and its focus on labor and the common man, right up to today's community-based murals, the works of art documented in this book deserve our close attention.

They are monumental expressions that give voice to people in our communities, their hopes for the future, their daily lives in all their wonderful complexity and their struggles to survive and prosper in a changing world. These murals can be seen nearly everywhere in San Francisco, and collectively have become a street-level gallery of international renown, showcasing the culture and creativity of our City for all the world to see.

Today, murals are an integral part of San Francisco's neighborhoods, a voice for community expression and a public forum through which we can better understand the struggles and aspirations of the many people who comprise our city. In these works local artists of different backgrounds articulate their traditions for everyone to admire. The mural painting process often brings together disparate people, and in doing so contributes to the creation of a diverse, multifaceted San Francisco community.

This book gives us a comprehensive guide to those creations, and I'm pleased, as the Mayor of San Francisco, to share it with you.

This book also gives us complete lists of the murals painted all around the San Francisco Bay Area, from South San Francisco down the peninsula to San Jose, and throughout the East Bay, providing in one publication a catalogue of the entire region's wonderful mural tradition.

Tim Drescher is perfectly situated to write this book because of his 25 years of involvement with the city's community mural movement. He was a member of the Placa Group that muralized Balmy Alley, a leader of the ILWU mural-sculpture project which graces the Embarcadero, among other projects – so he knows what he's talking about.

Mr. Drescher offers not only insight and information, but context and perspective. This book places the San Francisco mural tradition into wider historical, and art historical, perspectives as the century draws to a close, confirming that our city is a leader in the worldwide community mural movement.

We are fortunate to have a book of this quality, sensitivity and clarity, as a record of our city's rich mural tradition.

Willie L. Brown, Jr.
Mayor

401 VAN NESS AVENUE, ROOM 336, SAN FRANCISCO, CALIFORNIA 94102
(415) 554-6141
RECYCLED PAPER

Introduction

This book surveys murals painted in the San Francisco Bay Area, south down the Peninsula to San Jose, and up the East Bay to Richmond. Information from the two previous editions (1991 and 1994) has been updated with murals painted since 1994 added to the lists in all locations. The San Francisco neighborhood maps have also been updated. The biggest overall change is the addition to the listing of nearly 125 murals located south of San Francisco.

The listings include murals from the turn of the century (1903), the 1914–1915 Panama Pacific International Exposition, the New Deal, and, especially, contemporary community murals painted from 1970 through 1997. Lists also include selected destroyed murals, which are marked with an asterisk. My belief that the community-based works and their creators deserve accurate documentation continues to be my motivation for writing this book. Selected commercial murals and school murals are included as examples as well as to underscore the difficulty in drawing a clear line demarcating one type from another. Children's murals deserve more attention than they receive here, and in particular, Ruth Asawa, "one of the godparents of the community mural movement," and the Alvarado Arts School Program deserve attention. I hope the examples included here will encourage others to pursue their proper documentation.

San Francisco's claim to being the "mural capital of the world" lies in both statistics and innovation. Compare San Francisco's 754 murals and its population of about 730,000 with the Los Angeles count of 1500 to 2000 murals for a population of over 3 million people. But San Francisco has always supported innovation and has consistently produced especially significant murals. To cite a few examples, Coit Tower was the prototype for the New Deal/WPA mural programs; the Mujeres Muralistas were an extremely influential women's mural group; muralists have painted collectively in Balmy and Clarion Alleys and on the ILWU Mural-sculpture; there are significant mural clusters such as the Minipark at 24th and Bryant Streets; and both sides of an entire building became murals when a group of women muralists painted the Maestrapeace murals on the San Francisco Women's Building. Other cities have also supported important and influential mural production, but none more consistently and more influentially than San Francisco.

The mural lists and the murals within them are ordered more or less geographically. Numbering down the Peninsula begins in the north and moves south to San Jose. The East Bay murals are given new numbers beginning with Newark and moving north to Richmond. In San Francisco, murals are arranged by neighborhoods, with consideration given to accessibility. For example, since it is often difficult to cross Market Street, murals to its north and south are put into separate sections. If a fanatic wanted to see all the San Francisco murals beginning with number 14 (the first thirteen are now destroyed), I believe that the order given is an efficient way to proceed. In this case, I also recommend beginning the tour at 5 a.m. on a Sunday morning. Otherwise you will be caught in traffic for the first five hours.

Photograph selection remains difficult, because so many murals are worthy of full color reproduction, but cost limitations prohibit anything other than a representative selection. I've tried to have the photos indicate the diversity of local murals, emphasizing the community works because others are covered elsewhere. The photos indicate the range of styles, themes, geographical areas, and artists. I've included a number of significant destroyed murals because they can no longer be viewed anywhere else (see "The Lost Murals of San Francisco").

I first began documenting murals in Chicago in 1971. In the seventies, Margo Bors and I studied several Mission District murals, and in 1980 Ruth Gordon helped with a list of East Bay murals of the 1970s. The present mural list is based on my earlier work, *A Checklist of San Francisco Murals, 1914–1986,* compiled with Victoria Scarlett and published by the Library of San Francisco State University. Nicole Emanuel's patient, thorough work helped me in compiling that material. It includes several revisions of the data on the pre 1969 murals contained in *A Survey of Art Work in the City and County of San Francisco* published in 1975 by the San Francisco Art Commission, edited by Joan Ellison, with additions by Joyce Konigsberg. Errors and omissions are of course my responsibility and corrections are appreciated. The murals and their artists deserve accuracy.

In addition to those with whom I have collaborated in preparing lists of local murals, many others have helped gather material for this book. The muralists have been unanimously generous in providing information about their works, and patient with my rechecking. At the Galeria de la Raza, Maria Pinedo, Rene Yanez, and later, Humberto Cintron were always helpful and supportive. At Precita Eyes Mural Workshop, Susan Cervantes, Ron Wheeler, Margo Bors, Tony Parrinello, Gary Graham, Cynthia Rojas, and the entire Precita Eyes family have made a special contribution to this book and to the vitality of local murals. At the Mural Resource Center, Kathie Cinnater and the current director Betsie Miller-Kusz, provided accurate information and encouragement. Ray Patlan and Eduardo Pineda, Josh Sarantitis, Johanna Poethig, Miranda Bergman, and Aaron Noble have been especially helpful among local muralists. Cecily Harris and Emmanuel Montoya helped in "discovering" and pointing out murals unknown to me. Jack Casbara provided valuable information about San Jose murals for the list.

The Peninsula list is a collaboration between Moira Harris and myself, and the San Francisco list is a similar collaboration between Cynthia Rojas, Precita Eyes Muralists, and myself. Each year PEM publishes a valuable listing of all mural-like works, to which I am indebted.

With so many more businesses than ever before supporting murals the line between community and commercial murals continues to blur (and it was not all that sharp to begin with). Businesses are commissioning mural-type paintings and signs for both interiors and exteriors of their establishments. It seems obvious that these would not have been painted if not for the community mural movement, whose ubiquity and quality provided legitimacy for the mural form. However, this does not mean that every commercial artwork in a business is a mural of interest to this survey. Sometimes the decision to include a piece rests on a subjective assessment of the painting, including its location

and its "spirit." No decision to exclude has been made without discussion with knowledgeable people. Those murals listed have some connection with more community-oriented works, either in content, process, or painters, i.e., some commercial murals are included because they were painted by community-based muralists as examples of their commercial work.

For the first edition of this book, Jim Prigoff shared his collection of San Francisco mural slides. Photos lent by him, James Dong, Susan Cervantes, Ray Patlan, Fran Valesco, Jean Constant Gindreau, Wilfredo Castano, James Pontiflet, and Susan Greene are gratefully acknowledged. Rodger Birt helped with slides of the first Western Addition murals. Permission from the San Francisco Recreation and Parks Department to use a photograph of Maxine Albro's *California* (#46) and from the San Francisco Art Institute to use a photograph of Diego Rivera's *The Making of a Fresco Showing the Building of a City* (#20), is also gratefully acknowledged.

Computer help, including the entering of initial listings, was provided by Shelly Kushner and by Stacey Callahan. Their expertise, advice, and good humor strengthened the project at every stage.

John Pitman Weber, Carol Kenna, Eva Cockcroft, Shifra Goldman, Enrique Chagoya, Jim Prigoff, and Jo Drescher read drafts of the text and their comments were invaluable in improving it.

My greatest appreciation is reserved for John and Moira Harris of Pogo Press, whose ongoing enthusiasm for murals has enabled this book to be published, and whose editorial and design expertise, as well as their knowledge of murals across the country, has become a major resource of mural studies.

My family has remained enthusiastic and supportive throughout the writing and expanding of this book. Sarah and Meagan have been spotting murals since they could talk, and have grown to enjoy last-minute searches for rumored murals. Their critical comments have also contributed to making this a better book.

Timothy W. Drescher
Berkeley, California
September 5, 1997

Murals: From Cave to Contemporary

Murals have been painted in many ways for many reasons under varying conditions—social, political, economic, aesthetic—for tens of thousands of years. Today, all previous styles and media are available (including fresco, abstraction, mosaic, etc.), but most murals are narratives painted onto walls. Some new possibilities, unknown in previous mural epochs, are also practised, such as extensive collaboration by artists with a mural's audience in its design and execution. Today's community murals are exciting partly because they embody this monumental art tradition, and partly because their world is our world; we can empathize with the paintings we see. I hope this book encourages readers to go see the murals themselves, hear the sounds around them, smell the nearby bakeries and restaurants, and talk to locals so that the entire mural, including its community, comes alive.

THE MURAL TRADITION

One thing today's murals have in common with paleolithic French and Spanish cave paintings is their role in the community. The murals were painted by members of the group which lived with them daily. The role of the cave painting in their societies is unknown, although theories from the hopeful to the plausible have been advanced since their discovery at the beginning of the twentieth century. Some appear to be part of daily community life while others are located in remote sanctuaries deep in their caves. Access to these was probably limited to special occasions. Besides being the product of their community, these murals share another characteristic with today's walls. They have an impact on the people who view them because, however removed they may seem from our lives, they also capture something in common with us, and we are often moved by that feeling of similar experience.

Of post-paleolithic murals it seems that the closer the civilization moved toward modern times, the less the murals retained of community immediacy. Aboriginal peoples in Australia, America and Africa painted murals on the rock walls of caves apparently as fully integrated parts of their daily lives, but in other parts of the world murals became associated with elite interests, decorating the tombs of Chinese emperors, Egyptian pharaohs, and Mayan kings. In several locations temples with painted murals or carved reliefs were open to the "public," such as those at Teotihuacan or Babylon, or Angkor Wat. These works were significant to their populations. Although hardly community-based, they are an important source of information about their cultures and history. Egyptian murals, for example, depict significant commerce between central Africa and the mighty kingdoms of the Nile at Karnak and Thebes. These images support Diop's contention that the early Egyptian civilization was a black culture.[1]

European murals, which are the more direct antecedents of today's urban expressions, divide roughly into religious and secular. The earliest walls were religious paintings in churches: mosaics for the wealthier orders, egg tempera and fresco when mosaic was too expensive. They depicted biblical scenes to the satisfaction of the church fathers and the awe and instruction of the illiterate churchgoers, a didactic function used to great effect in the twentieth century by Diego Rivera. Fresco is a process of applying colored paint pigment to wet plaster. When the plaster dries, the painting becomes a part of the wall itself. It requires skill and confidence, because it cannot be painted over or erased. By the end of the Middle Ages the development of painting techniques included greater use of modeling, making Christian scenes increasingly realistic. Throughout this period, European murals were Christian and the church was almost the sole patron of muralists.

With the coming of the Renaissance, patronage and thematic content shifted, although the religious murals have never died out. Because of the significance of Catholicism, church murals were public art. As Europe moved from religious-dominated feudalism to commodity-dominated capitalism, the favored media of expression kept pace. Techniques of perspective were developed, and oil painting came to dominate plastic expression because it best allowed the newly accumulated secular possessions to be exhibited for what they were: tangible, portable commodities.[2] Oil paint displays the textural richness of the possessions of the wealthy along with their myths and portraits. Earlier murals were not commodities (you could hardly buy or sell a church ceiling, let alone move it to your palace), but with the development of secular wealth, patrons were merchant, rather than religious or hereditary, princes, and their taste demanded subject matter inappropriate for church walls. So from the Renaissance until today, both strains of the mural tradition that split in the late fifteenth century have continued in parallel traditions, one private and secular, the other public and religious. From that time on, not only were churches painted with appropriately devout imagery (by Michelangelo, for example), but murals were painted in dining rooms and living rooms of private palaces and every other portion of the baroque estate. Murals "went public" again in the nineteenth century, decorating public buildings in Europe and the United States. For the community muralists of today, however, a more influential line stems from Mexican murals.

MEXICAN MURALS

There is a direct line from European, specifically Italian, Christian frescoes to the contemporary mural movement in the United States. That line runs through one of the Tres Grandes of the Mexican Mural Renaissance. Diego Rivera, after studying in France and Spain but prior to returning home to Mexico in 1922, toured Italy and viewed first hand many Italian frescoes which taught him a great deal about the use of architectural space in monumental painting. When he returned to his native Mexico, Rivera began painting murals at the behest of the education minister, Jose Vasconcellos, to educate the largely illiterate population, and recover indigenous history (much as contemporary community muralists often try to emphasize ethnic cultural traditions in their imagery). He began applying the compositional lessons he had observed in Italy along with those of his cubist studies in France to the walls of government buildings. Rivera was also influenced by indigenous pre-conquest figurines and, especially, by the codices, which recorded ancient Mesoamerican societies in vivid pictures.

Rivera was soon joined by Jose Clemente Orozco and David Alfaro Siqueiros. Together they were Los Tres Grandes, the Three Great Ones of Mexican muralism, and their works are a major inspiration for today's muralists, particularly in their commitment of their artistic skills to the struggles of indigenous peasants and workers.

It should be noted that there have been many other important Mexican muralists, among them Pablo O'Higgins, Juan O'Gorman, Jose Camarena, and Rufino Tamayo. Jean Charlot brought a significant knowledge of fresco techniques to the Mexican muralists in the 1920s. Many community muralists in the United States have studied in Mexico, either formally or on their own, observing the works of this great tradition. In recent years, the work of Arnold Belkin and others has begun to be known in the United States, and U.S. work has also begun to influence mural painting in Mexico. The main source of Mexican influence for contemporary muralists in San Francisco has been the Tres Grandes.

All three of the Great Ones were politically active and leftist. Siqueiros and Rivera were members of the Mexican Communist party, although Rivera, with strong Trotskyite leanings, was often in official disfavor. When a reactionary administration gained power in the 1930s, all three came to the United States to paint, Orozco in the east and at Pomona College in southern California, Siqueiros in Los Angeles and New York, and Rivera in New York, Detroit and San Francisco, where he painted four frescoes. So the link between the Tres Grandes and San Francisco is direct, and the sources of influence are visible not only in Rivera's works, but in the New Deal murals executed during and after his visits here, and in the contemporary murals as well.

Diego Rivera significantly influenced San Francisco muralists. The New Deal artists watched him paint in person, and sometimes worked as his assistants. Subsequent muralists learned about his murals and those of other Mexican masters by visiting the walls themselves or through reproductions in books. Technical and stylistic aspects were thus passed on to later generations. Above all, the Tres Grandes demonstrated that public art and political commitment were bound together.

Rivera painted a mural at the Art Institute of San Francisco in 1931 (#20). In 1934, muralists painting the interior of Coit Tower were influenced by Rivera's piece just a few blocks away.[3] His other murals were a small fresco painted at the Atherton home of Mrs. Sigmund Stern, now in the downstairs lobby of Stern Hall on the University of California's Berkeley campus (#EB 85), a mural painted on the main stairwell outside the members' dining room of the Pacific Stock Exchange (#79), and a large fresco painted on Treasure Island for the 1939–40 World's Fair, now relocated in

Diego Rivera's enormous engineer-worker in his fresco for the San Francisco Art Institute (20) served as inspiration for Chuy Campusano in the Bank of America mural, *Homage to Siqueiros*. Rivera's monumental engineer becomes Campusano's "The New Chicano" which was also painted as if concealed by scaffolding in this mural-in-progress mural. (294)

the foyer of the Little Theater of the City College of San Francisco (#197).

Rivera's influence is also clear in some community murals, such as Chuy Campusano's *Homage to Siqueiros* (#294), in which he revises Rivera's Art Institute image of the construction of a worker into the construction of a model Latino. Rivera's vision of California's wealth coming from natural resources and labor is also found in the Coit Tower murals and in a number of community murals showing Latino migrant farm laborers.

NEW DEAL MURALS

While Coit Tower was not, strictly speaking, a WPA (Works Progress Administration) mural project, its sponsor, the PWAP (Public Works of Art Project), was the forerunner of the WPA program that sponsored thousands of murals nationwide from 1934 until 1946, and which became the model for the CETA program of art sponsorship in the 1970s (see "Funding"). New Deal murals have been covered in several excellent

publications (see "Bibliography"). WPA murals in San Francisco span the entire period of the New Deal from 1934 through the final WPA mural, the panels at Rincon Annex post office (now Rincon Center) painted by Anton Refregier from 1946–48 (#221). During these years murals were painted in public buildings such as post offices, government buildings, the court house, museums and school libraries throughout the city. These murals were public art, executed for official buildings, not generated by the community in the way that today's murals are.

Today's community muralists saw the WPA murals on the walls of their schools, or when they mailed letters at post offices, or when they visited Coit Tower. This mural presence also included the ubiquitous Italian restaurant Venetian gondola paintings, and murals in meat markets and movie theaters, suggesting to them that murals could be a viable means of public artistic expression. When the mass political activities of the 1960s focused artistic energies on social issues, a model for one form of expression was already in place.

The north side of the *I.L.W.U. Mural-sculpture* by the muralists known as M.E.T.A.L can be seen here. (220)

Sometimes the connection was made directly between community murals and their New Deal forerunners. Some muralists who had worked on Coit Tower also worked with younger artists. Emmy Lou Packard, a well known printmaker who had worked with Diego Rivera, served as an advisor on Chuy Campusano's "Bank of America" mural (#294). Several muralists became friends with Coit Tower painters Edith Hamlin and Bernard Zakheim. The style and to some extent the content of the *I.L.W.U. Mural-sculpture* (#220) were selected as a gesture of admiration for Anton Refregier, whose Rincon Center murals are diagonally across Mission Street from the 1986 work. Lucienne Bloch and Stephen Dimitroff, both of whom worked with Rivera, continue to give fresco workshops.

After over fifty years New Deal murals, despite their locations indoors, show signs of damage. Any water leaking into a building eventually damages a fresco so that both its pigment and plaster are apt to fall from the wall. Before attempting to restore the Coit Tower murals, the city had to have workers clean the building and rebuild the roof. In 1990 conservators Anne Rosenthal, Constance Silver, Jim Bernstein and Gregory Thomas completed restoration of the first floor murals. Those murals found upstairs in Coit Tower remain to be treated. Rosenthal and Thomas also restored the Labaudt mural in the Beach Chalet in 1988. The Beach Chalet mural (#182) and those in the Mother's House at the San Francisco Zoo (#186–#189) suffered from dampness and water damage which causes the paint to flake and mosaics to loosen.

Although the original federal groups which sponsored the New Deal murals in the 1930s no longer exist, mural restoration funds have been given to the city by the NEA, the California office of Historical Preservation, and the National Paint and Coating Association, a trade group.

CONTEMPORARY COMMUNITY MURALS

The major political issues of the late 1960s—Civil Rights, the women's movement, education, and above all the Vietnam War—caused millions of people in the United States to become politically active. Many visual artists committed themselves to the social practice of their skills, making posters, silkscreens, book illustrations, leaflets, dances, performances, happenings, music and. . . murals for the general public. These media traditionally have been the means of expression for poor and working class people, and especially people of color who were disenfranchised from access to mass media.

The communities to which these people turned usually meant "neighborhood," but also often included union halls, schools, women's centers, workplaces, etc. "Community" here has a social, not merely a geographical definition. It refers to any group of like-minded people. Including "community" in "community murals" makes these artworks different from any others, and that is why it helps to make a distinction between "community art" and the more general term "public art." Public art is art done for a general, undefined population (although some sort of middle class standard is probably assumed). It is for the most part commissioned by official bodies, governments, corporations and the like. Community art is created by or with a group of people who will interact with the finished artwork. Its standard of satisfaction is determined by its acceptance to the community from which it springs, not by any outside audience. Community arts can include performance arts, film, theater, dance, posters, etc., but the key factor is the work's creation with or by a group of people. The "with" includes projects done by an individual or group in consultation with a community, but in which the community does not actually paint (or dance, or act, or whatever).

Local people sometimes like artworks done "for" them, but their involvement with the work is then very different from one on which they have worked themselves. In both cases the artwork lends prestige to its location, but in community-based arts, its status as art (and relative survival) is dependent on public acceptance, not the reputation of the artist.[4]

Community murals may be painted by groups of individuals (see "Process"), but they are always closely related to those who live or work near them.[5] The relationship of community artworks to their communities is dynamic, intimate, extended and reciprocal. In a real sense, the immediate "support group" of a mural project, its "community," determines the work's meaning. Consciously or not, the image-makers articulate their communities' wishes. If representatives of hotel owners, world's fair organizers, a YWCA, a government bureaucracy, a union, school or neighborhood produce a mural, then that mural will articulate their ideas. Some of these uses are not what we normally mean by "community," and there are exceptions, of course, but the general rule holds. Of all members of a community, the most important is the artist or group. So it is probably more accurate to say that mural art is always an intersection of social and artistic contexts (influences), with some participants playing more important roles than others, depending on specific circumstances. But (especially with murals), the "community" is always a crucial aspect of the work's process and effect: hence the subtitle of this book.

Out of the Closet was the title given to a series of four panels painted inside the Women's Building by muralists Johanna Poethig, Selma Brown, Claire Josephson, K. Bucklew, Ariella Seidenberg, and Deborah Greene. (270)

Flags, relevant faces and books are placed around the doors and windows of *The Socialist Bookstore* mural by Susan Greene and Pedro Oliveri. Photograph by Susan Greene. (307)

13

Today's community murals represent the coming together of social (historical) and artistic traditions. While this is true of the artwork of any period, it seems more obvious in this case because a) the history is ours; we've lived it or are living it, and b) the murals usually take that experience as their subject, one way or another. Also, we find the often collective, interactive process more compatible than previous generations did.

The earliest community murals in the United States were painted in the mid 1960s in Colorado and California, and in Chicago and New York. Chicago became the focus of the early movement because of the vitality of its mural images, the skill of its artists, and the publicity their work received in national media. All these early works were community expressions generated by political activism.

The earliest corresponding murals in the Bay Area were executed at Grove Street Community College in Oakland in 1968–69 by a group of artist-activists (#EB101). At about the same time artists began painting murals in San Francisco across the Bay. In no time at all (historically speaking), the movement had come to "everybody's favorite city," expressing on its walls the aspirations, problems and hopes of its multiethnic population.

Because of its ethnic diversity, small geographical area (San Francisco is only 49 square miles), the proximity of Mexican and New Deal models, and most of all its concentration of skilled, creative and prolific artists, San Francisco soon became one of the leading mural centers in the world.

Process

There are many ways of painting community murals. At the heart of each one resides the relationship between artist(s) and the social community which will be the audience for the finished painting. The simplest process is when an individual artist paints a mural alone. This kind of work becomes a community mural only if the artist lives or works in the community, or has "done his/her homework" with the community.

The most complicated process is when a group forms within the community or contacts a group of artists to work with them in creating a mural. In this case, the meetings, discussions, sketches and arguments can continue for prolonged periods of time; more than a year or two is not uncommon.

But a community mural process can consist of any variation in between these examples: a group contacting a community group, a community group contacting an individual or separate artists or an established mural group (from within or outside of the community), and so on. The basic characteristic in all cases is the extensive participation with the people who live/work with the mural. Typically, an artist or group has a particular wall in mind, and usually a subject, too. They then speak with people around the site, and in many cases these "locals" will be instrumental in suggesting ideas for or modifications of the original proposals. By the mid 1980s, however, in order to comply with increasingly demanding civic funding requirements, artists were focusing more on satisfying "downtown" bureaucratic requirements than on working with communities.

The basic question for a muralist to ask the community is "What is important to you?" People know what matters to them, and they are not reticent about telling you. Artists, trained in visual expression, then can give form to the things mentioned by the folks with whom they talk. Sometimes, the question asked is, "What would you like to see?" This sounds good, but too often elicits visual cliches from untrained people, cliches such as an advertising image or a record album cover. Once suggested, such images take hold rapidly because they provide something "pre-approved" and already widely accepted. Such images produce weak murals.

Whatever the details, community-interactive processes lead to artist(s) working out tentative design ideas, presenting them to locals or appointed groups, and listening to suggestions (sometimes in the form of, "Gee, I'd like to see a. . . in the picture," sometimes in the form of "Can't you remove that. . . ?" and sometimes in the form of, "This is terrible. Who do you think you are?"). Design meetings can be heated, but they are an inescapable part of a community interactive process, and of a perhaps unique opportunity for community involvement by artistically untrained members, all of which contributes to the role of the mural in the (social) community from which it stems.

Once agreed upon, the design is ready to be painted. If the site is an outdoor wall, it must first be prepared, which is not terribly exciting, at least after the initial thrill of climbing up on scaffolding and seeing the neighborhood from a new angle. Walls must be sanded, scrubbed, cleaned, sealed and primed before they can be painted. Poor surface preparation leads to an early death of the mural. Almost anyone can help in this work. It mostly takes a desire to help get the mural painted correctly, and a lot of elbow grease.

There are three methods of transferring the design onto the wall. In a few cases the artist simply draws on the wall. More often, the design sketch has

been drawn to scale (1″ to 1′ is common, although any scale is possible), and with a surveyor's snap line one foot squares are drawn onto the wall so that each square foot on the wall corresponds to a square inch of the sketch. Then, after triple checking to be sure the squares are right, nearly anyone can transfer an inch of sketch onto a foot of wall without too much trouble. A trained artist can come along later and make changes for consistency, etc.

The third method of design transfer is to use either an opaque projector or slide projector to project the sketch onto the wall. Then the lines are just traced. This is certainly the quickest method for a large wall, but it is best done at night, and sometimes the space available in front of the wall is not sufficient to allow the image to be fully projected onto the wall. Muralists have had some nasty run-ins with traffic while backing up to get the right distance between projector and wall.

Once the sketch is up, the painting begins. Again, nearly anyone can put basic paint on the surface of a

Two student assistants are shown at work on *The Fire Next Time I*. (423)

A parade celebrated the completion of the murals of Balmy Alley in 1984. The musicians are shown walking past a portion of the mural *Culture Contains the Seed of Resistance* by Miranda Bergman and O'Brien Thiele. (347)

Two children at play are painted on the wall of the Baptist church overlooking the Chinese playground in this untitled mural by James Dong. The girl's swing casts the shadow of a phoenix. Photograph by James Prigoff. (69)

wall. It only requires following the lines of the design and asking for help when it gets confusing. Trained artists can mix the colors and finish it all off, giving the final modelling, shading and stylistic contributions necessary for a unified image. In several cases, a decision was made that "participation" on a mural meant that everyone would paint some final portion of the wall, or their design suggestions would be included, regardless of coherence. This often results in an image which looks like it has been painted by several different people of different levels of ability. We should try to keep in mind in such cases that the social element of participation is at least as important to the group as the "professionalism" of the final image.

What this adds up to, no matter what particular process is involved, is an amazing amount of work on the part of the muralists. The actual painting of the mural, which can itself take a year or more, takes place only after endless weeks or months of exhausting, ine-

fficient, time-consuming meetings and planning sessions. Ideally, efficiency in painting is not a consideration for people working with necessarily complex groups of people, but pressures of families, other jobs, other projects frequently place enormous burdens on the muralists. Certainly it's all part of the game, but it helps to understand the sheer quantity of work that goes into creating a community mural.

We should not forget the final event in the process, the dedication ceremony. "Ceremony" is too formal a word here, because the dedication is usually more of a party, the moment on a sunny afternoon when the street in front of the mural is closed off and local residents and admirers from all over the city join to enjoy local bands, dancing, and donations of food—both homemade and from nearby restaurants. The dedication is the celebration of the entire community in honor of its new addition, and the mural's role in that community continues afterwards.

Aesthetics

One person's "subtle" is another's "blatant," to be sure. So we must be clear about our purpose in assessing community murals. If the goal is to try to grasp the work in its many simultaneous relationships with its community, then we must take that community into consideration. The goal of this book is to help the reader understand enough about murals to help him or her do exactly that. Some observations may help. In addition to learning (or asking) about the immediate community surrounding a mural, it often helps to be aware of influences so that you can get an idea of "where the artist is coming from." In San Francisco murals, influences include ethnic location and background of artists, other artists, folk arts, the Tres Grandes, other murals, "fine" arts, photographs, posters, underground comix, and current political issues.

It also helps to understand that community murals are unique in certain ways, when compared to other art forms. First, because they are often so large, community murals have the potential for unique manipulations of scale (both the relationship of the sizes of things within the painting and also between the painting and its audience.) Because of the large size of murals, these opportunities are not usually available to easel paintings. Second, murals can utilize the architectural environment, which includes not only the architecture of the buildings on which they are painted, but the entire visual area seen by a mural's audience. When executed well, a two dimensional painted surface becomes three dimensional and the entire mass of the building on which it is painted contributes to the effect of the painting. Third, a community mural can involve a public process. The images painted "on the streets" are different from the individual artistic expressions of easel artists working alone.

Finally, there is a group of "contexts" which can be utilized in a mural's design. Every mural can be said to exist in several "places," such as architectural (noted above), geographical, historical, and social. A few murals grasp this thoroughly, and become truly astonishing expressions of all these elements.

Windows were thrust forward with vigor by a figure in this detail from the destroyed *International Hotel Mural* by James Dong. (73)

Josie Grant's mural, *Ode to Rousseau*, expands the landscape setting of the Page Street Minipark through its clever use of sky, clouds, and castles in the air. Photograph by Jean Constant Gindreau. (142)

1. See Cheikh Anta Diop. *The African Origin of Civilization: Myth or Reality*. Westport: Lawrence Hill & Co., 1974. This material helps explain the numerous images of Tutankhamen, Egyptian pyramids, etc., in black community murals.

2. John Berger. *Ways of Seeing*. New York: The Viking Press. 1972.

3. See Masha Zakheim Jewett. *Coit Tower: San Francisco, Its History and Art*. San Francisco: Volcano Press, 1983. This definitive study is authoritative and readable, with excellent photographs.

4. I am indebted to John Pitman Weber for this observation. He suggests a multiple distinction based on the different intentions of community artists, audiences, and funders versus those of "fine" artists, audiences, and funders. For example, fine art objects are selected by "experts," while community arts are developed with local audiences. On the whole, some distinctions are useful, but precise denotations are always debatable.

5. In this case, the traditional art theoretical disjunction between Subject (artist) and Object (the painted) crumbles to dust.

San Francisco Murals

THE MISSION DISTRICT

Why are there so many murals in the Mission District? The answer lies in San Francisco demographics and history. The earliest Europeans to visit San Francisco (then unnamed, of course) founded Mission Dolores, which gave its name to today's Mission District. While Latinos always lived in the area, it was not until 1934 that the area began to shift from primarily Irish to primarily Latino in ethnic population. Chicanos had lived on Rincon Hill, but were evicted when the western base of the Bay Bridge was placed there. They moved up Mission Street into the core of the Mission District. A change in immigration laws in the 1950s brought thousands more from Latin America, and although most of the Latino residents are from Central American countries, many people are from Mexico. They brought their tradition of monumental public art, and in particular the history of the Mexican revolutionary muralists. Murals had always been a part of the Mexican community in meat markets, saloons, and restaurants, so when the contemporary mural movement began, the District was ready, with centuries of tradition already in place.

An early significant Mission District community mural was painted in 1973 by a group of artists in the Jamestown CYO center at 23rd Street and Fairview (#309). It is important because it was early, and because it was a group effort; several artists working together created not only a mural but a precedent for subsequent projects. The artists were Patricia Rodriguez, Ruben Guzman, Chuy Campusano, Consuelo Mendez, Tom Rios, Jerome Pasias and Elizabeth Raz. Jamestown was a proclamation that community murals were not the same as individualistic easel paintings, and that the subject matter was, as the artists were, part of the community itself. Jamestown's murals were political, to be sure, because they depicted the human ravages of the Vietnam war, police harassment of local youth, and the notion that drugs corrupt not only a human body, but the body politic of native people, La Raza, as a whole. It was also a celebration of Latino youth and roots.

Jamestown was an interior group of murals, lining both sides of the second floor corridor of the building. The following year, 1974, a number of other murals "went public" in a big way, being painted outside or in more accessible locations.

As part of its heritage from the 1960s, San Francisco became a center of underground comix. This inheritance found its way onto the walls of the city in the Mission District. Early in 1973, along with Ruben Guzman and others, Robert Crumb, the most famous and influential underground comix artist, executed his only mural, on the Mission Rebels in Action building on South Van Ness Avenue (#275). In 1972, Spain Rodriguez (best known for his underground hero, Trashman) and others painted a comix-like panel of local scenes on the Horizons Unlimited storefront on Folsom Street (#304), and Michael Rios painted the *MCO* mural on the side of the Mission Coalition Organization at 22nd and Folsom Streets (#305). Rios' scenes were enacted by rats-as-humans, "Because that's how we're treated here," Rios explained. While painting a scene showing police as pigs, Rios was arrested for an outstanding parking ticket, and beaten up, he says. Upon his release, he returned and finished the scene as he had begun it. All these muralists continued to draw and paint, but Spain alone among them has retained his comix style.

In June of 1974, Jesus "Chuy" Campusano and his coworkers dedicated the "B of A" mural, *Homage to Siqueiros* (#294) in the Bank of America branch office at 22nd Street and Mission. Although it is an interior mural, it can be seen from the sidewalk through the bank's windows. At the dedication reception in the bank, while the bank officials handed out glossy brochures about the mural, the muralists handed out dittoed statements attacking the bank's policies and quoting Diego Rivera in defense of their having painted the mural in such a "bourgeois" location. The mural offers a series of scenes of the Mission District, ending above the corner teller's window with a vision of illuminating hope for the future. A few feet to the left, the mural had shown a serpent-like BART writhing out of downtown into the predominantly Latino Mission District, and to the left of that, a campesino handing an open book across a fallen crucifix. In the book are printed the words, "Our sweat and our blood have fallen on this land to make other men rich." Interestingly, the Bank's brochure included a photograph of this detail with the pages blank. It is likely that the bank's photographer took the photograph before the lettering had been added, and before the mural was completed or installed (it was painted on panels in an unused bank building, then mounted on the wall above the tellers' windows). Cynics, recognizing the profits the bank makes from the local population, suggest that the mural was probably listed under "insurance" by the bank's accountants, not under artworks. However the bank thinks of its mural, it inspired one of the assistants, Michael Rios, to begin painting the *Minipark* at 24th Street near Bryant that same summer.

Campusano also continued to paint murals, the most spectacular of which is the 1986 *Lilli Ann Mural* (#258) at 17th and Harrison Streets. Its brightly colored geometrical abstractions suggesting fabric swatches cover a huge south-facing wall in an industrial area. The mural is a reminder of Tomas Belsky's earlier piece at Potrero and 24th Street, *My Tis of Thee* (#381), but Campusano's is notable for its size, its brighter, acrylic, colors, and for its suggestion that, since it was painted in 1986, it might mark a new direction for Mission District murals.

Another early Mission muralist was Carlos Loarca, who worked on one of the earliest murals in Balmy Alley in 1973, taught classes at the Mission Cultural Center, and in 1978 with students painted *Homage to Woman* (#407) inside the Cultural Center on the second floor. In 1982 he joined with Manuel Villamor and Betsie Miller-Kusz in painting the immense exterior of the building. Their mural portrays Native American Mexicans (#405) in a stylized manner extending around the northeast corner of the building. Villamor's borders are executed in a contrasting style which is much more hard-edged and tightly controlled. The combination suggests the variety of cultures indigenous to Mexico, and that in turn suggests the variety of events and activities available inside the Cultural Center.

The original idea for the *Minipark* murals was Ralph Maradiaga's. Maradiaga was one of the three co-directors of the Galeria de la Raza, half a block away. He was a man filled with joy, artistic vision, and a tremendous dedication to helping his community. Rios took over the idea, and in 1974 observed that Latino children came from wonderfully rich cultural traditions which they were not studying in school. He

remembers being punished for speaking Spanish in grammar school, and never learning about his family's traditional culture, so he set about painting the three walls surrounding the *Minipark* with images from Latino cultural traditions (#357). He, Richard Montez and Tony Machado, who worked on several mural projects with Rios, began on the east front wall by painting Quetzalcoatl, the feathered serpent, chiseled from rock with children frolicking over him amid tropical plants and bubbling waterfalls. Toward the rear of the *Minipark*, two other murals were painted, and on the rear wall they painted a vision of a Latino future filled by learning and a strong sense of community (#365).

Rios' concept was given form on the west walls by the Mujeres Muralistas, who painted *Fantasy World for Children* (#363), but was also joined by an anomalous semi-surrealistic mural (#364) painted by Domingo Rivera which became a focus of ongoing controversy because its theme did not fit in with the other murals in the *Minipark*.

Over the years, Rios returned to repaint and maintain the first panel, while others replaced faded murals with newer visions. Murals were painted by Jerry Concha, Miranda Bergman, Olivia Montez and Emmanuel Montoya, all in keeping with the theme of the *Minipark* and all more or less administered by the Galeria de la Raza located just half a block away. The Galeria, along with local merchants and other community representatives, successfully pressured OCD (the Mayor's Office of Community Development) for funds to enable Miranda Bergman to refurbish the murals in 1990.

Two problems arose in the course of these changes through 1990. The first, in about 1980, concerned the city's Parks and Recreation Department which wanted to plant a New Zealand willow tree in front of the rear wall. At a meeting between the Department and members of the Minipark's community, the shift in cultural make-up of San Francisco was played out in crystal-clear terms. The newer residents, mostly Latino, wanted to paint murals for the benefit of the *Minipark*'s users, and they did not like the tree's location in front of one of "their" murals. The old-line, mostly Irish, civil servants of the Parks and Recreation Department responded by denigrating "murals" as just paint and chemicals, "but a tree is a living, growing thing, and a beautiful thing for everybody." No one disagreed with this, or wanted to harm the tree, but there was a strong feeling that murals were expressions of living, breathing people who used the Minipark. . . and so it went. In the end, nothing was done about the tree, which within a year or two burst into maturity covering most of the rear right wall and providing a large shady area for park users. When the rear image was repainted by Emmanuel Montoya in 1983, the wall was simply painted a bright, friendly yellow, with designs along only the bottom, under the tree's branches, and at the end of the left-hand wall. The Parks and Recreation Department removed the drinking fountain in the *Minipark*, and refused to pick up the overflowing trash containers more often than once a week, so the struggle for *Minipark* maintenance continued, led by the determined efforts of Rene Yanez and the Galeria de la Raza.

The other problem occurred in 1980 when Domingo Rivera's abstract mural, which everybody seemed to think inappropriate in content, was badly in need of repair. Finally, Rivera gave permission for it to be painted over and it was replaced by Rios. He painted giant *ABC* blocks (#365) surrounded by people of all ages, and images of education and learning and achievement, all of which were appropriate to the young clientele of the Minipark and the original conception of its murals. The problem of whether anyone ever has the right to paint over someone else's mural without permission, even if it has become an eyesore, was averted by Rivera's giving permission. In the case of the nearby Garfield Park (#388) mural which he also painted, and which was in terrible condition for several years, the Art Commission refused to allow repainting

because it lacked written permission to destroy or replace it. For several years its disgraceful state continued as a reminder of an impasse between community needs, artistic intransigence and governmental bureaucracy. It was finally painted out in 1988.

The *Minipark* has been inspirational, both in San Francisco and beyond. I have spoken with visitors from Europe, Australia and Mexico, all of whom had heard about the Minipark and wanted to see it for themselves. Within the city, it has been a reference point for other projects, such as Balmy Alley in 1984. Rios' contributions to the murals of San Francisco include an anti-Vietnam War mural (now destroyed), a mural for the Bicentennial Show at the San Francisco Museum of Modern Art, the *BART* (Bay Area Rapid Transit) mural (#312), and the Santana mural, *Inspire to Aspire*, of 1987 (#301).

BART had been pictured as a snake in the Bank of America mural just a block from the corner subway entrance at 24th and Mission Streets, and at first glance one might think that Rios' *BART* mural (#312), painted with Montez and Machado, repeats the depiction of the mass transit subway as a viper threatening the low property values of the Mission District. The question arises in terms of the mural's imagery: does it show BART riding on the backs of the people or does it show that the people support BART? The answer de-

Three apartment buildings form the canvas for *Inspire to Aspire: A Tribute to Carlos Santana* by Michael Rios, Carlos Gonzalez and Johnny Mayorga. The mural honors a local resident who is flanked in the mural by images evoking the community's Mexican and pre-Columbian heritage. Photograph by James Prigoff. (301)

An early flower and plant mural by Patricia Rodriguez and Graciela Carrillo covered this garage in Balmy Alley. (345)

directly into the stairway entrance to the BART station itself.

In 1972 Patricia Rodriguez and Graciela Carrillo painted their first mural on a garage across the alley from Rodriguez' apartment. Then, joining with other women artists they knew, they embarked on a major mural project, *Latinoamerica* (#402), painted on the side of the Mission Model Cities program headquarters building. They called their group Mujeres Muralistas, "Women Muralists." *Latinoamerica* was painted by eight women (four artists, four assistants), and the difference in their native cultures is evident in the mural's images. San Francisco's barrio differs from Latin American areas in other cities by virtue of its predominantly Central American population. Its images and traditions are different from the Puerto Rican influence in New York City, or the Mexican and Chicano domination in Los Angeles, for example. The mural has a Bolivian dancer and a Peruvian pan pipe player along with images from Venezuela and, of course, a significant presence of Chicano culture and Mission District mixtures, too. The work, as with many community murals, takes on a didactic function, educating its audience about the diversity of Latino influences in the Mission District. For passersby already aware of the references, a specific image can be a warm reminder of childhood in a distant homeland.

The significance of the Mujeres Muralistas cannot be overemphasized. Muralists, and most especially women, were struck by the fact that a group of Latinas was painting bold, striking murals, and working without men. The group was known and admired throughout the country, and in particular in Latino neighborhoods. The Mujeres painted in various configurations, but the key members were Patricia Rodriguez, Graciela Carrillo, Consuelo Mendez. Others included Miriam Olivas, Xochitl Nevel-Guerrero, Irene Perez, Ester Hernandez and Susan Cervantes. In addition to their joint work, they have painted murals in several locations. Carrillo painted *Humanidad* (#260) at the Mission Neighborhood Health Center in 1976, and a small mural on a bakery two years later. Perez has painted several murals in the East Bay and in Fresno. Hernandez has painted in the East Bay, and did a striking piece at the SFAI mural show in 1986.

Patricia Rodriguez has painted more than a dozen murals. In addition to her work with the Mujeres, she has worked on *Women's Contribution* (#272) on the exterior of the Women's Building in 1982, and *People We Knew, The Beauty of Life, and Dreams and Fantasies* (#306) at the Mission Mental Health Center in 1983.

In 1974, the same year that *Latinoamerica* was

pends on your analysis of BART's role in the community. After a couple of years of informal poll-taking on the site, when I asked Rios which it was he laughed and replied, "I think BART does both. It has raised rents around here and that hurts a lot of people, but it also provides good transportation to downtown. I guess I was ambivalent when I painted it." In either case, the mural is an example of the excellent use of environmental space by a well-designed image. The BART train in the mural begins at the left and curves across the long, narrow length of its wall until it executes a single, lovely swoop at the far right, taking the viewer's eye across the mural and then down, off the wall and

The Bolivian devil dancer was part of the South American section of the destroyed mural *Latinoamerica* painted by the Mujeres Muralistas. (402)

painted, Graciela Carrillo and Consuelo Mendez undertook to paint the fence in the parking lot adjacent to Paco's Tacos, a taco stand at 24th Street and South Van Ness Avenue. The commission to the Mujeres came from the owner, a local realtor who, the muralists said, wanted to establish his taco stand's identification with the Latino population before a McDonald's was built two blocks away. The mural, *Para el Mercado* (#313), showed the gathering, harvesting and transporting of food to market in traditional American settings. The two muralists were busy that summer and lacked the time to get together to fully integrate their design, so they decided that each would paint one half

of the fence. Carrillo asked Susan Kelk Cervantes to help work on an overall color scheme which unites the two portions otherwise clearly drawn by different hands. The taco stand was destroyed by a construction project in July of 1990, but Cervantes has rescued at least part of the fence on which it was painted. The Mujeres continued to paint after 1974, and produced *Fantasy World for Children* (#363) at the *Minipark* and other projects before disbanding at the end of the decade.

Susan Cervantes had worked with young children painting a mural at the corner of Balmy Alley and 24th Street (#345). After the Paco's Tacos fence she initiat-

Ray Patlan's mural, *Venceremos*, occupies the main stairway wall at the New California College of Law. Dramatically placed figures, flags, and a distorted bridge overcome the problems presented by the mural's location. (106)

ed a project at the Precita Valley Community Center, *A Day in the Life of Precita Valley* (#400), and went on to paint the monumental diptych, *Family Life* and *The Spirit of Mankind* (#397) on the south side of the Leonard R. Flynn School (formerly LeConte School) at Harrison and Precita Streets, facing Precita Park. Both designs are based on a spiral, with the right side of the diptych, *The Spirit of Mankind*, developing East Indian motifs and the left side, *Family Life*, portraying neighborhood residents, the people who use the park and for whom it has become, as depicted in the mural, a center of neighborhood social life.

In 1977 Cervantes founded Precita Eyes Muralists. It is one of the oldest ongoing mural workshops in the city. She had been a CETA muralist and Precita Eyes Muralists was founded as a portable mural workshop with people who had worked together on previous projects. The goals of the workshop include trying to educate the community about the mural process, and to encourage participation, to sponsor mural walk-

ing tours, and so forth. Regular classes are conducted in the group's storefront studio on the south side of Precita Park. Participating artists include Margo Bors, Tony Parrinello, Denise Mehan, Judy Jamerson and many others. Members have painted twelve murals, including the perfectly appropriate sea-scene on the south front of the Garfield Park swimming pool (#390) which combines images of ocean life, phases of the moon, Jacques Cousteau's ship Calypso, and assorted mythological symbols (a typical element in Precita Eyes' work). Perhaps most typical of their work is the group of six portable murals at the Las Americas school at 20th and Harrison Streets. The murals were painted in the workshop and erected later, after the site was found. These murals, *Reflections*, *Celestial Cycles*, *The Unicorn's Dream*, *Every Child Is Born To Be A Flower*, *Suaro's Dream*, *Masks of God/Soul of Man*, were painted from 1977 through 1982 (#282-#287). Their life-affirming spirit transforms the otherwise conventional stucco walls of the bungalow-style school.

24

Through her work as the central figure in the Precita Eyes Workshop, her unrelenting advocacy of murals to city officials, her organization of mural tours and lecture series, and most recently her murals with Juana Alicia, Cervantes has proven herself to be one of the central figures in San Francisco muralism.

Judy Jamerson, who worked with Precita Eyes, painted two murals at Mission High School in 1981. One showed students with a lamp of knowledge, which, unfortunately, was not popular among local youth (#265). The other, adjacent to it, was a relatively simple silhouette mural showing youth, cars and general high school-type activities (#266). Painted in dark blue and bright orange-yellow, it has remained untouched for a decade. Jamerson also was a major participant in the *Family Life* and *The Spirit of Mankind* murals in Precita Park.

In the late 1970s Ray Patlan moved to the Bay Area from Chicago, where he had been a participant in the early days of the community mural movement. Patlan came with exceptionally powerful artistic skills and years of mural painting experience, having studied and painted in Mexico, Vietnam and Chicago. Besides painting important murals in the East Bay, he was mentor and inspiration to innumerable local artists. In fact, his influence extends beyond the relative-ly small number of murals he has painted himself.

Each of Patlan's murals has something worthy of close study, from the Orozco-influenced cartoon-like characters in the monochrome *Prime Time/No Time* (#104) at the New College of California School of Law, to the manipulation of a complex stairwell space in *Venceremos* (#106) at the same location, to the innovative design of *Y Tu Y Yo Y Que* (#367), where the mural is composed of snapshots of local residents which are replaced periodically by images of new residents and activities. Working with students at San Francisco State University, and giving them major control over the images, he directed three murals on campus, including the large complex *Communiversidad* (#193). In 1982 Patlan worked with local youth at a Mission District playground called Folsom Park. A city official drove by and criticized the project for exposing young women to the roughness of the playground, but in fact Patlan's achievement was that this was the first time local girls had ever been allowed to use the facility. He was a member of the M.E.T.A.L. group that painted the *I.L.W.U. Mural-sculpture* (#220) in 1986. He worked with Eduardo Pineda at the Flynn School in 1989 and in 1990 in Healdsburg where they painted a mural dealing with the role of Latino laborers in the history of the California wine industry.

Ray Patlan and Carlos Gonzales transform their mural *Y Tu Y Yo Y Que* by changing the photographs of neighborhood people in the angled sections of the mural. Photograph by James Prigoff. (367)

A garage door provided the space for Juana Alicia's now destroyed mural *We Hear You Guatemala* in Balmy Alley. Photograph by Wilfredo Castano. (337)

Perhaps the most influential of Patlan's mural projects is Balmy Alley. The project was his idea, as was "*PLACA*", the name of the loose group that formed to paint the murals. A "placa" is a graffito tag symbolizing the writer, noting his presence, claiming an identity; an image calling for a response. The group named PLACA sought to do that on a larger scale by painting as many murals as possible in Balmy Alley (officially Balmy Street) in the Mission District. Balmy runs from 24th to 25th Streets between Harrison and Treat Streets. The alley was historically significant in the local mural movement as the location of both an early children's mural and of the Rodriguez-Carrillo garage mural painted before they founded the Mujeres Muralistas. A half dozen others had been painted in the mid seventies, too. In 1983, after several months of discussion and planning and drawing, $2,000 was donated by the Zellerbach Family Fund. Nearly three dozen people created 27 murals in the alley during the summer of 1984. Their efforts generated a spectacular block-long outdoor art gallery which has received notice in foreign countries and throughout the United States. The dual themes were opposition to U.S. involvement in Central America and celebration of Central America's indigenous cultures. In the summer of 1990, the murals were restored and several new ones added. (PLACA inspired a similar project in New York's lower east side (Loisaida) two years later called *La Lucha Continua*.) A walk through the alley gives the viewer the chance to see the most murals "per step" of any place in the world.

Ray Patlan is the Executive Director of Creativity Explored, an art therapy workshop where trained artists, some of them local muralists, work with developmentally disabled clients. In 1986 Susan Greene directed a mural project with them in which four muralists painted portraits of the clients, while the clients designed and painted the overall mural. It is located at 20th and Folsom Streets, and is titled *New Visions by Disabled Artists* (#281).

From her arrival in 1983 through 1990, Juana Alicia's mural output was tremendous. Working alone, with partners, groups, or collections of community residents, she painted over a dozen murals in San Francisco, Sonoma County to the north, and in Nicaragua. At the same time, like several other muralists, she led workshops, worked as an artist-in-residence at La Raza Graphics Center and in schools, and taught courses at local colleges. She worked with a large group of local residents and three other muralists (Raul Martinez, Susan Cervantes, and Emmanuel Montoya) on *Balance of Power* (#276) in 1985 at the Mission Swimming Pool. Two years later, in 1987, working with Cervantes and Martinez, she painted *New World Tree* (#277), which is a variation on the tree of life theme in keeping with its swimming pool location, and is extraordinarily well integrated with its architectural environment. The design works with the building on which it is painted, and thus enlists the entire mass of the structure on behalf of the image. Painted tree limbs repeat roof angles, the mural image centers on the main door at the center of the building, and foliage in the painting merges with landscape plantings next to the building. In this, *New World Tree* raises San Francisco murals to a new technical level.

Painting alone, in 1985 Alicia created *Las Lechugueras/The Women Lettuce Workers* (#368) dealing with the exploitation of women workers in California's lettuce fields. An interesting comparison can be made between this mural and a panel in Coit Tower painted in 1934 by Maxine Albro (#46). Albro's image depicts New Deal workers, perhaps dustbowl refugees, picking oranges and glad to be working. It is idyllic, even if quasi-industrial. Alicia's image, much greater in scale and outdoors, boldly declares the problems of subsequent migrant agricultural workers, such as being sprayed with toxic pesticides, spied on by company bosses, and controlled by company-run machines. It is a curious contradiction that a mural treating such harsh themes is so beautifully painted, but, then, viewed in this way many murals articulate the tension between creativity and destruction/exploitation. The destruction of many murals exemplifies this most clearly (see "Lost Murals of San Francisco").

In 1985 a joint committee of local residents and San Francisco Mime Troupe members selected Alicia to paint the history of the Mime Troupe, the neighborhood, and of the Troupe's building, which had been the studio of a Mission District recording company (#290). The resulting mural shows the Mime Troupe's location in the community, with scenes from several of its plays and a surrounding audience. Visually, as in life, neither the audience nor the image is passive, with "layers" of the design interacting in a dynamic fashion. Three years later, troubled by the horrendous human costs of ongoing war in Central America, she painted *Alto al fuego/Ceasefire* (#295) at the bus stop adjacent to Cafe Nidal on Mission Street. It shows a young boy simply holding out his hands against an onslaught of guns, with a lush mountainscape in the background.

In the fall of 1990, Alicia and Susan Cervantes completed a major work at Hawthorne School (#302)

Chilean-style mural painting was seen in this now destroyed mural on the *Casa Sandino*. The mural was one of several painted in the Bay Area by the members of the Brigade Orlando Letelier. (315)

on Folsom Street. The mural has complex images painted on the entranceway and two other supporting buttresses, all against a bright blue repainting of the school building itself. In panels across the long structure are painted letters from Roman, Chinese, Arabic and American Sign Language alphabets, and an image of an object that begins with the letter for the panel. The conception of the whole mural, and its excellently executed integration with the building's architectural configuration, makes it a spectacular addition to San Francisco's murals.

Alicia says that much of her inspiration comes from a belief in education. She sees a big part of her work as passing along various traditions to the youth of her audience, "especially third world people," who thus are given a chance to have an impact on the public environment through their presence in her murals. It is remarkable that, after a decade and a half, the vision of this muralist is so close to the vision of earlier muralists such as Michael Rios, who expressed almost the identical view when he began painting the *Minipark* in 1974.

Larger than lifesize images of children from the doorway to Hawthorne Elementary School where the *El Lenguaje Mudo del Alma* mural by Juana Alicia and Susan Cervantes begins. (302)

HAIGHT-ASHBURY

The Haight-Ashbury is the San Francisco neighborhood most prominently associated with the 1967 Summer of Love, with hippies, psychedelic drugs, free sex and a "no-hassle" lifestyle. It borders on Golden Gate Park, and Haight Street runs parallel to it two blocks away for over a mile. Artists were among the freespirited youths who crowded into the area in the late 1960s, and, as one later put it, "Since we'd been painting the insides of our apartments in all kinds of psychedelic designs it wasn't much of a leap to begin painting outdoors."

The earliest community mural in San Francisco was begun by Joana Zegri in 1967. It was never formally titled, but was called *Evolution Rainbow* (#160) because as the colors of its rainbow design progressed from dark to light, details within each color depicted the evolution of animals from early protozoa through dinosaurs up to modern species. Other murals were painted inside businesses shortly afterwards by Gary Graham and others and have now been destroyed, but Zegri's, in a troubled lifespan typical of community paintings, has withstood two serious challenges.

The first pause came when the artist, in the middle of painting the mural, took time off to give birth to her first child. After several months she completed the mural, and even restored it in 1981 with stronger paints. In 1982, the business on the wall of which the mural was painted changed hands, and the new owner had the mural painted out. This is an example of a common problem with community murals: the art is public, but the wall is private, and without special arrangements, the wall's owner is also owner of the mural (see below, "Legalities"). In this instance, the destruction catalyzed community forces in a way that indicates the role such murals play in forming social communities (or at least in focusing them). Protests, petitions, complaints by the store's customers, letter writing campaigns, and meetings late into the night followed. It is difficult to ascertain exactly, but the popular belief "on the street" is that someone called the store's insurance company and suggested that the store's window was not a good risk. When the insurance company cancelled its coverage, the store owner contacted Zegri and asked her to repaint the mural, thereby regaining insurance and community respect simultaneously.

The most prominent murals in the Haight-Ashbury were painted by a group called Haight-Ashbury Muralists, which in the spirit of the times sought a new way to organize itself into a unified artistic group. Members were Miranda Bergman, Jane Norling, Arch Wil-

liams, Jo Tucker, and Thomas Kunz. They painted a group of significant murals in the area, all of which depicted a belief in the struggles of poor and working people to better their lives and the need for new cultural organizations as part of that struggle. In *Rainbow People* (#156), a multi-racial, multi-generational, sexually mixed group of people was shown cutting off the greedy tentacles of a monopoly corporate octopus which had as its head the combined faces of President Ford and Vice President Rockefeller. The head had originally been Richard Nixon's, but after Watergate's scandal drove him from office, his successors' faces were substituted. Behind the tentacled terror a peace

Evolution Rainbow, painted by Joana Zegri, with its figure-filled bands of color was San Francisco's first community mural. (160)

Signs of protest carried by 1960s marchers were seen in this detail from the destroyed mural *Our History is No Mystery* by the Haight-Ashbury Muralists. (151)

"Kill Commies" was the spraycan message written across the native Californian section of *Our History is No Mystery*, the very long mural painted by the Haight-Ashbury Muralists. (151)

Figures around a campfire are watched by faces emerging from a window in *Each Come Together in Perceiving of Yourself* by Selma Brown and Ruby Newman. (158)

demonstration marched down Haight Street. The original mural was painted to commemorate such an anti-war march in 1972, but the paints were not strong enough to withstand the weather, and the surface was not prepared properly by the neophyte muralists. They repainted the mural in 1974 with several changes. To the right was depicted a countercultural scene of farming and musicmaking, out of which grows a rainbow. Two of the people working in the garden have necklaces with gay/lesbian symbols, and when the mural was attacked, these were one target. The other was the overall idea of the mural, or of murals in general. In foot-high letters, "Fuck people's art," was written across the center of the mural. The mural was restored and eventually was relocated indoors at the Haight-Ashbury Natural Foods Store across the street from its original location.

The largest work done by the Haight-Ashbury Muralists was *Our History Is No Mystery* (#151), which stretched down a low retaining wall at the John Adams School on Hayes Street until it was some seven feet

30

high at the corner of Masonic, where it turned and continued for another two hundred feet along the wall. It "read" from right to left, and showed a school history lesson about the working class in San Francisco. After beginning with Native Americans, the mural shows the gold rush, racist treatment of Chinese, the earthquake and fire of 1906, struggles for education for all citizens, a funeral in the Depression (with some famous muralists and some friends of the muralists helping carry the coffin), the internment of Japanese-American citizens during World War II, a generic march representing the 1960s demonstrations for peace, jobs, civil rights, etc., a section (symbolic of the ravages of urban renewal) depicting the struggle to save Chinatown's International Hotel and its mural from demolition, and finally, at the corner, a scene showing men and women of several races working together to create a society based on a vision of peace and productivity. On the Hayes Street side is a schematic hand pointing at the earth which bends around the corner itself.

One might think that people would appreciate this mural, whose theme and images were taken from a questionnaire circulated at the site by the muralists, and in fact it received a warm reception for years. But shortly before its completion in 1976, it was attacked by a single individual who, as he later explained in a letter, was distraught at losing his girlfriend, and had been drinking the night he defaced the mural. This attack was met with an outpouring of support for the mural by local people, dozens of whom helped restore the mural by cleaning it with special solvents. But in the 1980s, the mural was attacked again, more thoroughly. As is usual in such defacements, the primary targets were people of color, whose faces were covered with spray paint, but in this case the defacement went further, covering large portions of the wall, and adding graffiti saying "Kill Commies," and the like. It has been speculated that the same hand was involved in defacements of both Haight-Ashbury Muralist works because of their themes. Such a right-wing bigot may have been the same person who rollerpainted over the Native Americans in Eugene Curley's 1976 pastoral mural (#161) at Haight and Carl Streets.

The nation's bicentennial came in the middle of a tremendous surge of mural activity in San Francisco, and it made $10,000 available to the neighborhood for "beautification." Although some merchants wanted to use the money to paint fire hydrants, the money was split between three mural projects: *Our History Is No Mystery*, the Paltenghi Youth Center mural painted by Charles Lobdell (#163), and the Park branch library

Faces occupy the corner of *Educate to Liberate* just as they did in its predecessor, *Our History is No Mystery*. The mural on a retaining wall of varying heights was painted by Miranda Bergman and others. (152)

mural, *Each Come Together in Perceiving of Yourself* (#158) painted by Selma Brown and Ruby Newman. The latter is a strong example of how considered use of architectural space can make or break a mural's effectiveness. The mural's focus is at the bottom of a vertical space, where (appropriately for the Haight subculture and its idealization of Native Americans) a group gathers around a campfire. Two stories above is a recessed window well. The muralists made this a strength of their mural by designing their image to take advantage of the otherwise awkward architectural configuration. They reasoned that they were talking about myth in the mural, so they used the recess as the location of a personified sun figure benevolently looking down upon the vision of togetherness below.

Both women have continued painting, and Brown has created a strong image of the history of metalwork in *Masters of Metal* (#421), located at a tool and die works. She also painted a large, stylized historical portrait of Ben Franklin (#118) at the Ben Franklin School in the Western Addition.

By the late 1980s *Our History Is No Mystery* had been cleaned a couple of times, but continued to be attacked and was in bad shape. The muralists, in response to many local residents who liked the mural, decided that the best course to follow was painting a new mural in the space, and after three years of effort, raised enough money to allow the painting of *Educate to Liberate* (#152) in 1988. While the new mural lacks the historical specificity of the earlier mural, it is still current in its depiction of the multiplicity of cultures of

31

A detail taken from Jane Norling's destroyed mural, *Sistersongs of Liberation*, has been used very successfully in this poster printed for International Women's Day. (236)

INTERNATIONAL WOMEN'S DAY
Día Internacional de la Mujer   يوم السيدات العالمي
PHỤ NỮ QUỐC TẾ   SIKU YA WANAWAKE WAMATAIFA

working people in the area shown opposed to inimical forces which would exploit them. The latter are painted in monochrome greys and blacks, while above them are the brightly colored cultures of the people who attend the Vocational School on whose wall the mural is painted.

Educate to Liberate was a special regathering of the Haight-Ashbury Muralists, since they had not painted together in over a decade. Still, they had all been active in the mural movement. Miranda Bergman painted in Chinatown, Nicaragua, Palestine-the West Bank, Balmy Alley, the *I.L.W.U. Mural-sculpture*, with Wallspeak! in Oakland, and elsewhere. She is one of the central figures in Bay Area muralism.

Jane Norling had a baby and works as a graphic designer, but found time to paint *Educate to Liberate* and a strong mural in Balmy Alley. Her earlier *Sistersongs of Liberation* (#236) was a brilliant utilization of its cramped indoor space and has since been made into a popular poster celebrating International Women's Day. The mural has since been moved to San Francisco. Jo Tucker continued painting murals, including a mural at CASARC (the Child and Adolescent Sexual Abuse Resource Center) at San Francisco General Hospital (#370). Arch Williams painted in Balmy Alley and executed a number of other murals, such as *Tools for Peace* (#409), the Bernal branch library (#411), and at the Francisco Middle School (#33). Collectively and individually, the group's murals remain a significant presence in the Bay Area.

A word needs to be said about mural defacements (although see below, "The Lost Murals of San Francisco"). The vast majority of community murals are designed and painted with the support of people who live/work with the image on a daily basis, and they approve of its presence in their lives enthusiastically. These murals are not defaced in any way. In fact, they are typically defended against every attack, from graffiti to destruction by urban renewal. Occasionally, especially in areas where graffiti tags are common, murals are "hit," but this is indiscriminate and not directed at the mural in particular; any surface will do. Most people raised with formal training in art history disapprove of this, but in a survey I conducted of California Latino muralists a few years back, every single muralist in the state said that the graffitists had as much right to put their tags on the walls as the muralists did to paint their murals on them. Most of us probably agree that the murals look better without the additions (although some are designed to incorporate graffiti), but it is a fact of life muralists accept. The general idea is that if you do the proper legwork before painting, if you work with the youth of the area, then they will not graffiti the mural. If a mural has been up for eight or ten years, however, the youth at that time have no particular connection with the wall, and it may receive less respect than previously. The sort of attacks that have been directed at the community murals in the Haight are rare, and apparently are the work of a very small number of troubled individuals. They attack images of women and people of color, and seem generally to resent depiction of any sort of cooperative or culturally affirmative scenes, which they label "communist."

HUNTER'S POINT-BAYVIEW, THE WESTERN ADDITION, THE FILLMORE

These areas comprise the main locations of San Francisco's black population. The Western Addition and the Fillmore are directly west of the extent of the 1906 fire. This made them the primary location for the construction of much-needed housing immediately following the conflagration, but in the haste to provide housing and make profits, substandard buildings were built which soon became tenements and were made available to black people settling in the city. Immediately prior to World War II the U.S. Navy decided to build a major shipyard at Hunter's Point, and this in turn brought the major black migration to the city to work there during the war. What was built as temporary workers' housing at that time remained to house the black community until finally replaced by newer housing projects in the late 1970s and 1980s.

Among the earliest black community muralists in San Francisco were Caleb Williams and Horace Washington, whose 1973 work in the Western Addition housing projects depicted indigenous African scenes and cultures (#129). Both have continued to paint in the city, working together in the Bicentennial Show. Washington works primarily as a sculptor of large masks, but was a member of the *I.L.W.U. Mural-sculpture* (#220) team in 1986, and in 1984 created a History of Black Americans (#428) which was installed in Hunter's Point. This mural is a series of glazed tiles comprising stylized portraits of famous black Americans. Also early in the community mural movement such artists as Camille Breeze and Bob Gayton painted in the Western Addition, but most of their works are destroyed, as is the delightful *Sgt. Henderson Park* mural painted by Sondra Chirlton in 1973. On the walls facing a vacant lot at Divisadero and Eddy Streets, she painted a landscape. At the left was Sgt. Henderson whose army jacket was clearly labelled with his name. He was the person who took care of the lot when it was converted into a minipark by residents. In the 1980s, a large housing project was built at the site, obliterating the mural (#116).

An influential black muralist has been Dewey Crumpler, both because of the scale of his works and the fact that they have been painted in several parts of the city, each involving a different set of conditions and interrelations with local community members.

In the late 1960s, Crumpler first learned about the work of the Tres Grandes. By the early seventies, he had visited Mexico to see for himself how Siqueiros, Rivera and especially Orozco, handled architectural space in their works. When the saga of the George Washington High School murals finally reached the point of allowing painting to begin, Crumpler was ready, having painted other murals in the meantime. The students at the school had for years passed by Victor Arnautoff's 1935 entry hall frescoes depicting the revolutionary war and slave society of the late eighteenth century. They felt an uneasiness about the depictions. It wasn't that they were historically inaccurate, but that black and Asian and Latino students felt the need for more positive depictions of their cultures. They respected the progressive elements in Arnautoff's murals, such as the figure of George Washington pointing westward to the future across the continent and directing explorers, mountain men, and pioneers toward it (#176). Arnautoff included the body of a slain Native American over which the "developers" had to step on their journey, along with a Native American conversing with explorers in a pipe ceremony. The

Ceramic tiles were used for Horace Washington's series of six portrait panels of black leaders and entertainers on the wall of the Martin Luther King Jr. Swimming Pool. Washington was assisted by Seitu Din and Kate Singleton. (428)

Dewey Crumpler designed a very large mural called *The Fire Next Time II* for two adjacent walls of the Joseph P. Lee Recreation Center. Flames and an African-style cloth link images of Africa with faces of African-Americans in the mural's two parts. (424)

students tried to convince the administration to sponsor another mural in the main building, but they met a bureaucratic stone wall. When Martin Luther King, Jr. was murdered, students carefully removed announcements from a hallway bulletin board and put up materials about black pride. When the school authorities responded with disciplinary measures, the students said they wanted their mural or they would destroy Arnautoff's work. The administration was not impressed, so the students tossed ink onto the frescoes, and this militancy eventually led to an agreement for the new murals. The students however, wanted Crumpler to paint the new murals while the school officials did not want a young black artist barely out of high school to receive such a significant commission. When they finally agreed on Crumpler, they offered him the insultingly low sum of $1,000 for the job. This was finally raised to $17,000, on which Crumpler lived for four years while he researched and painted the three panels of the mural.

One panel is of Native American and Latino figures with cultural symbols such as the great pyramids in Mexico, the eagle and serpent, Cesar Chavez, and so on. Another shows the Asian American heritage, including for example, not only famous figures from Chinese history, but also a pile of army helmets, one with "442" written on it. Students who pause to find out what this means learn that this mural, like many murals, has a strong didactic content which can teach viewers about their own and others' histories. In this case, the "442" stands for the 442nd Regimental Combat Rifle team, the Rainbow Division which fought in Italy during World War II and which was the most heavily decorated division in the U.S. Army. Most of the soldiers' Japanese-American families were locked away in detention camps while their sons were fighting. The central panel of the mural is a depiction of African American history, with the building's huge supporting beams effectively incorporated into the mural design, and an honor roll of famous black people coming out of the center, below an image of black rebirth. Crumpler's idea was to suggest to students that they too might have their names added to the list some day (#180).

This theme of the relationship between African and African-American cultures has persisted in Crumpler's work, and is the main idea of his next two major projects. In *The Fire Next Time* (#423) at the Joseph Lee Recreation Center in Hunter's Point-Bayview, Crumpler depicted three aspects of black people's lives in the United States: education, religion, and culture. The contemporary figures, a teacher and student, athletes, and dancers, are watched over by exemplary portraits of Harriet Tubman and Paul Robeson. Above them are two Senufo birds, which are mythical beings in Africa but here oversee the cultural and creative lives of the community. Two incidents during the painting of this project demonstrate how community relationships can interact with murals. In one case a young man came up to Crumpler and asked who the two portraits were, and when told, the young man listened and then responded by saying that "They don't live here, man. You should put up a couple of locals like Richard and Edwina. They're a stone couple." Crumpler tried to explain, but the young man would hear none of it. Several weeks later, he returned, and told Crumpler that he was right, that black people needed to know more about important leaders so they could have somebody to respect, and besides, Richard and Edwina had broken up.

In the other incident, a group from a local church came to question the propriety of the two nude figures in the center of the design, and in flames. Crumpler explained that the figures symbolized duality, which was important in Dogon and other African religions, and also in the Bible, as were the flames. The neighborhood had been a site of riots and burnings in the late sixties, but the mural showed flames not only as destructive but as purifying, their common meaning in African religions and the Book of Revelations. This satisfied the church delegation, and after a decade the mural remains untouched by any sort of marking (although the City of San Francisco has planted a tree and erected a tall light pole directly in front of it, reminding us of the discussion about the willow tree in the Minipark some years before). It was my privilege to work as Dewey's assistant in this project.

By 1984, Crumpler continued the mural on the adjacent gymnasium at the Recreation Center (#424). More stylized than the first part of the mural, it continues the same visual motifs, with large portraits of black leaders and a background of dualistic flames.

Dewey Crumpler poses beside the Oni of Ife figure in the center of his mural, *The Fire Next Time II*. (424)

Wrapped around the northern corner is a hand holding a quilt from Alabama. Up Newcombe Street is another hand, but with a section of cloth with an African textile design on it. The manipulation of architectural space obliterates the corner, and brings the mural into a dynamic unity. Between the two hands is a giant replica of a 16th-century Ife bronze figure against a background of Egyptian and United States figures: King Tut, Muhammed Ali, Willie Mays, Wilma Rudolph, Arthur Ashe. The second part alone measures over five thousand square feet.

In the same year, with the assistance of Kemit Amenophis, Bonnie Long and Sandra Roberts, Crumpler painted *A Celebration of African and African-American Artists* at the Western Addition Cultural Cen-

Two figures in outline leap into the intricate African-inspired patterns of James Phillips' *Sunflowers of Nature*. Photograph by Ted Pontiflet. (422)

ter (#135). This, too, is a huge wall, even larger than the one at Hunter's Point. The mural design incorporates a number of difficult architectural characteristics of the building (primarily large screen-covered windows), and is anchored by a large stylized portrait of Duke Ellington. He is surrounded by artists in music, dance and painting—a perfect theme for the use of the center and the cultural heritage of the location.

In 1976, David Bradford painted a spectacular wall of respect for black leaders on the WAPAC building in the Western Addition (#112). It stood as a beacon in an area on the verge of urban renewal until the mid 1980s, when it was removed. In the late 1980s two other murals were painted in Hunter's Point. One was a geometrical design by James Phillips. The other, *Tuzuri Watu/We Are a Beautiful People* (#425), was painted by Brooke Fancher two blocks away from *The Fire Next Time*. It is a beautifully painted tribute to Afro-American culture inspired by black women writers. The design shows scenes of black peoples' lives, rural and urban, with a strong emphasis on community and family life. Quotations from the works of five black women authors appear throughout the mural. Fancher explains her choice of location and topic by saying that "A lot of people don't even know about black women writers. Their work is a part of the self-affirmation of people learning about their culture, and the mural seems a good place to proclaim it."

THE BICENTENNIAL

In addition to the three Federal Bicentennial Neighborhood Beautification Fund murals painted in Haight-Ashbury, two other multiple mural projects were produced in 1976.

The Bicentennial Show at the San Francisco Museum of Modern Art (SFMMA), was curated by Rolando Castellon, a man whose abilities and enthusiasm opened the doors of that august edifice to community artists of color. This show, devoted entirely to murals, was the first such exhibit at any San Francisco museum.

The murals for this show were painted with acrylics on plywood panels, and most measured eight feet high by twenty feet wide. The show provided the public with a chance to observe the work of a significant number of the most influential community muralists of San Francisco at that time, without having to go into the poorer neighborhoods where the muralists' work was usually located. Some found this a favorable development, some deplored it because of the lessening of impact murals have when wrenched out of their social contexts. The murals were *Two Hundred Years of Children's Toys and Games*, directed by Shoshana Dubiner with the Creative Arts Workshop at Bessie Carmichael Elementary School (#240); Horace Washington and Caleb Williams' *Crispus Attucks: The Boston Massacre, March 5, 1770* (#154); Dewey Crumpler's untitled piece showing working people nurturing a living plant from the bonds of racism (#132); the Haight-Ashbury Muralists' *200 Years of Resistance*, which was later mounted on Uganda Liquors at the corner of Masonic and Haight Streets (#155); Jim Dong and Nancy Hom's International Hotel mural, *The Struggle for Low Income Housing* (#406) which measures 14′ x 22′ in a "V" shape; and Robert Mendoza's *The Struggle of Native American People for Sovereignty*, a rare Native American mural depicting traditional images alongside contemporary scenes of alcoholism, drug abuse, and Indians occupying Alcatraz and fighting against U.S. government attack forces. On the lower right is a "holy" Native American family, including two smiling, happy children and two parents armed with guns.

Perhaps the most shocking image was Michael Rios' and Tony Machado's depiction of fascist pigs dragging an American flag on the ground (#408). It has a swastika in place of stars. It was titled *Esta Gran Humanidad ha Dicho Basta!/This Great People Has Said Enough!* (an image ironic by the late 1980s, since Rios has become a serious student of Buddhist pacifism).

Next to it was Graciela Carrillo and Irene Perez's untitled piece showing a dual image of Latino/Native American people engaged in traditional food gathering/preparing and also holding rifles in preparation for armed struggle (#EB31). These murals are only twelve feet wide.

Several of these pieces found their way into community display after the show closed, but some remain untraced.

The other bicentennial mural production was located at Fort Mason, in an abandoned military supply warehouse now used as part of a cultural activities center run by the Golden Gate National Recreational Area. Inside local artists painted thirteen 10′ x 35′ panels just below the ceiling. Since they were located between large windows, they were difficult to see clearly. The images depicted a wide range of San Francisco scenes, from early Golden Gate Park and Chinatown, to the building of the city's skyscrapers. The styles tended more toward the artistic expressions of the artists than to any community involvement, and few other murals were painted by these artists. All the murals were destroyed in 1987 in an "upgrading" of the space (#1–#13).

A CHANGE OF TONE: THE LATE 1970s

In the late 1970s, community murals changed. The struggles and the concerns of many of the early muralists were generated by their political activism and resulted in collectively developed images. Potentially volatile themes still remained, but became muted. The early muralists were growing older, setting up house, having children, sometimes getting tired of living hand to mouth. Also, the mass political activity of the previous decade waned, (with a solid shove from the government) and many political organizations expired, their issues no longer having mass appeal. As one disgruntled veteran of the 60s put it, "We may have been beaten, but we weren't wrong. The causes still exist and the problems will be back again in some form or other." In short, there was a lack of civil rights, antiwar and feminist actions to which a community muralist could relate. The issues' publicity (not the issues themselves) receded, and muralists' work became accordingly less volatile. To this must be added the gentrification of San Francisco neighborhoods and a change in mural financing. As relatively upscale residents moved into older, physically upgraded neighborhoods, early murals were painted over or destroyed in renewal projects. Funding sources narrowed to the point that the Mayor's Office of Community Develop-

Michael Rios and Anthony Machado painted *Esta Gran Humanidad ha Dicho Basta!* for the Bicentennial Mural exhibition at the San Francisco Museum of Modern Art. Their mural, painted on panel, is seen on display in the museum. (408)

ment (OCD) was almost the only source available to local muralists except for an occasional foundation grant. What is more, as with everything else, the costs of painting murals rose.

One other reason for this shift in mural images is the direct result of the early murals themselves. People had come to accept them. When trying to gain permission to paint on a wall it was no longer necessary to justify the idea of a mural, only to satisfy the wall's owner that a particular image would not have anything objectionable in it, and then to receive design approval from the Visual Arts Subcommittee of the San Francisco Art Commission (sometimes a daunting prospect). Murals were OK. Younger, "second generation" muralists came onto the scene as murals became an acceptable art form, an approved forum for expression. This and the lack of concurrent political activity (hence lessened opportunity to learn to think in political terms) contributed to the increase in numbers of "apolitical" images. Since murals were OK, a young artist could turn to community walls for self-expression, and some commented privately that this was their road into the galleries, which otherwise were not interested in their easel work.

The proliferation of images made each image seem less significant than before. It took something special to get people's attention. The mural movement as a whole had developed three separate currents. At

37

its heart remained the socially active artists and processes (the community muralists). However, a growing number of artists did not see murals as a part of a larger social process, but rather as vehicles for self-expression. A third well publicized strain developed commercially, as businesses hired muralists to paint attention-getting images for them. Still, community-based works continued to be produced, and competed with some potentially significant innovations.

THE EIGHTIES

In 1982 the Galeria de la Raza sponsored a show titled "In Progress." Twenty San Francisco muralists painted fourteen murals on panels of various sizes in the gallery space, which was open to the public during the painting. The show then travelled to Sacramento, to the Social and Public Art Resource Center in Venice, and to the Centro Cultural de la Raza in San Diego, where local artists painted their own pieces for the show. At every site the show was exciting for artists and the public, who were able to witness the process of painting in person. Some of the images were very strong politically. But that the murals were painted in gallery spaces suggested a shift from the earlier artworks "on the streets."

In 1986 the San Francisco Art Institute (SFAI) sponsored a similar show called "The Murals Project" in one of its galleries. Since the Art Institute had not been known for its support of muralists in the past, some said the artists were making a statement by working in a location where their mural work has not been traditionally accepted. The idea was that the meaning of this show could be extended to society as a whole, i.e., people initially turned to murals because their art and cultures were not acceptable in the mainstream. Now even mainstream institutions were recognizing their significance. This was continued at the end of the decade as SFAI sponsored a series of excellent forums on the problems and potentials of artists of color.

Many murals continue to be painted, and if we look back on the past two decades of community mural painting in San Francisco, we can see that in one way or another the city has continued to support murals, in spite of a complex and often infuriating bureaucracy that has driven some muralists away from seeking its help. OCD (sometimes referred to at the end of the decade as "MOCD," recognizing publicly the mayor's titular position) has the best record in the country of recognizing that communities can be developed by means other than massive construction projects. In its con-

tinued sponsorship of community murals OCD demonstrates that it has recognized the importance of culture and the existence of social, not just geographical, communities. Also, the role of the Mural Resource Center (MRC) cannot be overlooked. It has developed from being engaged in a constant fight for existence to acting as the major facilitator of city murals, especially in its function as administrator of the OCD mural projects. From its earliest days under the leadership of Kathie Cinnater to its present director Conrad Okamoto, it has grown in stature.

One muralist, Johanna Poethig, is difficult to place in a particular district because she has painted murals in several. She has painted with Southeast Asian refugees in the Tenderloin (#86), youth in the Mission District, a wall in honor of slain gay Supervisor Harvey Milk (#146), and a stunning multi-cultural mural, *Artifact*, at the South of Market Cultural Center (#248). She is perhaps best known for her work with the Filipino community. She has painted their history on Dimasalang House, a residence for elderly Filipinos

Johanna Poethig titled her mural of Filipino history, *Descendants of Lapu-Lapu*. It was painted on Dimasalang House by Poethig, Vic Clemente and Presco Tabios. (225)

(#225), and *Lakas Sambayanan* (#431) which deals with the coming to power of Corazon Aquino, painted near the intersection of Highways 101 and I-280. Fluent in Tagalog, tall and very fair-skinned, Poethig is a striking presence among groups of Filipinos, but that too is emblematic of the mixture of cultures in San Francisco's varied population.

The middle of the decade saw the creation of Balmy Alley and the *I.L.W.U. Mural-sculpture*. Although the latter had OCD funding, most of its cost was raised from union donations. That example and the subsequent increase in foundations' willingness to fund mural projects suggests the development of a new direction for funding in the nineties.

In 1990 a group of new murals was painted in Balmy Alley to replace those which had been destroyed. Patlan had plans to gain sponsorship for a similar project in the next alley to the west, Lucky Alley, and in addition he refurbished the PLACA murals in Balmy. The summer of 1990 saw Miranda Bergman begin restoration of the *Minipark* at 24th and Bryant Streets, too, with official funding.

The news was not all good. *Community Murals Magazine* had been edited and published by local muralists since 1978. It had become a respected and authoritative source of information about murals, written by muralists for each other. It was collected by libraries, universities and individuals. At the end of 1987, due to lack of funds, it ceased publishing. It was one of many arts publications to bite the dust in the decade, and represented a loss to muralists internationally as well as locally. Suitably, its demise was publicly announced when three of its editors created an altar at the annual Day of the Dead ceremonies at the Mission Cultural Center. The altar paid tribute to *CMM* and other arts magazines which had recently passed away.

In the Mission District, Chuy Campusano's massive abstract 1987 mural at 17th and Harrison Streets was a departure for the Mission District, at least in scale (Tomas Belsky had painted an abstract mural at the other end of the inner Mission District in the early 70s). Johanna Poethig, Susan Cervantes and Juana Alicia continued to produce spectacular murals. Alicia and Cervantes worked together on two in particular, *New World Tree* (#277) on Linda Street at 19th Street, and a truly massive project at Hawthorne School. *El Lenguaje Mudo del Alma/The Silent Language of the Soul* (#302), was painted on Shotwell Street between 22nd and 23rd Streets in 1990.

In 1989 Keith Sklar completed *Learning Wall* (#107) on the west side of the San Francisco Unified School District building on Franklin Street at Hayes.

Children of various ages painted *My Journey*. Muralist Johanna Poethig can be seen watching their efforts. (228)

Fittingly, this is the building in which the offices of the Alvarado School Arts Project were located at the beginning of the 1970s. Sklar's wall is so highly stylized that it borders on being abstract, and in several places is completely non-representational. The bright narrative panels, extending some fifty feet up the building, are placed within arches which Sklar has extended from ornaments on the building. The result, bolstered by art historical references within the mural (e.g., Michelangelo's "Cumean Sybil" from the Sistine Chapel frescoes) is a stunning combination of classical and modern—perhaps the muralistic equivalent of postmodern. In any case, it shows that the muralists have learned from their traditions, and that we can learn from their work on San Francisco's community walls.

FUNDING

Significantly, neither the Balmy Alley murals nor the *I.L.W.U. Mural-sculpture* were sponsored by the normal city-oriented community development process. The Balmy Alley project was completely ad-hoc, involved dozens of people who live/work in the immediate area, obtained permission only from owners whose fences or garages were painted, and held its own meetings to discuss designs. Suggested changes in designs were shared at these meetings, and changes were often made, but the city's official bodies had no role in the project. Muralists worked for free, however, putting in time after work or on weekends, or during their yearly vacations from regular jobs. One wonders if such a project, with such a theme and diversity of styles and technical levels of participants could ever have received approval from all necessary committees, or, if so, how many years it might have taken.

The I.L.W.U. project did receive OCD funding, but from a different part of its budget than was normal for murals. The key to the project's success was support from the union, both administratively (through the efforts of Director of Communications Danny Beagle) and through the donations of the rank and file membership. It received official approval of the design by both the Parks and Recreation Department and the Art Commission and was administered financially by the normal city arts channels in a frustrating, Byzantine manner.

In the mid 1970s, block grant money from Housing and Urban Development funds (HUD) became available to mural projects through the local Mayor's Office of Community Development (OCD, or MOCD). The specific agent was the Neighborhood Improvement Initiative Program (NIIP), which paid only for materials through the San Francisco Art Commission. The grants were small, only one to three thousand dollars, but supported about a dozen murals/training programs a year.

From 1975 until 1980, the Comprehensive Employment and Training Act (CETA) enabled muralists to receive salaries for conducting training programs, and thus CETA artists could apply for NIIP grants to paint murals. In many ways, CETA was modelled on the WPA of the 1930s. CETA artists' salaries were around $700 per month. When the CETA funding drew to a close at the end of the decade, muralists requested a follow-up, and this led to the establishment of the Mural Resource Center (MRC) which was funded by CETA until 1981. The MRC began to administer the OCD funds, and to move away from the Neighborhood Arts Program as the NAP was phasing out mural projects and putting its resources into the Neighborhood Cultural Centers, of which there were five in the city. This relative centralization put money into neighborhood centers, but reduced more widely-dispersed funding which had supported a wide variety of small projects throughout neighborhoods. Because of this shift in priorities by NAP, and because it was obvious that community mural projects in fact did develop communities, especially if one understood by "community" a social, not just a neighborhood grouping, OCD became the major mural funder in the city.

When CETA ceased to exist, OCD undertook on a cost per square foot basis the funding of materials and salaries, beginning with $1.75 per sq. ft. in 1975

and moving up to $5.75 per sq. ft. in 1986, where the figure remained through 1987. The current breakdown, as understood by muralists, was $3.25 per sq. ft. for materials, $2.50 per sq. ft. for salaries, but this was never made a clear policy, and OCD has resisted paying any salaries. Beginning in 1983, muralists are classified in a category that prohibits their being paid salaries. For reasons such as these, muralists and groups prefer to gain funding outside official city channels, continuing to search for independence. The MRC itself was always under pressure to raise its own funding, even after moving under the autonomous umbrella of the Friends of Support Services for the Arts, the governing body of the South of Market Cultural Center, where the MRC is located. This pressure kept the MRC's director working on funding the MRC instead of developing murals.

There is a built-in difficulty in the tension between truly community murals, independent funding for the MRC (which is virtually non-existent), the requirements of governmental funding groups such as OCD, and the MRC's acting as an agent for commercial jobs. These are not, of course, mutually exclusive, but establishing the proper balance has been difficult. If the MRC administration is supported by city funds released for mural projects, those funds are deducted from already underfunded muralists, while increasing commercial activity removes the MRC from the sort of advocacy and administration of community projects. Amid such problems it is easy for muralists to grouch about being ill-treated, which they are. But it is also important to keep in mind the admirable fact that there are an MRC and an OCD which have continued to support community murals for over a decade. Only Los Angeles provides comparable mural support.

In the 1980s there were few non OCD-funded murals in San Francisco, of which Balmy Alley is the leading example. Some of Precita Eyes' projects, for instance, have been corporately funded, some privately. The city's Department of Parks and Recreation has also been a steady source of mural support over the years. The MRC's involvement differs according to the project, sometimes acting as fiscal agent, sometimes as a technical resource, but always being available to bring muralists in contact with potential sponsors. Funding has ranged from $40,000 per year to around $186,000. In general, it is accurate to say that there is a tension between community-based murals, independent funding for the MRC, and commercial agentry.

As community muralists increasingly look "downtown" for funding, one problem has been the amount of unpaid work the current procedures demand. For community artists, it is particularly difficult to explore a community, develop a design, and prepare the presentation for free. It requires months, even years of meetings, design alterations, research, more meetings, etc. Official agencies have a tendency to approve a project on Friday and want to see paint on the wall on Monday. For the process to be as inclusive as possible, the muralist should begin the process of development only after some financial support frees him or her from other jobs.

LEGALITIES

When OCD took over paying salaries upon the withdrawal of CETA mural support, a contract was developed between muralists and the city which has served as a model for similar contracts elsewhere. At considerable personal sacrifice, the city's muralists fought for the retention of copyright, allowing the city to use images for non-commercial purposes. This was a small acknowledgement of the lack of adequate financial support given muralists. Also, provision was made that muralists must be notified if their works needed restoration or in case of proposed alteration or destruction. Unfortunately, the city unilaterally dropped these latter provisions in 1987.

The execution of a formal contract in itself tells us something about community murals and the law. On the one hand, increasing bureaucratic requirements are imposed as a matter of course when official agencies take a greater role in funding and administration. This in itself is a recognition of the murals' significance in the city. On the other hand lies the reality of muralists' inability or disinclination to support a formal legal challenge to any breach of contract or of law. Many muralists believe that their work belongs not to them but to the public, to the community, and they consequently believe that the image is not theirs to copyright. Others simply do not want any involvement with the legal system. Still others believe that it is important to copyright their work to protect it from a use opposed to their purposes for the project.

The basic motivation for copyrighting a mural image is to protect the artist's financial interests. While many muralists formerly believed that publication of a photograph of a mural image somehow meant the author or publisher was making a lot of money, most have come to realize that while this is not true, still, there is a principle involved saying that someone should not benefit financially from others' work without their permission. Copyright is a means to that protection. It is always ethical and appropriate, therefore, to get the permission of the artist before using images of his work.

In one instance, a member of the Haight-Ashbury Muralists discovered an airline's in-flight magazine in which their mural was portrayed as representing the cultural diversity of San Francisco. After numerous letters, the airline paid the muralists a total of $500. In another case, a textbook company used a detail of a mural for the cover of one of their texts, and paid a similar amount.

In addition to copyright protection, the California Arts Preservation Act (Civil Code Section 987) declares that "there is a public interest in preserving the integrity of cultural and artistic creations." This law gives muralists certain rights concerning protection of their work, and codifies several legal remedies if it is destroyed or damaged without permission. I know of no case yet which tests this law, although there are tests underway in two other states with similar laws.

CENSORSHIP

The question of legalities raises the problem of censorship. Censorship is illegal and abominable. But what exactly constitutes censorship, and what might be done about it? Asking these questions exposes a distinction that has played an uncomfortable role in San Francisco mural history. Speaking generally, muralists understand censorship to occur when an official demands alterations of an artist's image for reasons of disagreement with content. I know of only one public instance in San Francisco. Privately, I have been told of several where the artists chose to accept the censorship because they needed the money from the project, or thought there was no way to gain approval of an image if the official was challenged. One muralist told me, "They never say, 'I don't like the content of that.' What they say is, 'On purely aesthetic grounds I wish you would change that figure (or remove it). Then the design will be acceptable.'" Officials always deny such intentions, of course, and it is extremely difficult to prove otherwise, which is why instances of proven censorship, here or elsewhere, are so rare.

Also worth noting is the artists' self censorship. This occurs when an artist "knows what they will accept," and alters a design before showing it to an official body. It has been argued that officials certainly cannot be blamed for something that existed only in the mind of the artist, and on one level this is so. But there may well be good cause for the artist to have such suspicions, and in any case this scenario evidences something other than encouragement of unfettered artistic expression of the sort that civic arts bodies are charged to promote.

The instance of blatant public censorship in San Francisco occurred in 1981, at the time of the opening of the Moscone Convention Center building. A number of artworks had been commissioned for the space, including what has become a cause celebre, a bust of assassinated Mayor George Moscone by Robert Arneson. It was declared unacceptable because of its "tasteless" references— revolvers, bullets, and Twinkies—all elements in the mayor's murder. What went relatively unnoticed was the San Francisco Art Commission's rejection at the same time of another piece it had commissioned for the building, a mosaic mural by Katherine Porter. "It makes a political statement and I don't think any kind of political statement is appropriate," a *San Francisco Chronicle* article of December 1, 1981 quoted Art Commission chair Dimitri Vedensky as saying. Porter had put eight names on her ten by twenty foot piece: Martin Luther King, Jr., Cesar Chavez, George Jackson, I.F. Stone, Paul Robeson, Dorothy Day, Emma Goldman and Wounded Knee. Vedensky is quoted as saying that this "Is a very bizarre and personal list of people." Also according to the *Chronicle* article, although other artists had made similar changes to their works without consent of the committee, "they objected to the aesthetics of Porter's new frame." Thus does censorship operate in San Francisco when it is overt. The piece was not placed in Moscone Center (and remains untraced).

It is worth emphasizing that "censorship" in the sense being used here refers to actions taken by officials or official bodies. This is vastly different in results and implications from influences/pressures stemming from people in the community acting without the clout of the government. In fact, responding to such pressures is at the very heart of the artist-community interaction of community visual arts. Timing is crucial here, with community involvement occurring at a point in the mural's design process before the image is completely developed. It is part of the development. Official censorship imposes a different set of criteria than the community's, and thus functions negatively. I believe that in trying to satisfy official agencies, muralists may allow elements of censorship to intrude into a mural's design, possibly without even being aware of it.

BILLBOARDS AND "BILLBOARD CORRECTIONS"

Occasionally, someone mentions how billboards deface communities, but the ensuing discussions do not use art terms because billboards are not considered art; cynics point out that they have too much effect on our lives to be considered art. The fact remains that they are large, carefully placed for visual impact on their audience, and they offer possibilities of scale and subject matter which muralists are well qualified to utilize.

In 1975 a group of artists at the Galeria de la Raza became fed up with the imposition of advertisements on their community, in particular ads for liquor and cigarettes across from schools, and in general ads for products where purchase would help a corporation but not the community. For years there had been a Foster & Kleiser billboard on the Bryant Street wall of the Galeria, at street level, and so some of the artists stepped outside and "appropriated" the space. What they painted was an "ad" for *Tin Tan*, an arts magazine produced and sold in the Mission District, featuring the work of local artists. More than an ad, the magazine and the billboard were celebrations of local culture, and that was the beginning of the Galeria billboard.

Since then, dozens of versions of the Galeria billboard have been painted by local (and occasionally guest) artists. For a few years, the practice was semi-clandestine and fraught with uncertainty. One day, for instance, a Foster & Kleiser truck pulled up in front of the billboard and two young workers got out. Some folks from the Galeria came out to meet them, and a crowd began to gather on the sidewalk in front of the billboard. Suffice it to say that the local residents convinced the workers that they should not paint out the current design to prepare for more ads, and the workers got in their truck and drove off. The director of the Galeria, Rene Yanez, tried unsuccessfully for over two years to talk with the billboard company, but telephone calls were not returned, or he was put on hold and then cut off. Letters went unanswered.

Finally, the company took the billboard down. Someone from the Galeria asked what they were going to do with it, and was told, "Probably throw it away." They responded by saying, "Oh, we'll do that for you," so the company gave the disassembled billboard to them and drove off. The Galeria artists then set about putting the billboard back in its place. At that point, the company responded to Yanez's efforts, and erected a frame on the building onto which plywood or masonite panels may be affixed, combining to make a full-sized billboard lacking only the frame of the original (and the company logo). The space is now used exclusively by community residents who have a particular image to share, sometimes of community-interest messages. The billboard usually announces the current show at the Galeria, a storefront gallery which has become not only an important part of Mission District community life over the years, but a significant model for Latino and community-based arts throughout the country.

Unfortunately, it is impossible here to reproduce color photographs of every incarnation of the Galeria billboard, which is the best way to let readers see for themselves the changes in style and content over a prolonged period of time. Some information on particular examples will have to suffice to give some idea of the billboard's relationship to the community.

The third billboard in the series was painted by Michael Rios. In many ways it represents the heart of the project: immediately understandable to the people who saw it on a daily basis, bright, positive toward its community, celebrating the Mission's own culture, it depicted a laid back, stylized guitarist, with the large slogan across the top, *Salsa Ahora* (Salsa now). Over the years, Rios painted many of the billboards, including the spectacular *Homage to Frida Kahlo* in 1978 and the *International Year of the Child* in 1979.

In 1976, Xavier Viramontes embarked on the longest series of "linked" billboards. The initial design featured a large portrait in the center, with a word balloon off to the upper left of the billboard. The day Viramontes completed the portrait, he left the balloon empty, intending to return the next day and put in the telephone tree number for those who were prepared to protest the imminent eviction at the International Hotel across the city in Chinatown, where over a hundred mostly elderly and mostly retired Filipino merchant seamen lived. The Hotel had been purchased by a Hong Kong corporation which planned to wreck the building. The hotel represented not only the last stand of its residents to continue their inexpensive lives together, but had been taken on by activists as a symbol of urban renewal and its ravages on poor people. When Viramontes returned the following day to his mural, he found that someone had already written in the balloon, with spraycan, "Que Viva Danny Trevino?" Trevino, as nearly everyone at that time knew, was a young Latino who was stopped by San Jose police and then shot eight times in the back of the head for "trying to escape," or some such excuse. There had been no particular reason for his being stopped, other than he was roughly similar in appearance to a current suspect, i.e., he was a Latino youth. Viramontes understood immediately that this alteration of his design was completely in keeping with the spirit of his work and the spirit of community arts in general, and he let it stay for several weeks, adding the I-Hotel telephone tree number only in the week before the actual eviction occurred.

Xavier Viramontes used the Galeria de la Raza billboard for some advice about health in his temporary mural, *Avoid Junk Food*.

Some weeks later, Viramontes returned again and, using the same portrait, changed the surrounding areas to depict 24th Street with a legend reading "It's your neighborhood, keep it clean, por favor." Finally, almost a year later, the billboard was repainted by another artist, and the current string of incarnations began.

Billboard variations have included some painted by visiting artists, such as ASCO, a punk performance art group from East Los Angeles ("ASCO" is Chicano slang for "vomit" or "nausea"). The group painted not only the billboard, but the entire interior wall of the Galeria in preparation for their weekend shows. The Border Art Workshop from San Diego also painted a billboard, continuing the design into the adjacent Galeria storefront window, complete with a chain link fence to announce their show focusing on issues of immigration and border control in their part of the state (and thus figuratively moving the Mexico-U.S. border into the Mission District).

Other Galeria billboards have included the *Homenaje a Frida Kahlo*, and the *Low n' Slow* billboard for a lowrider art show (designed by fourteen year old Derrik O'Keefe). Billboards have been painted by Native Americans (for the American Indian Movement

photography show), by Graciela Carrillo for *La Mujer Nueva/The New Woman* show, and a Day of the Dead altar for victims of the Mexico City earthquake, Ralph Maradiaga (who had died suddenly that year), and AIDS victims (a courageous gesture by the Galeria in a neighborhood which had often been hostile to gay and lesbian people).

The notion of changing billboards takes another form as more and more artists and activists have "corrected" advertisements on prominent advertising billboards throughout the city. The trick here is to alter the advertising image as elegantly as possible so that the ad's own message is turned against it. Sometime, new words are added to the billboard to change the message people glimpse as they drive by. A cigarette ad showing a cardboard box was quickly "corrected" when red dots were put on the face of the smiling portrait and the wording was changed from "the Box" to "the Pox." Another cigarette ad was changed by the beheading of the man shown relaxing with a smoke. A concern with alcoholism motivated the correction of the slogan "The Silver Bullet," to "The Liver Bullet," and so on.

In 1977 the Eyes and Ears Foundation sponsored a group of 14 billboards in the Embarcadero-Fisher-

Billboard corrections change the intended message of a cigarette company.

man's Wharf area. These billboards were each painted by a single artist, a few of whom were muralists. The project reflected more of a gallery-orientation than a community perspective, since they were divorced from any community input. When asked what it was these billboards were advertising, one observer answered, "Billboards."

The use of billboards for non-advertising has been discovered in other cities in the United States and Europe, and billboard corrections are popular in England and Australia as well as here.

LOST MURALS OF SAN FRANCISCO

In the two decades since the inception of community murals in San Francisco, many have been destroyed. In some cases, this was planned or at least expected because the images were in a space such as the *Minipark* on 24th Street near Bryant where it was understood that they would be replaced periodically. The Galeria billboard mural is the most extreme example here, but Bill Wolf paints murals on his studio at 14th and Natoma Streets every 18 months.

In some cases murals have been destroyed by "routine maintenance." After a mural has been painted out, the landlord/owner defends the action by saying the destruction was merely the result of regularly scheduled painting. Although it is rarely possible to discover for certain, most muralists believe that many such cases are political attacks. They believe that when property owners or administrators don't like the politics of a mural they have it painted out. Important murals which have been destroyed include those painted at the city jail by Mosher and one painted by Ray Patlan and students in the central stairwell of the Humanities building at San Francisco State University. (Statewide, school administrators have been responsible for painting out dozens of murals, often in the early weeks of August, when virtually everyone is away on vacation or preparing for the beginning of the school year. At San Francisco State, the mural was ordered painted over by the Dean of the School of Humanities).

Most other cases of mural destruction stem from gentrification, or from real estate transactions where a building changes owners, and the new owners, having no obligations to neighbors, residents, the community, or the artists, simply choose to paint over a mural on one of "their" walls. This is perfectly legal unless there is a formal agreement specifying that a mural may not be covered or removed without the artist's permission. Since such agreements encumber the title to their property and hence make it more difficult to sell, property owners are understandably reluctant to enter into such agreements unless they plan to retain title themselves well into the foreseeable future.

In some instances, entire buildings have been demolished, and their murals along with them. The LULAC building (#394) at Folsom and Army Streets is an example, as were the mural on the front of the African-American Cultural and Historical Society (#102) on McAllister Street near Gough, and the mural at Hunter's Point II school (#427). Perhaps the most publicized of such destructions was the demolition of the International Hotel and its mural (#73). As the photographs show, destruction of murals by wrecking balls often provides a striking, albeit momentary, literalization of the destruction of poor and working class neighborhoods and communities by developers.

Sometimes the murals are not actually destroyed, but another building is constructed so close to the mural that it can no longer be seen. Neighboring buildings now prevent viewing of the Puerto Rican mural on Mission Street near Valencia (#410) as well as James Dong's Chinese American mural (#111) at 1834 Sutter Street.

Sometimes, the reasons for a mural's destruction involve complex community forces. Each such incident mirrors the vitality of our city, and the nature of conflicting interests. Some examples will help give an idea of the variety of forces interacting around community murals. One is Domingo Rivera's mural at Garfield Park (#364). According to local residents who frequent the park, the reason it was covered with graffiti when adjacent murals are left untouched is simple. Local people had no say in the image, never liked it, felt that it did not in any significant way pertain to them, and found it an arrogant visual imposition. The basic feeling seemed to be, "If the artist doesn't care about us, why should we care about what happens to his mural?" But this mural is more than simply an example of what can happen when community members are not adequately involved. It is also an example of a difficult and very real problem: under what circumstances should a mural be painted out? In the previous examples the murals were obliterated on the orders of a single authority. In the Garfield Park case, the muralist was unwilling to allow another mural to be painted on the wall. In spite of surveys of residents who saw the wall every day, it was not painted out until 1988. The artist's integrity, even though it was destroyed in the attacks on the wall, held priority over the expressed desires of the community audience.

Curiously, however, there was no such difficulty

Fran Valesco's two panel mural in Balmy Alley called *The Contest between the Sun and the Wind* was defaced by a spraycan-wielding vandal. (344)

when the art commission wanted to paint out a mural on the top of Twin Peaks shortly before the Democratic National Convention. The mural depicted a history of San Francisco (#208), and was painted on a service building at the base of the Sutro tower. Since no one staffs the building or regularly patrols the parking lot, the mural was a natural target—interesting but not on anyone's "turf." Or, it may have been the building itself, against which a series of fires were set. At any rate, the artist agreed, reluctantly, to allow the mural to be painted out under the condition that she be given support for another project. The mural was painted out. The convention came and went, and the artist has not received the promised support to date.

In 1980, murals were painted at the Holly Courts housing project (#413) after extensive discussions and design sessions with residents. At the dedication, the muralists experienced a tremendous outpouring of gratitude for their work and for the murals themselves. But within a couple of years, new leadership was selected for the tenants' group, and apparently as a demonstration of their power and of their need to "start with a clean slate," the murals were painted out. Five years later, another mural by one of the artists, Mike Mosher, was destroyed at Albion and 16th Streets, without notifying the artist or the art commission, for reasons of "routine maintenance."

Two other cases of calculated defacement are worth noting. As we have seen, the Haight-Ashbury seems to harbor one or more people politically opposed to community murals. They are apparently unable to organize a project articulating what they do like, and their only response to others' murals is destruc-

tion. Thus have two Haight-Ashbury murals and Eugene Curley's Native American landscape been systematically defaced over the last decade. This includes the red-baiting, racist attacks on *Our History Is No Mystery* (#151), and an earlier attack on *Rainbow People* (#156). A third mural was also attacked. It was originally painted for the Bicentennial Exhibition and titled *200 Years of Resistance* (#155), but subsequently retitled *Uganda Liquors* when erected on the side of a liquor store by that name at the corner of Haight and Masonic streets. In 1986, someone completely covered it with thrown paint, destroying it. The mural had been instrumental in causing removal of an unsightly billboard which was originally adjacent to it. The owner of Uganda Liquors had even installed lighting to illuminate the mural at night, which was certainly a contribution to the enjoyment and safety of the area. There is no recourse for this sort of destruction other than to repaint the mural or to paint another mural in the same location. But the 1980s are more difficult economically for community artists than the 1970s, and what cost a few hundred dollars to paint then would undoubtedly cost several thousand to paint now, and so the corner remains without decoration of any sort save the dark brown paint on the side of the building.

Generally speaking, if a mural is the product of its immediate community, it will not be defaced, let alone destroyed. The most active enemy of community murals is gentrification, the "upgrading" process when a building changes owners. Political destructions are frequently masked as "routine maintenance," although there have been blatant attacks on some murals, almost always motivated by pig-headed racism.

What this adds up to is the fact that we live in a society/socio-economic system that values several things more than art or cultural expression. Until we can create a society in which all cultures are accepted, in which all people have the chance to develop self-confidence and sensitivity, the destruction of murals (not to mention other forms of cultural expression) will, sadly for us all, continue.

When chronicling the sad tale of mural destruction, we should end by remembering the experience of Balmy Alley. About two weeks before the murals were to be dedicated, several were defaced with pro-Nazi slogans and symbols. The muralists repainted their works within a week, but even before they could repair the damage, local children who had been a constant audience for the muralists, borrowed paints from them and wrote in front of their favorite murals a warning to any future vandals. The children's assertion of community support was simple: "No touching these."

Technical Considerations

At the most basic level, a mural is simply a painting on a wall. It makes a difference, however, what the wall is made of and what type of paint is used on it. Failure to prepare the wall surface properly or the use of incompatible paints may lead to an early demise of the mural through flaking, peeling, fading, or falling off the wall through weathering action (usually of water) beneath the paint. What follows is a brief outline of technical aspects of mural painting as practiced in San Francisco.

SURFACES

Walls are made of stone, brick, plaster, stucco, wood, concrete, or sometimes a combination, including even glass and tile in some instances. Basic wall preparation insures that the paint will adhere properly to the surface, and that normal aging of wall and paint will not cause problems. No matter what the surface, it must first be checked to be sure it is structurally sound, and that repairs will not have to be made to it or its drainage system once the mural is painted. Then, the wall must be thoroughly cleaned, using trisodium phosphate or some other cleanser followed by a thorough rinsing. If the surface is wood, careful filling and sanding are required. The surface is normally sealed with a clear sealer, then painted with a white gesso to give the most luminous background to the color.

PAINTS

Ancient cave painters made their own paints, grinding pigments for color. Today, muralists buy their paints. In between, paint technology continued to provide the "right paint for the job." New Deal artists worked mostly in oil paints and sometimes in fresco (a process of applying colored pigments to wet plaster which makes the final image literally part of the wall). Of the Mexican muralists, Siqueiros was a great experimenter, trying such innovations as airbrushes and automobile paints (for longevity and brightness).

Windows, doors, and heating vents are among the structural devices confronted by a muralist when he designs his painting. Dewey Crumpler is seen standing on the scaffolding next to his mural, *The Fire Next Time II*. One figure in the mural seems to be lifting a heating vent into the flames. (424)

San Francisco muralists have occasionally executed frescoes, and have tried other media, but the vast majority of local murals are done with modern acrylic paints. Until the late 1980s, when the local distributor went out of business, the brand of choice was Politec, which, like all acrylics, was easy to work with

A wood frame apartment building above the House of Brakes offered the setting for the mural, *Carnaval*. (314)

In *Carnaval* the walls of the apartment building are tranformed into city blocks. Between the houses the Carnaval parade explodes down each imaginary street. The mural was designed by Daniel Galvez and painted with the assistance of Dan Fontes, James Morgan, Jan Shield, and Keith Sklar. (314)

and terrifically durable, even in the California sunshine. It was specially formulated, with additives that help the colors resist fading due to the ultraviolet rays of the sun. Politec was developed in Mexico by Jose Gutierrez and had been sold locally since 1973. An advantage of working with acrylic paints is that as long as they are wet, they are water soluble, so spills and "errors" can be corrected easily (a major consideration when working with children or inexperienced painters). Once dry, the paint becomes plastic and resistant to nearly every kind of attack. Since the demise of Politec, muralists tend to work with Novacolor or, sometimes, Liquitex, both of which are excellent acrylics.

The murals are normally coated with clear sealer after they are finished as a final protection against the elements and graffiti. (If graffiti is put on the mural, it can be washed off with the right solvent without removing the mural paint itself. Manufacturers are searching for an ideal "graffiti protection" covering, but as of mid 1990, no product has found general acceptance among muralists).

Some artists have used oil-based paints, mostly because they are familiar with them from their easel painting. Any moisture beneath the paints, however, will cause them to peel. This familiarity has obvious advantages for the artist, but the oil paints will crack, however, and not weather as well as the acrylics. Still, Bulletin sign painter's colors have been used with great success in other parts of the country, especially in Chicago, with its harsh winters and hot, humid summers. (In Chicago, sometimes the paint holds up well, but the wall beneath deteriorates and crumbles away beneath the mural, destroying it). In Chicago these days, the medium of choice is Keim Paints, made in Germany, which are exceptionally durable, second only to fresco. They have been used sparingly in San Francisco, perhaps because of difficulty in availability.

Cynthia Grace's *Tactile Mural* is a fabric collage intended to be touched by those who come to the Rose Resnick Center for the Blind. (94)

The entire community (children, their parents, and the buildings in their neighborhood) was presented in this mosaic mural by Nancy Thompson at the *Alvarado Elementary School*. (216)

OTHER MATERIALS

For some reason, San Francisco muralists are curious and experiment with different materials. In 1984, Horace Washington installed a series of mural panels at the Martin Luther King, Jr., swimming pool (#428). Each panel consisted of individually painted and fired tiles. Several tiles made up the portrait of a figure. Although painted tiles and even mosaics had been used in community murals elsewhere, this is the first such instance in San Francisco. Tiles have the special value of being virtually immune to weather, and will retain a high gloss for decades.

Another unusual material was used for the *I.L.W.U. Mural-sculpture*, a group of three panels made out of 3/8″ structural steel with a narrative mural painted on both sides. The type of paint used was polyurethane epoxy. Extremely bright and durable (it is commonly used to paint automobiles, trucks, and airplanes), it should weather for an extended period of time. The drawback to using it is that it is a cumbersome medium to mix (short pot life of about four hours) and extremely toxic. Protective garments, such as respirators, gloves, goggles, and earplugs must be worn at all times when working with it. "Normal" paints, especially acrylics, are much more user friendly.

PORTABLE MURALS

In San Francisco, muralists have painted backdrops for rallies and speeches, and more permanent backdrops for stages. Also, many "portable" murals have been painted. These are usually painted on 4' x 8' masonite panels, or sometimes on marine plywood. The panels are then grouped into, commonly, an eight foot by sixteen or twenty foot rectangle, about the size of a small billboard, painted in a studio space, and then erected wherever an appropriate location is found. This style of working has the great advantage of not being subject to weather while being painted, and the relative calm of a studio environment.

Portable murals also have a tendency to be little more than large easel paintings, and often seem imposed on their exterior sites since they are rarely painted with a particular architectural (or social) environment in mind. In a few instances, portable murals have been executed in "unusual" shapes. Jane Norling created a portable mural in an accordion shape made by placing panels in a zig-zag pattern. This gave the structure a depth that created a visual variety not possible on a flat rectangular surface. There is no reason plywood cannot be shaped in virtually any way, and this has in fact been done by Leo Tanguma in Denver and Raul Valadez in Austin, Texas. Their inevitably small scale (they can be disassembled and stacked in the back of a station wagon for transport) also limit their potential as murals.

All of the M.E.T.A.L muralists needed to wear protective masks and clothing while they worked on the *I.L.W.U. Mural-sculpture.* (220)

Folding screens show the possibilities an artist can utilize in creating a portable mural. This untitled work with its effective sense of depth was painted by Jane Norling.

Introduction to East Bay Murals

The "East Bay" consists of towns and cities on the eastern shore of San Francisco Bay. Like San Francisco, most were founded in the nineteenth century and grew up as the gold and silver booms brought expansion to the area. Few New Deal murals were painted in the East Bay, although there were some public art projects, especially at schools, including the massive University of California campus in Berkeley. Still, the impetus for mural work came in the 1960s in the midst of the political activism for which the area is so famous. Nor were murals the only form of public visual expression of the times. Especially notable were the hundreds of posters announcing political events, and silkscreens dealing with ethnic or political themes which led to the Bay Area becoming the preeminent poster/silkscreen production center in the country.

The first political murals in the Bay Area were painted in 1968–1969 by students at Oakland's Grove Street Community College (#EB101). Murals were painted celebrating black, Latino, and multicultural concerns of the student population. They were painted by Shirley Triest, Wilma Bonnett, Joan X, David Salgado, David Bradford, Manuel Hernandez and Malaquias Montoya. These murals were admired by activists and activist artists throughout the area, and encouraged others to turn to public walls for artistic expression.

The most prolific of East Bay muralists has been Malaquias Montoya. Montoya's primary medium is silkscreen, and examples of his work are seen on office and apartment and home walls throughout the area. As a teacher of Chicano culture and art at several local colleges his method was to work collectively with students. In the seventies they produced a group of outstanding murals, such as: *The Limits of Tyrants* (#EB37), *Nuestra Historia* (#EB32), *No Hay Rosas Sin Espinas* (#EB33).

Other Latino artists active in the late seventies included Ray Patlan and Patricia Rodriguez, who worked with groups and painted murals in the Latino neighborhood of Fruitvale and East 24th Street in east Oakland. Rodriguez and Patlan also taught a course together at the University of California which generated a handful of murals close to the university campus.

In Berkeley the most influential group was Commonarts, the members of which were Osha Neumann, O'Brien Thiele, Patlan, and Anna de Leon. They painted half a dozen murals, such as *Winds of Change* (#EB114), and the spectacular *Song of Unity* (#EB99) at La Pena Cultural Center. *Song of Unity* is a magnificent example of a community mural. It was executed by a group of artists working in conjunction with the immediate community and the staff at La Pena. It is executed on plywood panels shaped at the top to conform to the outline of the images in the mural, giving the piece a dynamic presence along an otherwise routine one-story roofline. On the right stemming from a ceramic eagle are figures in U.S. culture, such as jazz and folk musicians. On the left, stemming from a South American condor, are figures of Latino culture, such as musicians playing Andean pan pipes and guitars. They come together at the entrance to La Pena, inviting everyone inside. On the larger left side is a figure of a guitarist in low relief (made of a wire armature and papier mache soaked in acrylic plastic sealer instead of paste). The musician is Victor Jara, a Chilean poet and folk singer whose hands were chopped off by Pinochet's police before they murdered him. The mural's concept is that Jara joins with artists and musicians from both continents in creating the culture inside La Pena. In 1986 the mural was refurbished, and a quetzal bird, symbolic of Central America, was added to the center in reference to the intensity of the current struggles there. Its painted tail spread down the mural and out across the adjacent sidewalk.

Another major mural of the seventies was *A People's History of Telegraph Avenue* (#EB79), located at the corner of Haste Street and Telegraph Avenue near People's Park. In it, Osha Neumann designed a political history of the area, much of which occurred at the site of the mural itself, from the Free Speech Movement of 1964 through the anti-Vietnam War and police riots of the early seventies. The mural ends on the right side with a scene of utopian frolic—and a life-size panhandler, who is often obscured by homeless people who stand on the spot asking for help.

The other well-known mural from the seventies is

Stefen's *Dutch Boy Mural* (#EB115), which was painted on the west-facing wall of a paint store at Milvia and University Avenues. It depicted a futuristic view of San Francisco Bay from Berkeley, a theme appropriate to the "new age" segment of the counterculture. Stefen included a figure on a ladder painting the wall, who looked at first glance like the Dutch Boy of paint advertising fame . . . or perhaps like Stefen himself. When the mural was destroyed in the process of renovating the building for a new tenant, many people in the community were upset, but the mural was not replaced.

Other muralists active in Berkeley and Oakland were George Mead, Gary Graham, Lou Silva, and Deborah Greene and Ariella Seidenberg. Of particular note among their work is *Oceanus* (#EB68), painted by Silva and Graham. Its underwater scene (excellently situated beneath a freeway overpass) contains drums of radioactive waste. This is a reference to the discarding of such waste near the Farrallon Islands, a marine life refuge just outside the Golden Gate. Strange, un-

The subject is education in this Oakland school mural by Malaquias Montoya and his mural students from the California College of Arts and Crafts. The Spanish title can be seen in this detail from *In Knowledge There is Liberation*. (EB36)

Detail from a destroyed mural painted by Malaquias Montoya and students from the California College of Arts and Crafts in Oakland. (EB59)

The hands and guitar of murdered musician Victor Jara emerge from the top of the La Pena mural, *Song of Unity*, painted by the Commonarts muralists in Berkeley. (EB99)

known plants, clearly mutations, are seen growing from the mural's drums.

The East Bay contains many examples of school murals, especially in high schools in Oakland, Berkeley, and El Cerrito. The Brigada Orlando Letelier, a Chilean refugee group, painted a mural at *Oakland Technical School* (#EB68) and another at *Berkwood-Hedge* School, an elementary school in Berkeley (#EB94).

In the eighties, Daniel Galvez painted three murals in Oakland using the popular photorealist style. He used photographs of local residents for his images, thereby linking the murals indelibly to the community. One of these murals, *Grand Performance* (#EB 53), by Keith Sklar and Galvez, is painted on a freeway underpass, and is a tribute to Bay Area artists including jazz pianist Mary Watkins, the San Francisco Mime Troupe, Oakland Symphony conductor Calvin Simmons, folksinger Malvina Reynolds, and muralist Ray Patlan. Both Sklar and Galvez have painted major walls in San Francisco.

Also prominent in the decade was Dan Fontes, whose animals painted on freeway support pillars gained instant popularity (#EB54, #EB55). A number of muralists have painted on both sides of the Bay, among them Miranda Bergman, Ray Patlan, Dewey Crumpler, James Morgan, Edythe Boone, Kim Anno, and John Wehrle. So has Eduardo Pineda, who has begun what may prove to be a major outpouring of community murals in Richmond.

In 1985 a group of artists who had worked on Balmy Alley in San Francisco joined with East Bay artists active in Art Against Apartheid and formed Wallspeak! (originally Oakland Wallspeak!). Over the next four years the group painted five murals in Peralta Village (#EB43-#EB47), a poverty-stricken housing project in west Oakland next to the Cypress Freeway. The murals all celebrate black pride or try to make a connection with conditions in the local housing projects and apartheid in South Africa (although in their effort to paint this observation the artists were constrained by interference from the Oakland Housing Authority, on whose walls the murals were painted). Still, the brightness, hope and generally positive feeling the murals impart to their locations is impressive. Members of Wallspeak! include Edythe Boone, Dewey Crumpler, Kim Anno, Miranda Bergman, Tim Drescher, Roi Brown, Karen Bennett, Sam Shuchat, Nzinga Kianga, Jimi Evins, and Joel (Phresh) Freeman (a spraycan artist who combines graffiti-style with more traditional community murals).

The cutaway interior of a synagogue forms the setting for *Mitzvah: the Jewish Cultural Experience* painted by Keith Sklar, Brooke Fancher and Dan Fontes in Oakland. (EB43)

Bay Area Murals in the Nineties

The nineties are a watershed in the mural movement. Murals are being painted in larger numbers than ever, there are many new faces in the movement, and a wide variety of media and ideas are being used in monumental community-based images, from hip-hop to poetry, to mosaics and ceramic materials and collage. The mural cluster, developed twenty years ago by Michael Rios in the Minipark project, finds its current embodiment in the Clarion Alley Mural Project (CAMP), while Lucky Alley, a block west of Balmy, looms on the horizon as the next alley waiting to be turned into an outdoor community art gallery. By 1994, community murals in San Francisco had established an important tradition of public works. For example, in 1991 the Muros exhibition at Capp Street Project included not only designs for unrealized mural projects, but actual panels from murals that had been taken down, including pieces of Paco's Tacos, *Para el Mercado* (313) and murals from Balmy Alley (1984). Murals from the early period, which in the Bay Area covered roughly 1968 to 1974 (the other two periods are 1974 through the 1980s, and the 1990s), are now viewed nostalgically as icons from an earlier age.

Unfortunately, there is no master plan for the preservation of these stunning works of community expression. Unlike Los Angeles, which has begun a systematic cataloguing of the conservation needs of all its thousand-plus murals, San Francisco is now just beginning to think about the importance of its more than five hundred-plus murals. All effort is going into painting new works, and in that regard the Bay Area is witnessing the greatest explosion of community murals in its history.

New artists with new attitudes toward murals are producing exciting work in addition to the new work by the "veterans." These veterans (artists such as Ray Patlan, Miranda Bergman, Johanna Poethig, Irene Perez, Horace Washington, Susan Kelk Cervantes, Ester Hernandez, Chuy Campusano, and Selma Brown) are all busy and earn enough money and satisfaction through painting murals (and from their day jobs) to keep them involved.

The politics have changed a bit, but monumental public images on community walls continue to articulate community concerns. Also, spray can pieces appear more often and need to be taken into consideration when assessing the area's community art. Bay Area muralists have already produced over 150 murals in the nineties. Although the first edition of this book ended with the murals created in 1991, that year is included again because it is now possible to assess all the murals painted in that year, as well as those produced in 1992, 1993, and some of the productions of 1994. This book remains the only complete guide to San Francisco and East Bay murals, but mural awareness has grown through articles in general magazines such as *Sunset, Travel and Leisure,* San Jose's *Artweek,* and even a feature on television's "Good Morning America."

Perhaps the most controversial mural in recent years was Senay's *Malcolm X* (585). Painted on a wall of the San Francisco State University student center it was attacked at its unveiling on May 19, 1994, the anniversary of Malcolm X's birth. University president Robert Corrigan ordered it painted over because of its anti-Semitic symbols. The overpainting was then washed away by students so the campus authorities had the mural sandblasted from the wall.

NUMBERS TELL (SOME OF) THE STORY

Since 1968, roughly 229 women and 294 men have painted on San Francisco walls. Many have worked on several projects over the years although exact figures are not possible because of uncertainty in the composition of some groups. In the nineties, approximately 87 men and 64 women have had leading roles on local murals, about half the murals were team projects, and half of those teams were multi-racial. Virtually all the teams include both men and women. In the East Bay, twice as many men are painting as women (47 and 23) in the nineties. One conclusion drawn from these statistics is that women have played a major role in designing, organizing, and painting murals. During the 1980s, with the exception of 1984, more women artists painted San Francisco murals than did men. It is to the

In *To Cause to Remember* (492) Johanna Poethig captures the bitter irony of current attitudes towards immigrants, homeless, and disenfranchised people. The Statue of Liberty, whose torch has left her outstretched hand, seems tired, suggesting that traditional notions of liberty may no longer be as respected as they once were.

Time After Time (483) faces a playground where its brightness and abstraction give a flair of visual excitement to the space. Betsie Miller-Kusz's mural is an example of the variety of images being painted in the city.

This Women's Building mural (528) is one of the most talked about murals in years, both because of the spectacular impact of the image, and because of the stunning team of skilled painters involved in the process. The mural celebrates the accomplishments and struggles of women today and throughout history, and proclaims a universal sisterhood.

credit of the mural movement and its motivating principles that its productions reflect so well the make-up of our society.

FUNDING

In the 1980s, funding for San Francisco murals came primarily from MOCD (the Mayor's Office of Community Development), which administers the federal Housing and Urban Development money. In the 1990s, the range of funding sources is much wider. MOCD still plays an important role, but private businesses, corporations, individuals and foundations are all expanding their support of mural projects. This is one result of the mural movement: the funders are aware now of what murals can offer to a community. The projected budget for the Lucky Alley mural project, a block away from Balmy Alley in the Mission District, is between $30,000 and $40,000. By contrast, in 1985 more than two dozen murals were painted in Balmy for a total cost of $2,500. Ray Patlan, who is leading the Lucky Alley project, says raising the money "shouldn't be a problem." This statement indicates the impact murals have made on many parts of our society.

Muralists engaged with their communities still need other sources of income (although Fresco and

Precita Eyes now receive enough funding to enable some members to live on it if they are frugal, and commissions/competitions are sufficient to sustain Oakland's Daniel Galvez). While all muralists have outside sources of income through regular jobs, many find funding support by working with students in schools, with Fran Valesco's *Quilt Mural* (460) or Johanna Poethig's William DeAvila School project (472) as examples. Mural work must be wedged into lives already occupied by "regular" jobs and families. In a project like the Women's Building (528) where seven artists comprise the painting team, the scheduling complexities are staggering, and the level of sacrifice rises to match the scale of the project. The women paint on Tuesdays, Thursdays, and all day Saturday, much as the dozen painters did on the *I.L.W.U. Mural-sculpture* (220) in 1986.

Funding in the second period of mural painting, from 1974 through the eighties, depended primarily on federal money, beginning with CETA, the federal Comprehensive Employment and Training Act which paid artists, among others, to teach usable skills to low-income residents, especially youth. In San Francisco, CETA monies supported 101 murals. When CETA was phased out (its last support is listed in 1982), the local Office of Community Development (OCD) stepped in and supported several mural projects every year. OCD, which became the Mayor's Office of Community Development (MOCD) in the eighties, works with federal HUD money which it administers locally. From 1979 to 1994, OCD supported 91 murals. The city's record of unbroken support for murals is unmatched anywhere in the world.

In the nineties, the biggest change in mural support lies in sources other than federal/MOCD: businesses and foundations, especially. In the nineties, over twenty private businesses have already contributed to mural projects, as opposed to only twenty-five for the entire decade of the eighties and twenty-one from 1968–1979. Clearly, businesses are realizing that mural projects can be a healthy part of maintaining a stable community. In the case of the Clarion Alley Mural Project, nearby businesses, owners of property in the Alley and residents all agree that an alley-full of murals will attract visitors and this increased attention to the area will encourage drug dealers/users to go elsewhere.

A similar funding pattern is true of foundations. In 1984, the Zellerbach Foundation contributed $2,000 to PLACA for the Balmy Alley mural project which painted over two dozen murals in a one block long Mission District alley. Three foundations supported mural projects in 1986, five in 1990, seven in 1993, and the number is already at six for 1994. Foundations, too, have seen that mural programs involving communities are worthwhile projects deserving their support.

Municipalities remain an important source of mural funds. In San Francisco, agencies such as the Mural Resource Center and the San Francisco Art Commission continue to support murals, and the recent availability of anti-graffiti funds administered by the Neighborhood Beautification and Graffiti Cleanup Fund (NBAGCF) have played a major role in funding recent murals (twelve since 1991). Significantly, the wider variety of funding sources in this decade has meant that individual projects are funded from several different sources. Whether this means muralists are freer because they are not beholden to a single funder, or whether they are even more constrained because they must not antagonize several funders, is yet a matter of discussion. But the relatively small size of the city and its tradition of support for community artworks does not appear to have greatly constrained the mural images themselves. While the muralists in the eighties had to "satisfy downtown," meaning MOCD, they nevertheless kept their focus on the communities with which or for which they painted. In the Bay Area, neither censorship nor lack of government funding have exerted significant limitations on recent mural work. What changes have occurred are due to shifts in, and lessening of, political activism.

TECHNICAL PROFICIENCY

The technical proficiency of the murals has improved over the almost three decades of the movement's existence. Partly this is due to greater artistic skills on the part of artists who have been painting now for ten to twenty years. Partly it is due to the higher expectations generated by constantly improving projects. Also, artists are now sometimes actually trained to paint murals in art schools such as the California College of Arts and Crafts in Oakland, or through workshops at Precita Eyes Mural Arts Center. In addition, artists have over five hundred local examples to study.

THEMES AND NUMBERS

Mural themes have remained more or less constant over the years. The two main topics have been destruction of communities by "urban renewal" or other gentrifying projects, and declaration of group identity, primarily ethnicity. In the nineties, too, these themes continue, but AIDS as a theme has appeared in three recent works. Ecological/nature themes continue to proliferate at an even greater rate.

Latino-theme murals have been painted at a rate of about half a dozen a year (except for Balmy Alley in 1984, when two dozen Latino themes were painted). The number of African-American images was comparable (from six in 1975 to ten in 1993). But, significantly, the number of murals with multicultural images has always been greater than those identified with a single group (again, with the exception of Balmy Alley). In 1976, eleven multicultural-theme murals were painted. There were six in 1990, ten in 1992, seven in 1993, and eight thus far in 1994. Of course, the actual numbers in this sort of survey will vary depending on individual definitions, but the primary fact remains: the themes of San Francisco's community murals reflect its multiethnic population.

There were three high points of mural painting over the years. First, recall that 1976 was the nation's bicentennial celebration, and unusually large amounts of money were available for communities to spend on art. In the Haight-Ashbury neighborhood, a battle raged for months between a group of merchants which wanted to paint fire hydrants red, white and blue, and another group which supported the painting of community murals. The group preferring murals won, so

In this mural Susan Greene and Meera Desai have captured Reverend Martin Luther King Jr.'s concern for the future and for commitment to moral principle and historical reality. Called *To Ignore Evil is to Become an Accomplice to It* (EB 183) the mural was painted in an underpass under Highway I-580.

Isaias Mata's *500 Years of Resistance* (555) is a spectacular mural wrapped around the corner of a Catholic church in the Mission District. The east wall shows the positive spirit of working people, their demands, and their heroes. Note the children in the lower corner, reminding viewers that the work we do is also for future generations.

three were painted, each receiving one-third of the $10,000 grant.

The next burst of murals came with the Balmy Alley project in 1984, in which all the images either celebrated Latin American cultures or opposed United States intervention in Latin America. The final highpoint in mural production occurred in 1993 with the *Clarion Alley Mural Project.* Twenty murals were painted in that year and another twenty are planned for 1994.

In the East Bay, the pattern is basically the same, but the numbers are smaller.

Let us take a quick glance at some of the most productive muralist groups over the past three years.

PRECITA EYES MURAL ARTS CENTER

The most prolific group of muralists over the past three years has centered around the Precita Eyes Mural Arts Center, located facing Precita Park on the northern slopes of Bernal Heights. Precita Eyes is led by Susan Kelk Cervantes. In addition to sponsoring mural workshops for participants of all ages, that workshop schedules regular lectures about all aspects of mural painting, and has developed Mural Awareness Week, held yearly in late spring to honor local muralists and help call attention to the beauty and variety of the city's community murals.

Part of the program at the workshop is called Precita Eyes Youth Artists or PEYA, which has forged a strong bridge between spray can artists and more traditional mural approaches. The integration seems to be working well.

Another of its contributions is the guided tours of Mission District murals (near the workshop's location) offered every Saturday, and on other days by special arrangement. These tours begin with a brief slide show on mural history and then visitors take a walking tour of several of the most exciting mural sites in the area, including Balmy Alley. Details and reservations are available by telephoning the workshop.

FRESCO

Taking a different approach, one of the leading muralists of the first generation of painters, Ray Patlan, has joined with muralist Eduardo Pineda to form "Fresco," a private partnership. Fresco provides consultation, slide shows, and most importantly, the painting of murals by the two professional community muralists. It is funded by businesses, MOCD, and foundations, allowing it the freedom to pursue its own

The giant tree in Susan Kelk Cervantes' *Keep Our Ancient Roots Alive* (579) soars above a school playground. Climbing the tree and behind it are students of various ethnic backgrounds. Framed by borders of masks, these motifs illustrate how the school helps students treasure their traditions while living and working productively together.

vision. Even though it is a professional endeavor, Fresco's orientation remains rooted in working with members of different social communities. In the past two years Fresco has completed over a dozen mural projects, ranging from large outdoor walls in Oakland, to relatively small portable murals for indoor locations.

CLARION ALLEY MURAL PROJECT

Of all the recent mural activity, the *Clarion Alley Mural Project* (CAMP) is among the most exciting. Inspired by the Balmy Alley project of the mid 1980s (itself inspired by Michael Rios' *Minipark* project of the mid 1970s), Clarion Alley was planned in October 1992 to take two years with twenty murals painted each year. CAMP is exciting for a number of reasons. Its concept

A good example of the work by Fresco artists Ray Patlan and Eduardo Pineda is *Universal Learning* (501). The diversity of people who see the mural as well as the many cultures represented by students at Marshall elementary school are stressed.

and execution are guided by a group of "new" artists, people who did not participate in the earlier periods of the mural movement, even though they were inspired by it. CAMP's original intention was that the work would be a "free field," but executed by people closely connected with either the North Mission area or the alley itself.

Funding comes from foundations, private donations, local businesses, and the city, but the group retains complete autonomy within the project. No problem is anticipated with Art Commission approval of any design, and if there were, it is likely the money would be refused rather than allowing funders to censor the artists. As one walks through the alley itself (somewhat warily because of the neighborhood) the variety of the artwork constantly surprises. If a piece is not to your liking, walk on a few paces and see what's next. CAMP includes spray can art as well as cartoon pieces mounted on large panels, traditional murals (Fresco and Precita Eyes have pieces in the alley), and even collages and poems. In 1992–93, CAMP had a "poetry curator" to help select the poems mounted in the alley. There is talk of continuing the project for another year or two and of painting portraits of local residents and denizens on the several doors into the alley.

CAMP counters the misinformed opinion that "murals aren't political anymore." They certainly are, perhaps especially when the focus is on members of the immediate community. CAMP incorporates much of what gave the community mural movement its strength for the first quarter century of its existence: the participants are ethnically and sexually mixed, the content is spontaneous and relevant to the visions and concerns of the people who live with the images on a daily basis, and it is supported financially by those same people. The variety of images, participants, and styles (from felt-tipped pen to spray can to paint and brush) is inclusive, not exclusive. CAMP speaks to the idea that we all now live in a multicultural world, a postmodern world where "everything is everywhere, all the time." CAMP exemplifies this reality by welcoming the diversity. Earlier mural cluster projects such as Balmy Alley, the Minipark, *La Lucha Continua* on New York's Lower East Side, or Chicano Park in San Diego had more focused themes which were appropriate to those times (and, sadly, still appropriate today). CAMP takes for granted much of what earlier muralists fought to legitimize, and moves on from there.

GRAFFITI/SPRAY CAN ART

Certainly a word is in order about graffiti/spray can art. Kids and lovers have carved their initials on trees or written them on walls seemingly forever, but today, such gestures of self declaration are more numerous than ever before, made possible by easy-to-handle, quick-to-dry, adhere-to-any-surface, spray can enamel paints. Its ubiquity demands attention, which, in the case of tags, is the whole point.

According to Martha Cooper and Henry Chalfant in *Subway Art* (New York, 1984), there are three types of spray can work. The simplest is the tag. Tags are

Is this escalator a way out of the deteriorated environment of Clarion Alley? Or is it a route into the alley from "up above"? Julie Murray's untitled mural (518) only suggests, but does not answer, these questions.

drawn with spray paint, felt-tip pens, magic markers, or pencils — anything which can quickly declare a writer's initials, "placa," or nickname. With tagging, the goal is to "get up" in as many places as possible, including walls, signs, busses, subway trains, mail boxes — any place to get your tag noticed. The Spanish word for tag, "placa," was the name used by the group that painted Balmy Alley, although in the original version only one piece was painted with spray enamel. Today, several Balmy Alley murals are spray can pieces. Nearly everyone finds tags unsightly, but to poor youths who see no other way of establishing a presence in their world, it passes for self expression, or at least a declaration of existence.

A name in large, quickly written letters done in one color with a single outline is known as a "throw-up." Large, multicolored, calligraphic tags, intricately lettered, and deliberately difficult (or impossible) to read, are known as "wild style." Many New York subway trains in the 1970s were covered with wild style spray can names.

The most aesthetically complex spray can works are "masterpieces" or simply, "pieces." They are often done with permission, since they require more time and space than other forms. Every city has locations which are at least tacitly permission spaces. Writers (all spray can/graffiti artists are known as writers) con-

gregate there to share ideas, and put up new works. In San Francisco, Silver Terrace Playground off Silver Avenue, and Psycho City, a series of interlocking parking lots on the south side of Market Street at Franklin, are major locations for spray can writers.

The artistic source for much spray can art is the comic book, in both style and content. The example of such spray can artists as Keith Haring and Jean-Michel Basquiat, who successfully moved their spray can work from subways to art galleries and museum exhibitions, is undeniable. Museums have continued to host shows of graffiti art, sometimes commissioning a site-specific example as San Jose's Museum of Art did when it sponsored a painting called "Fascinating Slippers" done by Los Angeles artist Gronk in 1992. In San Francisco, Brett Cook-Dizney, Twist, Reminisce, Estria, TWS, Neon, Krash, Benz, Nate, Omen, EFX, and Dug all gained tangible artistic reputation through their spray can work. Each is an accomplished artist, and some of them continue to execute "non-permission works," as Cook-Dizney calls them.

Anti-graffiti campaigns, whether initiated privately by irate property owners or sponsored officially by municipalities, often enlist racist stereotypes and become civic excuses for harassing or sometimes beating up youths who have been caught with spraycans. Graffiti, especially tags, are surely attacks on either

Rigo's mural is the third to grace this fence in Balmy Alley. Called *Colors* (546) its title refers to both the variety of racial groups in the neighborhood and to the way in which spray can artists bring color to otherwise blighted areas.

Twist's unmistakable figures elicit smiles whenever you run into them throughout the city. This untitled work (508) can be seen in Clarion Alley.

public or private property. This lack of discrimination seems to lessen any subversive effect the graffiti might have, although that is probably irrelevant to the ego-motivation of the taggers. But official outcries against spray can-using youths appear just as self-serving and hypocritical when the same voices are not raised against, for example, urban renewal programs which obliterate entire neighborhoods. The "solution" to graffiti is clear enough—build a society in which even poor youths can see hope for a decent future and a life with dignity instead of degradation, so that the writers might choose other venues than busses and walls. Unless this occurs, rampant tagging will continue. As a lifestyle and as a commentary on the decay of civic (but not of individual) spirit in our cities, spray can art will continue until youths recognize another outlet for their self-expression.

In the spring of 1994, a young tagger was caught in the act of writing in the Richmond District and charged with committing over $5,000 worth of damage. If convicted, he faces possibly years in jail and, when released, hundreds of hours of "community ser-vice" erasing tags. Significantly, newspaper and TV stories identified him as a "muralist."

"TEMPORARY" WALLS

In the first decades of community murals, construction fence paintings were sometimes sponsored by contractors who wanted something more visually palatable on the fences surrounding construction sites than handbills and graffiti tags. In the past few years, construction fence murals have become part of the planning of large projects. Competitions are held and images are planned long before the fences actually are erected. The fences are often painted by classes of school children. These murals often remain in place for two or three years, sometimes longer. Then the fence murals are returned to the muralists or taken to previously selected locations for permanent installation. In San Francisco, recent construction projects included Yerba Buena Gardens (490), and the Muni turnaround at Mission and the Embarcadero (489). In Oakland, similar fences currently surround buildings

Spray painted on a fence surrounding an empty lot is Brett Cook-Dizney's 1993 mural, *Confused, Frustrated, Vandalized, Misguided, Active, Poor, Need Love, Gato, Desolate* (493). The people portrayed live, often homeless, in the immediate area, and the words are what they feel about their lives. The mural provides a public respect rarely given to those depicted.

damaged by the earthquake of 1989, and construction sites near City Hall. City-block length fences with works by several artists thus become temporary street galleries of community-inspired mural art. In any city these days, if you have an interest in murals, take a glance at large-scale construction projects.

EAST BAY MURALS

Several East Bay projects have already been mentioned, but it is important to note that there, too, community murals are undergoing a renaissance in the nineties. Numerically, the most murals painted in any previous year was eighteen in 1978. In 1992 and 1993 eighteen and seventeen murals were painted. Reasons include the rising popularity of community murals as a form of expression (perhaps particularly in a depressed economic period), a prolific and increasingly serious group of young spray can artists, and the support of two government funded sources, the Public Art Program of the Division of Cultural Afffairs of the City of Oakland, and the East Bay Conservation Corps' Project YES (Youth Engaged in Service).

Project YES painted five murals in tribute to Reverend Martin Luther King, Jr. during the summer of 1992. The painting teams were each directed by an experienced muralist, and consisted of students from five local middle and junior high schools. Project YES has also sponsored several other projects, each involving students as painters. The Cultural Affairs murals are more formally produced, but nevertheless are always placed in locations beneficial to the general Oakland community. This demonstrates admirable support and enlightened understanding of the potential role mural projects can play in building and maintaining a strong sense of civic pride.

A further indication of Oakland's concern for its public spaces and communities is a major competition held to select muralists to paint three murals inside Oakland City Hall, which has been extensively renovated after serious damage in the 1989 Loma Prieta earthquake.

Seyed Alavi worked with high school students for months in designing four murals to be located at I-580 underpasses in Oakland. The task was to have the students articulate what was most important to them and then to reduce the ideas into words. *eRacism* (EB 186), created with outdoor paint and glass highway beads, is one of the powerful results of this process.

Phresh, Krash, Poem, Vogue, Dream, WIM, and Raevyn are examples of an increasingly sophisticated group of spray can artists working primarily in the East Bay. Each has also begun receiving formal commissions.

In Berkeley, while the City has not been sponsoring mural work, the People's Park area (see EB 192) has continued to be the location of ongoing, non-permission mural work. Murals were painted on the public bathrooms almost as soon as the walls were up. What these works lack in trained artistic skills, they offer in vitality. As spontaneous projects, they have also remained untouched by spray can tags for over two years.

OUT OF TOWN WORK

Local mural production would be even higher if several muralists had not been busy painting major projects in other locations. Sometimes this is because of funding inducements, but sometimes it is because an opportunity arises to paint in a particularly interesting location. Susan Kelk Cervantes, for example, painted a large project in St. Petersburg, Russia, in 1989, and expects to paint in the former Czechoslovakia in the summer of 1994. Foreign projects are painted in collaboration with local artists, and they, in turn, paint with Precita Eyes when they come to San Francisco. Thus do community murals continue to be painted by a widening community of artists.

The value of "expatriate" projects accrues both to the city where the murals are painted and to the Bay Area. Visiting muralists talk with other muralists, see other works, toss around new ideas about art, society, materials and techniques. In this postmodern world, murals and their ideas are everywhere in a continuing cross-fertilization. A 1991 mural in Belfast, northern Ireland, for example, was based on an international Women's Day poster which featured a detail from Jane Norling's *Sistersongs of Liberation* (236), a mural originally painted in Berkeley in 1975, but later relocated to San Francisco.

Fresco has accepted commissions in the wine country north of San Francisco at the Gundlach Bundschu Winery, where they painted a history of wine industry fieldworkers. The four women of the *Break the Silence Mural Project* (296) have painted on the West Bank of Israel/Palestine as well as in San Francisco, articulating a theme that everyone deserves a homeland, a place to put down roots. Johanna Poethig won a major competition and last year painted a spectacular mural on Main Street in Los Angeles. This project was administered by the Social and Public Art Re-

source Center in Venice, and was one of a dozen murals painted in Los Angeles under its auspices. And Oakland's Daniel Galvez has spent considerable time in the past few years painting murals in Massachusetts, New York and Santa Monica.

BAY AREA MURALS, 1994–1997

With the addition of listed murals extending south from San Francisco down the Peninsula to San Jose and north up the East Bay to Richmond, for the first time it is possible to place the murals of any given Bay Area location into the context of overall mural work. The two main periods of mural production are the New Deal and the Contemporary Movement. The latter began in the area around 1969-70. This expanded edition also includes several older interior murals, such as those at 465 California Street in the city, and one representative residence on the Peninsula, Filoli in Woodside, which was originally a private residence, but is now open to the public. Here, as elsewhere, the type of mural painted tends to reflect the class nature of its location. San Francisco's demographic diversity encourages a wide range of styles and themes. South of the city few murals are concerned with social issues. Instead murals there tend to be trompe l'oeil or decorative paintings. They are nonetheless vital and occasionally surprising, as in the cluster of murals at Stanford's Casa Zapata (Lucie Stern Hall) dormitory, which includes not only Latino-theme murals, but a delightful piece by

By helping to sponsor WAVES OF WISDOM, the San Francisco Water Department hoped to educate local youth about the problems of dumping oil into storm drains. A poem about recycling and repeated "recycled" images appear in the mural by Catalina Gonzalez and guest artists Elba Rivera, Marta Ayala, and Gregory Macias. Acrylic on stucco. 1850 Mission Boulevard, San Francisco. (658)

Far Side cartoonist Gary Larson showing a flock of sheep grazing in a meadow with one standing on its hind legs saying, "Wait! Wait! Listen! We don't all have to be sheep, you know." The Peninsula listings are introduced by Moira F. Harris' special essay.

Earlier editions of this book divided community murals into three time periods. This has now been changed to four periods because of the significance of the CETA murals painted roughly between 1974 and 1981. The periods of mural painting for the entire United States (and the Bay Area) are thus:

First Phase, 1965–c.1974

Second Phase (CETA), 1974–1981

Third Phase, 1981–c. 1987

Fourth Phase, 1987–to the present

In San Francisco, the themes of murals painted since 1994 (in fact, since the Third Phase) are less socially engaged than in the earlier phases of the mural movement. To be sure, socially-engaged murals continue to be painted, but even among those one can see that times have changed. Recent murals honoring Cesar Chavez and Malcolm X transform them from political activists into icons to be worshiped. Respectful representation of the diversity of local residents continues to be a major mural theme. Concern for technology and its effects on humans, and environmental themes are also popular mural subjects. Themes celebrating specific ethnic groups continue to be chosen, but there are fewer than before, with more murals presenting views/celebrations of diversity than of identity (although the two are not exclusive). This may in part be due to the pressures of funding tied to working with "at risk" youth who come from mixed ethnic backgrounds.

In GOLD MOUNTAIN Ann Sherry celebrates the history of California's immigrants. A place of honor in her mural is given to the first Chinese American woman to own a car and hold a driver's license in California. Acrylic, wood, stucco, concrete. Romolo between Broadway and Vallejo, San Francisco. (595).

There have been a handful of major mural projects executed from 1994 to 1997. One is the Redstone Building, where a group of murals focusing on labor themes were painted in 1996–7. The Redstone Building was for many years known as the Labor Temple as it was home to the offices of several Bay Area trade unions. While the murals are supposed to relate to the former building tenants, the styles and themes are widely divergent, with artists using spray enamel, ballpoint pen, and light pastels to create works from social realist to minimalist in style. The murals at the building entrance and in the first part of the foyer portray important moments in San Francisco labor history.

Many of the same artists who had worked in Clarion Alley painted at the Redstone Building, a project administered by Aaron Noble. Clarion Alley itself continues to expand in innovative directions and by 1997 offered some forty works in a single cluster, including

Kenneth Huerta designs in collage, using the distortions of that medium in his final painted image. His 1994 piece for Clarion Alley, WHAT WERE YOU THINKING?, was revised two years later for the same location and is now called MOJO MAN. Clarion Alley, San Francisco. (676).

FRISCO'S WILD SIDE is a long celebration of the natural environment in varied media by Josh Sarantitis, assisted by Claire Bain, Deirdre Weinberg, Peter Collins, Chris Kirby, Estria and SPIE. Acrylic and spray paint on concrete with cast concrete. Langton Street off Folsom, San Francisco. (652).

poems and sculpture, recalling the variety of Los Angeles' wonderful St. Elmo's Village.

In the South of Market area, Johanna Poethig continues to work on collaborative projects with local youth and other artists, including poets. One of her recent works, *Health,* involved a series of ceramic figures placed in mural-like settings on area buildings, demonstrating a sense of scale appropriate for both the sites and the viewers. Dan Fontes, who has worked for years in the East Bay, created his first major work in the city, the very large Bethany Center mural. Josh Sarantitis, Jan Cook, and Salvadorean muralist Isaias Mata combined to paint *The Dreamers Among Us Still Look to the Sky* (1997) on the rear wall of Bryant School. The mural demonstrates a strong sense of space, scale, and especially utilizes the building's architectural features in its design. Cook is a recent arrival to the area, having worked previously in Los Angeles; her political orientation is immediately apparent in her work, notably in the powerful *United We Stand* mural she painted at Thurgood Marshall High School.

Sarantitis collaborated with Emmanuel Montoya and Carlos Loarca on their 1994 work, *Carnaval,* a mammoth mural which covers a 300 foot long wall on Harrison Street with a delightful panoply of dancers,

actors, and local residents. *Carnaval* frequently appears as the backdrop for local television news reports. In 1995, Sarantitis directed another large mural which covers the side of a building on Langton Street. Aided by advice from Chicago's pioneer muralist Caryl Yasko, Sarantitis used cast and shaped concrete, spray can enamel and acrylics in his multimedia piece, *Frisco's Wild Side.* In 1996 and 1997 Eric Norberg was especially active as a muralist, crossing and sometimes blurring the line between spray can graffiti and traditional murals.

Precita Eyes Muralists (PEM) continues to be the most prolific producer of murals in the area (and one of the most prolific in the entire country), and continues to expand its programs in response to community needs. PEM offers the Youth Mural Painting class, Urban Youth Arts, the Mural Painting Workshop, and, on occasion, both Kids' Art (an afterschool program) and Toddlers' Art classes. In addition to offering year round mural tours, PEM sponsors Mural Awareness Month in the spring. Expanded from a weeklong event begun in 1990, Mural Awareness Month now offers lectures, forums, award presentations, and tours. These events bring muralists a good deal of positive publicity thanks to the perseverance of Susan Cervantes and her dedi-

To the tags of writers SPIE ONE, Buter, Chief, Rios, Tase, Rigs, and I.C.P.-IRIE were added a portrait of Che, the late Cuban revolutionary, and a banner remembering his life in CHE, VIVA CUBA, 1996. Mission Street between Russia and Onondaga, San Francisco. (744).

Sign-murals sometimes helpfully indicate the unexpected as does BIRDS AND CARS by Rigo '97 with Juan Jalbuena and Gonzalo Hidalgo. 16th and Bryant, San Francisco. Acrylic on wood. (706).

cated staff. The award categories indicate the recognition PEM's effort gives to community murals: Best Youth Muralist, Best Youth Mural, Best Collaborative Mural, Best Urban Mural, Most Innovative Mural, Best New Mural, Lifetime Achievement, and Master Muralist. Although these categories adopt a competitive format which some feel is inappropriate to community-based artworks, the awards are an important form of public recognition for the muralists, benefiting both them and the city they serve. After renting storefront space for two decades, in 1995 PEM began raising money to purchase the building it occupies. Buying a building demonstrates not only the stability of a program, but attests to the organization's leadership and its fund-raising ability. The latter is usually a daunting prospect for a community-based group.

In the East Bay, Daniel Galvez' mural, *Twist of Fate,* painted on the construction fence which surrounded City Hall during the months it was undergoing repair from earthquake damage, has been "recycled" to another construction site where it continues to provide a view of a bright and growing Oakland. Galvez also completed a magnificent mural for the Malcolm X Memorial at the Audubon Ballroom in New York City. *The Firestorm Community Mural Project,* consisting of over 2,000 ceramic tiles installed at the Rockridge BART station, captures the intensity of that 1991 conflagration. In the variety and authenticity of the emotions expressed on the tiles, it is one of the most moving memorial walls in the area.

A new mural at Calvin Simmons High School (*Calvin Simmons' Ancient and Future Hip-Hop Symphony*) is notable as the first production of the Institute for Urban Arts at Laney College in Oakland. This mural program continues the tradition of local school-linked mural training which was begun at the California College of Arts and Crafts by Malaquias Montoya in the early Third Phase. The program, directed by muralist Juana Alicia, promises many future mural productions as well as providing an integrated curriculum which can lead students to four year colleges and graduate studies. In the Simmons High School mural, it is evident that the instruction is of a high quality: note the sense of scale, place, and rhythm in the design. Yet, the style of the instructor is not obvious, indicating that Alicia encourages students to develop their styles and abilities.

In Berkeley, of all places, the Unified School District obliterated almost all of Osha Neumann and

CULTURE AND COMMUNITY is the title of Keith Williams and Dan Fontes' Oakland mural. Williams often works with other artists and local children, yet his murals retain his individual style—-and joy. San Pablo and 63rd Streets, Oakland. (EB114).

Daniel Galvez' 1980 mural, *Intersections,* leaving only a few isolated square feet visible at the upper corners after covering the entire wall with institutional pink paint. "Routine maintenance," was, as usual, the reason given for the destruction, But, uniquely for destroyed murals, it was repainted in September, 1997. A few blocks away from *Intersections,* Edythe Boone produced *The People's Park Mural* in collaboration with dozens of Park users. The mural is the only thing in the area not instantly attacked with graffiti, which is a testament to the involvement of local Telegraph Avenue street people in the project.

Events such as Mural Awareness Month receive news coverage, but so do "regular" mural dedications.

Not all murals are permanently attached to a surface. Miranda Bergman's WHO HOLDS THE MIRROR? WOMEN'S LIVES, BREAST CANCER AND THE ENVIRONMENT of 1997 is a portable mural whose images encompass many experiences of Bay area women in the ongoing fight against a terrible disease. (EB222).

An earlier mural on the wall of the Toot Sweets Bakery in Berkeley presented a trompe l'oeil vision of San Francisco Bay. In the untitled work from 1994 John Wehrle once more presents the viewer with the mudflat landscape of the East Bay, now adding birds that seem to fly on and off the wall. Keim silicate on stucco. 1277 Gilman, Berkeley. (EB221).

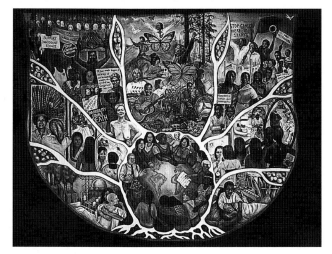

Most of the original INTERSECTIONS of 1980 was painted over. After protests, what remained was preserved in a redesigned mural painted by Osha Neumann and O'Brien Thiele in the fall of 1997. Acrylic on stucco. Willard Junior High School, Telegraph at Ward, Oakland. (EB 168)

After more than two decades of mural activity, local news media have realized that mural images are strong and colorful, and provide local interest stories for the evening news. Newspapers now routinely cover mural dedications, which indicates not only better PR work by mural sponsors and muralists, but also a greater recognition of the significance of murals to the community. Perhaps the best recent example was the dedication of *Now and Then* at Rosa Parks School. Mrs. Rosa Parks attended, and the dedication, with the mural shown prominently, was given wide coverage on both local and national television channels.

More murals were restored or received repairs than in previous years. This shows the recognition of their importance and is also the result of ongoing efforts by Ray Patlan, especially in Balmy Alley. As the listings indicate, a number of Balmy Alley murals have been restored and a number of new ones painted. Susan Cervantes has been negotiating with the San Francisco Unified School District to include mural restoration as part of the school district's regular painting maintenance program—a farsighted proposal. The San Francisco Art Commission has begun exploring guidelines for the care of other city murals as well.

The mid-1990s were not without controversy in the mural world. A new Afrocentric unilaterally nationalist *Malcolm X* mural replaced the hateful images previously painted at San Francisco State University. *Intersections,* as noted earlier, was defaced by school officials in Berkeley. Eric Norberg painted a mural with permission in the outer Mission district, only to have local police insist that it be painted over the next day. Juana Alicia's *Regeneracion/Regeneration,* commissioned by MACLA (Movimiento de Art y Cultura Latinoamericana) for their San Jose cultural center remains unmounted due to a series of snafus and lack of concern. But the response to the destruction of Neumann and Galvez' Berkeley piece indicates a public support for murals which was underestimated by authorities.

San Franciscans have willingly spent money to preserve and restore older murals and the successful results can be seen at Coit Tower and the Beach Chalet. On another occasion, whose final result is unknown at the time of writing, the preservation of a series of city-owned murals has became a source of controversy. In 1929 Gottardo Piazzoni was commissioned by the San Francisco Library's Board of Trustees to paint a series of murals along the main library's grand staircase and Great Hall. Piazzoni painted fourteen large canvases for the library, called *The Sea and the Land.* But in the 1990s San Francisco's cultural institutions began to move. Both the library and the San Francisco Museum of Modern Art built new buildings and moved out of the old building at the Civic Center. The Asian Art Museum was then scheduled to move in, leaving its former quarters in Golden Gate Park. Therein lay the problem. Directors and staff members of the Asian Art Museum didn't feel the Piazzoni murals should remain in place. Emily Sano, museum director, commented that they were "Western paintings, so they don't reflect the work of any Asian artist. Therefore, they are not consistent with our mission. It's my position that in order to preserve the murals and serve the public, it's better to put them in a different context, because we're changing the context in the library" (*San Francisco Chronicle*, February 25, 1995, 1,6). Others felt just as strongly that the Piazzoni murals should stay where they were, as moving them could damage them beyond repair, and they are part of San Francisco's cultural heritage. The discussions about the murals began long before the library moved out and still present a thorny problem to city administrators.

With profound sadness we record the passing of several master muralists. Stephen Dimitroff, who died in 1996, worked with Diego Rivera from the time of his Detroit Institute of Art murals. With his wife Lucienne Bloch, Dimitroff taught fresco classes to artists throughout the country. Dimitroff and Bloch were one of the links between Rivera's United States mural work and the contemporary community muralists, especially the fresco painters, because they taught the fresco techniques to a new generation of artists.

In the summer of 1996 Arch Williams died. He was one of the Haight-Ashbury muralists, and was committed to using his artistic skills for social change, both as a member of that group, and in numerous other projects after its breakup. Shortly before his death, he was honored with a Lifetime Achievement Award at Mural Awareness Month, and his *The Right of Education/The Seed of Freedom* was restored by Fran Valesco.

The director and painter of many of the murals at Casa Zapata on the Stanford University campus, Jose Antonio Burciaga, also died in 1996. Burciaga was a teacher, writer, and illustrator, as well as being a muralist.

Chuy Campusano, one of the earliest Mission District muralists, died early in 1997. His 1974 *Homage to Siqueiros* in a Bank of America lobby was a very influential work. In later years his style changed completely, and he designed the spectacular *Lilli Ann Mural* in geometric shapes.

Alice Campbell, director of the sixty-five women who painted *Women in Art Make the Difference* in San Leandro in 1994, also died in 1997. This mural project remains as a testament to her integrity, perseverance, and spirit.

In the course of updating the mural lists for this edition of the book, a number of older, pre-New Deal murals have been "rediscovered." All of them are interior works, and their rediscovery fills in some gaps in the mural history of the Bay region. The oldest mural is one located in a bank lobby at 465 California Street. Titled *Northwest Passage*, it was painted by Nils Hagerup between 1903 and 1906. It was installed in its present location after the 1906 earthquake and fire, along with five others painted by William Coulter between 1909 and 1920. All are seafaring scenes. When new owners acquired the building on California Street in 1997, still other early murals were discovered in lower level rooms. They were painted by Jose Moya del Pino in the 1930s, shortly after he had arrived in San Francisco from his native Spain. Moya del Pino was one of the Coit Tower muralists, and painted other murals in Redwood City, San Francisco, and San Diego.

Down the Peninsula, the listing notes murals by Victor Arnautoff, well known for his San Francisco work at Washington High School and Coit Tower. Across the Bay Arthur Mathews, whose murals painted in the old Main Library were thought to be the oldest in the area, was found to have painted an earlier series on canvas for the Greene branch of the Oakland library. Those murals are no longer at the now closed branch library, having been removed for storage. There may well be other old murals, perhaps in churches, but the point is not to discover "the oldest" mural, but to build as complete a list as possible to establish the area's mural history.

MARIN MURALS

Several murals were painted in Marin County on the North side of San Francisco Bay during the New Deal: by William Hesthal at Tamalpais High School and by Maurice del Mue at the College of Marin. There is also a mural in the County room of the San Anselmo Town Hall. Moya del Pino painted murals in a San Anselmo pharmacy and at Ross School. The famous intersection in San Anselmo was once the location of the *Famous Women* mural painted by Claire Josephson and Monica Armstrong. Their eclectic group included Golda Meir, Eleanor Roosevelt, Mother Teresa, Harriet Tubman, Clara Barton, and Helen Keller.

Perhaps the best-known mural in Marin was located on Sam Frankel's Frosty Acres building to the east of Highway 101. Painted in 1976, the mural of-

Above a laundry once stretched portraits of a pantheon of leaders. Claire Josephson and Monica Armstrong chose Golda Meir, Eleanor Roosevelt, Mother Teresa, Harriet Tubman and others for their 1982 mural, *FAMOUS WOMEN. Acrylic on wood. Fourth Street, San Anselmo. Photograph by Moira Harris.

fered a bicentennial greeting in Van Gogh-style to the thousands of commuters who passed it daily. Portraits of Washington, Franklin, Jefferson, and Lincoln faced the freeway, while an American flag was painted on the north side and a landscape on the south wall of the building.

The most impressive murals in Marin are not accessible to the general public. They are located inside San Quentin prison, and while a couple of the walls are typical of the contemporary mural movement, two are especially notable. One is an abstract, flat-color landscape of the Marin hills outside the prison. It was painted by Hilaire Dufresne on the wall below which prison activist George Jackson was shot to death. Inside the main cafeteria at the prison are three very large walls, each approximately twenty feet high and sixty feet long. Across all six walls stretches a sepia panorama of the San Francisco Bay Area, painted by an artist who clearly knew the work of Diego Rivera, as he quotes specific passages in his landscape and owes his organizational strategies to the Mexican master's style. The same idea of a panoramic history was created by another prisoner-artist in his mural at the nearby Vacaville Correctional Medical Facility. As prisoners move through the correctional system, it is not surprising that their murals share such influences.

Below the handholding, silhouetted figures in HOPE IS ALIVE, their symbolic champion attacks a cluster of freefloating AIDS viruses. The mural was painted by O'Brien Thiele, Sharon Siskin, people living with AIDS, and their friends. Acrylic on stucco. Shattuck Avenue at 59th Street, Oakland. (EB 156)

Peninsula Murals

by Moira F. Harris

The Peninsula lies between San Francisco Bay and the Pacific Ocean, linking by its highways two of northern California's major cities, San Francisco and San Jose. Two dozen towns and cities dot the Peninsula, creating the urban congestion now characteristic of its three counties: San Francisco, San Mateo, and Santa Clara. While once residents of the more rural Peninsula looked to their San Francisco connections, today their focus is more local as befits the Peninsula's new identity as Silicon Valley.

While many murals painted in private homes are beyond the scope of this book, those painted by Ernest Peixotto for Filoli, the home of the William Bournes in Woodside, should be noted. Peixotto was a San Franciscan by birth, but his art studies took him east and to Paris before 1900. His career was spent mainly in New York as teacher, arts administrator, and muralist. In 1921 he wrote in *Scribner's* magazine that muralists needed to change their sights. He suggested that those who, in the recent past, had painted murals in public buildings such as courthouses, libraries, city halls, and expositions, should consider private homes as possible locations for their work. Peixotto took his own advice and accepted a commission for the ballroom walls at Filoli. The scenes he painted suggested the Bournes' Irish heritage as they dealt with Muckross Abbey and the Lakes of Killarney. The artist visited Ireland to sketch the scenes he planned to use, but did not return to California until he was ready to install his oil on canvas paintings. To aid him in his work he created a small maquette of the ballroom. In his will the maquette was bequeathed to a nephew who had no idea what it represented. Years later that nephew happened to see the movie "Heaven Can Wait," which was filmed at Filoli. Realizing that the maquette represented the ballroom, seen in the movie as an elegant exercise room, Peixotto's nephew contacted the National Trust which administers the estate and donated the model to the Filoli collection.

MURALS OF THE 1930s

Murals are not as numerous on the Peninsula as they are in either the East Bay or San Francisco. The oldest public murals are those which resulted from the art programs of the 1930s. Some were federal public works endeavors such as the murals in the new post offices built in South San Francisco (1942), San Mateo (1937), and Redwood City (1937), while others were private projects that resulted in frescoes such as those at the Palo Alto Medical Clinic (1931) and the Allied Arts Guild in Menlo Park (1932). Not surprisingly, several of the artists whose work was commissioned— Maxine Albro, Victor Arnautoff, and Jose Moya del Pino,—had already worked on other Bay area projects, such as Coit Tower.

Mr. and Mrs. Garfield Merner began the Allied Arts Guild on property they bought in 1929. Spanish-

In a niche facing a fountain and gardens is Maxine Albro's proud symbol of CALIFORNIA, LAND OF ABUNDANCE. Allied Arts Guild, Menlo Park. (P25). Photograph by Grant Wilson.

Small grisaille panels contrast the ancient with the modern in Victor Arnautoff's murals on THE HISTORY OF MEDICINE. Here Euclid is seen at work. 300 Homer Avenue, Palo Alto. (P70). Photograph by Joan Jack.

style buildings were designed by Gardner Dailey to house artists' studios, shops, gardens, and a lunchroom. Pedro de Lemos, the director of the Stanford Art Museum, directed the design of the Guild property which included frescoes by Maxine Albro and mosaic murals by de Lemos, his wife, and daughter. The lunchroom was first run by a volunteer group and in 1951 that group, the Woodside-Atherton Auxiliary, purchased the entire Guild complex. The Auxiliary still manages Allied Arts which benefits the Lucile Salter Packard Children's Hospital at Stanford.

Not far away in Palo Alto the director of a medical clinic decided to commission murals for the entrance of a new building on Homer Avenue. The frescoes, painted by a former patient and Stanford art professor named Victor Arnautoff, illustrated in four large panels the work of famous physicians (Emmett Holt, an American pediatrician, Sir William Osler, a Canadian internist, and Harvey Cushing, the Boston neurosurgeon). Below these panels were smaller, horizontal frescoes with grisaille figures shown performing primitive methods. Subject matter had been suggested by the Clinic director, Dr. Russel V. Lee, but one panel caused initial furor. The artist depicted a clothed male physician examining a partly dressed female patient and that, according to local newspapers, made traffic slow to a crawl as Palo Altans came to be shocked. The murals were restored in 1980 and the original Clinic building (de-

signed by Birge Clark) has been granted landmark status, its use to be determined by the city which received it from the Palo Alto Medical Foundation.

Probably the most famous muralist to work on a Peninsula wall in the 1930s was Diego Rivera whose *Still Life and Blossoming Apple Trees* was painted in 1931 for the Atherton home of Mr. and Mrs. Sigmund Stern. That mural can now be seen in the foyer of Stern Hall on the University of California campus in Berkeley.

CETA MURALS OF THE 1970s

During the 1970s many communities used CETA monies to hire muralists. Nationally, those murals have not always survived. In Palo Alto, Greg Brown's CETA-funded murals have not only been repainted in situ, but redesigned for other locations when demolition of building walls made such transfers necessary. The community enjoyed his nine "California Street People" murals which he began painting on the exterior walls of downtown businesses in 1976. Each was a single figure set against a plain background, cheerfully doing something unusual: a pair of cat burglars trying to rob the second story of a business, a nun flying a paper airplane, a woman walking her pelican, and a secretive spy standing in his trench coat with a bird on his hat. The whimsy of his portrayals found approval and their trompe l'oeil style clearly influenced other muralists in the area.

Brown continues an active career as a muralist and in 1990 was chosen to represent Palo Alto in an exchange of artists with its sister city of Linkoping, Sweden. Brown painted a mural there and the Swedes gave Palo Alto an example of Swedish brightly-colored wooden outdoor sculpture. In the Swedish sculpture titled *Fjarran Vanner* (or Foreign Friends), a couple sits on a bench with a small dog at their feet and a street lamp behind them. The sculpture was placed in a small park on Embarcadero Road at Waverley Street. For some unknown reason various residents took an instant dislike to *Foreign Friends* and subjected the painted wood sculpture to various bits of vandalism (chopping off the heads of the figures, for example) until it had to be removed from view for repairs.

SCHOOL MURALS

Peninsula schools are often designed as several one-story units with long concrete walls unbroken by windows or student lockers. Such walls offer inviting large areas to be covered with murals as a part of classwork in art and art history. Terri McMahon, an art teacher at

Hillview Middle School in Menlo Park, invited Greg Brown to talk about his work to her students in 1992. That was the beginning of an ongoing mural display at the school on Santa Cruz Avenue, resulting to date in twenty-two separate murals on both exterior and interior walls. Brown's influence is clear, in the sometimes whimsical single figures usually set against plain backgrounds. Subjects of the Hillview murals are often the student artists themselves as well as their teachers and a few stray kangaroos, dinosaurs, and other unlikely friends.

A different approach to art, art history, and murals was devised by Michael Durkett, a Los Altos art teacher, in 1972. In the two year program at Georgiana P. Blach Middle School seventh graders studied famous artists, composers, and writers; as eighth graders they painted a mural reproduction of a masterpiece by one of the artists studied. The *Mona Lisa*, Grant Wood's *American Gothic*, and George Bellow's *Dempsey and Firpo* are among the sixty-six masterworks reproduced on the walls of the Blach buildings. The award-winning program, directed by Russell Hoffman since 1980, has even expanded. Chris Halmo and Clay Cahoon who had worked on the Blach school murals, developed a mural program for high school students called "Covington Musee." Twelve murals painted by students in those classes can be seen on the walls of the school district building. Durkett was recruited out of retirement to initiate a mural program at Egan Middle School with the support of both the school and the PTA.

The most extensive mural program in a Peninsula area college was begun by Jose Antonio Burciaga at Stanford University. Burciaga had already directed and painted several murals on Latino themes in Redwood City while he was a teacher at Cañada College. In 1984 he was asked to join the Stanford faculty as an art professor and to live with his family as a resident fellow in Casa Zapata, the Chicano student dormitory. Nineteen murals can now be found in Casa Zapata: on exterior walls, in stairwells, and in lounges, most painted by students in mural classes. The largest and most complex mural is Burciaga's own *Mythology and the History of Maiz* in the dorm's dining hall. It covers three walls with episodes tracing the development of corn from its PreColumbian past to the present. The central area is a version of The Last Supper with the participants reflecting Chicano sensibilities. In fact, Burciaga conducted a poll to learn who should sit around the table and the top vote-getters were Emiliano Zapata, Benito Juarez, Sor Juana Inez de la Cruz, Martin Luther King, Jr., Delores Huerta, Cesar Chavez,

Experiments may have gone awry in the Life Sciences lab at Hillview Middle School. Teachers are seen preserved in jars while odd creatures rule the room in this student mural. Acrylic on concrete block. Santa Cruz Avenue, Menlo Park. (P31). Photograph by Moira Harris.

and Che Guevara. Like some of Burciaga's other murals, this one aroused controversy, but, as Burciaga said to a reporter:

"You find my work in the local news pages, not on the art page. But that's fine, because it's art for the people, not for the art dealer. But at the same time, I realize there's a balance between aesthetics and political statements. If it becomes too political, it's propaganda. And if it becomes more decorative . . . Even decorative art is political because it's elitist. Who can afford that art?" (*San Jose Mercury News*, June 2, 1989, 17E).

MATERIALS

The materials used to create Peninsula murals reflect not only the technical skills of the artists, but changes in what is available on the market. Artists of the 1930s who knew how to work in fresco chose that medium. Another permanent way of bonding an image to a wall is mosaic, using small pieces of glass or ceramic set in concrete. Millard Sheets used mosaic for many of his commissions for branches of the Home Savings of America bank. His Peninsula example is in Mountain View. In San Mateo the glittering façade of the A.P. Giannini branch of the Bank of America was designed in glass mosaic by Louis Macouillard. And in Menlo Park the de Lemos family created their murals for the Allied Arts Guild with tile set in carved concrete. Newer works in mosaic are Maria Alquilar's mural for the San Jose airport and Lin Utzon's mural for the façade of the McEnery Convention Center in San Jose. Most

Two of the six panels which Johanna Poethig painted for the Episcopal Sanctuary in the South of Market neighborhood as part of her mural, A PLACE TO DREAM, can be seen in this photograph. Acrylic on stucco. Eighth and Folsom Streets, San Francisco. (655)

other muralists use latex or acrylic paints for their murals with an extra protective coating applied afterwards.

Very few murals in spraycan technique are found in Peninsula cities. Spraycan tags so annoyed people that most spraycan work is erased and removed as soon as it is noticed. Cupertino, Palo Alto, San Jose, and Mountain View have established anti-graffiti programs which depend on quick reporting of tags on public property. Technicians are dispatched in trucks stocked with graffiti-removal substances suitable to eradicate unwanted markings from any surface. Tags made on private property are left to property-owners to remove and volunteer efforts have responded to that need. A neighborhood group called the Beautification and Barbecue Corps of Central San Jose has worked diligently since 1994 to keep their area graffiti-free by sponsoring murals in various locations that had previously been tagged. A San Jose man was so determined to make tags vanish that he became a graffiti-busting vigilante, cleaning up and painting over tags sometimes without asking if homeowners wanted his help (*San Jose Mercury News*, March 19, 1995).

SPONSORSHIP

Although Peninsula cities may have art commissions, there do not appear to be any large-scale civic programs in support of murals. Rather most murals are one-of-a-kind efforts. Mural consciousness has been raised, mural awareness exists, but sponsoring a mural is left to individual businesses and institutions. Some muralists, like Greg Brown, John Pugh, and Noel Consigny, live and work in the area, while others—like Juana Alicia and Johanna Poethig—work on projects throughout the Bay area from their homes in San Francisco and Berkeley.

In the list of Peninsula murals which follows, communities are listed as if one encountered them on a drive south down the Peninsula from San Francisco to San Jose.

List of San Francisco Murals

If a visitor is pressed for time, the most murals can be seen in the briefest period by walking from 24th and Mission Streets (a BART stop) down 24th Street to York, then turning to go up and down Balmy Alley, next stopping at the Galeria de la Raza/Studio 24 at Bryant Street, and then visiting the Minipark just past Bryant Street.

Longer tours will find an automobile useful. The murals are listed in a reasonable order for driving tours.

The Mural Resource Center at 934 Brannan Street has a lot of information on the murals, and coordinates most of the mural painting in the City. Precita Eyes Mural Workshop offers information, workshops, and tours (285–2287). The Galeria de la Raza/Studio 24 has information, and is located in the heart of the Mission District murals (826–8009). All these resources have up-to-date information on current mural projects.

The information for each mural is presented in the following order:

Title [unofficial titles in brackets]. An asterisk indicates that the mural no longer exists.
Date completed
Funding source
Location
Size, medium and wall type [height precedes width. Sizes are often approximations]
Artist(s)

FORT MASON

1 *SAN FRANCISCO CHINATOWN 1890, 1976 (destroyed 1987)
CETA; NAP; National Park Service
Pier 2, Fort Mason
10′ x 35′, Politec acrylic on concrete
Judy Helsing

2 *SAN FRANCISCO'S GOLDEN GATE 1890, 1976 (destroyed 1987)
CETA; NAP; National Park Service
Pier 2, Fort Mason
10′ x 35′, Politec acrylic on concrete
Angela Berlingeri

3 *SUMMER REFLECTIONS, 1976 (destroyed 1987)
CETA; NAP; National Park Service
Pier 2, Fort Mason
10′ x 35′, Politec acrylic on concrete
Vincent Droney

4 *SAN FRANCISCO SKYLINE, 1976 (destroyed 1987)
CETA; NAP; National Park Service
Pier 2, Fort Mason
10′ x 35′, Politec acrylic on concrete
Richard Brown

5 *SAN FRANCISCO ORIGINAL LANDSCAPE, 1976 (destroyed 1987)
CETA; NAP; National Park Service
Pier 2, Fort Mason
10′ x 35′, Politec acrylic on concrete
Hilaire Dufresne

6 *SAN FRANCISCO MISSION DOLORES, 1976 (destroyed 1987)
CETA; NAP; National Park Service
Pier 2, Fort Mason
10′ x 35′, Politec acrylic on concrete
Adolfo Castillo

7 *1906 EARTHQUAKE, 1976 (destroyed 1987)
CETA; NAP; National Park Service
Pier 2, Fort Mason
10′ x 35′, Politec acrylic on concrete
Eileen Nelson

8 *BATTLE OF GOLDEN GATE, 1976 (destroyed 1987)
CETA; NAP; National Park Service
Pier 2, Fort Mason
10′ x 35′, Politec acrylic on concrete
John deLorimer

9 *CULTURAL PATTERN, 1976 (destroyed 1987)
CETA; NAP; National Park Service
Pier 2, Fort Mason
10′ x 35′, Politec acrylic on concrete
Diana Losch

10 *FLOATING CITY/BAY AREA WILDERNESS, 1976 (destroyed 1987)
CETA; NAP; National Park Service
Pier 2, Fort Mason
10′ x 35′, Politec acrylic on concrete
Lawrence Johnson

11 *SAN FRANCISCO RISING, 1976 (destroyed 1987)
CETA; NAP; National Park Service
Pier 2, Fort Mason
10′ x 35′, Politec acrylic on concrete
Louie LaBrie

12 *CALIFORNIA NATIVE AMERICANS, 1976
(destroyed 1987)
CETA; NAP; National Park Service
Pier 2, Fort Mason
10′ x 35′, Politec acrylic on concrete
Pamela Maxwell

13 *BRIDGES, 1976 (destroyed 1987)
CETA; NAP; National Park Service
Pier 2, Fort Mason
10′ x 35′, Politec acrylic on concrete
Jack Frost

14 TEOTIHUACAN MURAL PROJECT, 1986
Citicorp; M. H. de Young Museum
Mexican Museum, Building D, Fort Mason
8′ x 16′, Fresco
Chuy Campusano with Stephen Dimitroff and Lucienne
Bloch

15 POSITIVELY FOURTH STREET, 1976
CETA; M. H. de Young Museum
Pier 3, Fort Mason
16′ x 60′, Oil on masonite
John Wehrle and John Rampley

16 SEA FORMS, 1939
WPA
National Maritime Museum (promenade deck),
Polk Street at Aquatic Park
14′ x 125′, Commercial glazed tile
Sargent Johnson

17 UNDERSEA LIFE, 1939
WPA
National Maritime Museum (main hall),
Polk Street at Aquatic Park
10′ x 100′, Oil on canvas
Hilaire Hiler

18 PSYCHOLOGICAL COLOR CHART & DR. OSTWALD'S
COLOR SOLID, 1940
WPA
National Maritime Museum (ceiling),
Polk Street at Aquatic Park
50′ diameter, Oil on plaster
Hilaire Hiler with Richard Ayer, Thomas Dowley,
Lawrence Holmberg, and Sargent Johnson

19 [SOUTHWEST SCENE], 1940
WPA
National Maritime Museum (women's bathroom),
Polk Street at Aquatic Park
6′ x 32′, Oil on canvas
Charles Nunnamaker

20 THE MAKING OF A FRESCO SHOWING THE BUILDING
OF A CITY, 1931
William Gerstle
San Francisco Art Institute (gallery north wall),
800 Chestnut Street
18′ x 32′, Fresco
Diego Rivera

21 ARTS OF MAN, 1936
Albert Bender
San Francisco Art Institute library,
(north wall on east side), 800 Chestnut Street
30″ x 68″, Fresco
Fred Olmsted, Jr.

22 ARTS OF MAN, 1936
Albert Bender
San Francisco Art Institute library,
(north wall on west side), 800 Chestnut Street
30″ x 68″, Fresco
Gordon Langdon

23 PRIMITIVE AND WESTERN ART, 1936
Albert Bender
San Francisco Art Institute library,
(east and west walls), 800 Chestnut Street
Two panels, 30″ x 68″ each, Fresco
Ray Boynton

24 ART AND FREEDOM (THE MAN CHAINED, THE
CREATIVE ACT, and MAN FREED), 1936
Albert Bender
San Francisco Art Institute library,
(center of south wall), 800 Chestnut Street
Three panels, 30″ x 68″ each, Fresco
Victor Arnautoff

25 ARCHITECTURE AND SCULPTURE, 1936
Albert Bender
San Francisco Art Institute library,
(east side of south wall), 800 Chestnut Street
Two panels, 30″ x 68″, Fresco
Ralph Stackpole

26 TWO ALLEGORICAL FIGURES, 1936
Albert Bender
San Francisco Art Institute library,
(west side of south wall), 800 Chestnut Street
Two panels, 30″ x 68″ each, Fresco
William Hesthal

NORTH BEACH

27 [SEA LION SCENE], 1981
NAP
North Beach Housing Project,
600 Francisco Street at Taylor
Approx. 35′ x 28′, Politec acrylic on concrete
Kym Sites

28 [LAKE WITH PYRAMID], 1977
CETA
North Beach Housing Project,
590 Francisco Street at Taylor
12′ x 30′, Politec acrylic on concrete
Horace Washington

29 [YIN YANG MAN AND WOMAN], 1976
CETA
North Beach Housing Project,
120 Columbus Avenue at Francisco
35′ x 15′, Politec acrylic on concrete
Carol Nast, Percy Chester, Paula Remkiewicz, and
tenants

30 *UNTITLED, 1976
North Beach Project
North Beach Housing Project,
Francisco Street between Columbus and Taylor
Approx. 12′ x 25′, Politec acrylic on concrete
Jackie Ortez

31   [FISH SWIMMING], 1986
      OCD
      North Beach Swimming Pool,
      Lombard Street near Mason
      16' x 135', Politec acrylic, Roy Anderson latex,
      Triangle varnish on cement and wood on concrete
      Fran Valesco

32   *TELEGRAPH HILL NEIGHBORHOOD CLINIC, 1975
      NEA
      Apartment, 550 Lombard Street
      10' x 100', Politec acrylic and sealer on wood
      Karen Ezekiel and Lee Hastings

33   THE RIGHT OF EDUCATION/THE SEED OF FREEDOM,
          1987
      OCD
      Francisco Middle School,
      Stockton and Francisco Streets
      20' x 80', Politec acrylic on concrete
      Arch Williams with Jose Antonio Ochoa, Anthony Senna,
          Jo Tucker, Selma Brown, and Leo Frances Stevens

COIT TOWER, TELEGRAPH HILL

(First floor murals were restored in 1990.)

34   ANIMAL FORCE AND MACHINE FORCE, 1934
      PWAP
      Coit Tower (inner north wall)
      10' x 36', Fresco
      Ray Boynton

35   CALIFORNIA INDUSTRIAL SCENES, 1934
      PWAP
      Coit Tower (outer north wall)
      10' x 24', Fresco
      John Langley Howard

36   RAILROAD AND SHIPPING, 1934
      PWAP
      Coit Tower (outer west wall)
      10' x 10', Fresco
      William Hesthal

37   SURVEYOR AND STEELWORKER, 1934
      PWAP
      Coit Tower (outer west wall)
      Two panels, 10' x 4' each, Fresco
      Clifford Wight

38   INDUSTRIES OF CALIFORNIA, 1934
      PWAP
      Coit Tower (inner west wall)
      10' x 36', Fresco
      Ralph Stackpole

39   NEWSGATHERING, 1934
      PWAP
      Coit Tower (outer west wall)
      10' x 10', Fresco
      Suzanne Scheuer

40   LIBRARY, 1934
      PWAP
      Coit Tower (outer south wall)
      10' x 10', Fresco
      Bernard Baruch Zakheim

41   STOCKBROKER AND SCIENTIST-INVENTOR, 1934
      PWAP
      Coit Tower (outer south wall)
      Two panels, 10' x 4' each, Fresco
      Mallette Dean

42   CITY LIFE, 1934
      PWAP
      Coit Tower (inner south wall)
      10' x 36', Fresco
      Victor Arnautoff

43   BANKING AND LAW, 1934
      PWAP
      Coit Tower (outer south wall)
      10' x 10', Fresco
      George Harris

44   DEPARTMENT STORE, 1934
      PWAP
      Coit Tower (outer east wall)
      10' x 10', Fresco
      Frede Vidar

45   FARMER AND COWBOY, 1934
      PWAP
      Coit Tower (outer east wall)
      Two panels, 10' x 4' each, Fresco
      Clifford Wight

46   CALIFORNIA, 1934
      PWAP
      Coit Tower (inner east wall)
      10' x 42', Fresco
      Maxine Albro

47   MEAT INDUSTRY, 1934
      PWAP
      Coit Tower (outer east wall)
      10' x 10', Fresco
      Ray Bertrand

48   CALIFORNIA AGRICULTURAL INDUSTRY, 1934
      PWAP
      Coit Tower (outer north wall)
      10' x 27', Fresco
      Gordon Langdon

49   SAN FRANCISCO BAY, 1934
      PWAP
      Coit Tower (elevator lobby, north wall)
      9' x 54", Oil on canvas in lunette
      Otis Oldfield

50   SAN FRANCISCO BAY, NORTH, 1934
      PWAP
      Coit Tower (elevator lobby, north wall)
      9' x 54", Oil on canvas in lunette
      Jose Moya del Pino

51   BAY AREA HILLS, 1934
      PWAP
      Coit Tower
      (elevator lobby, east and west walls)
      Two panels, 9' x 54", Oil on canvas in lunettes
      Rinaldo Cuneo

52   SEABIRDS and BAY AREA MAP, 1934
      PWAP
      Coit Tower (elevator lobby, south wall)
      Three semicircular panels, approx. 2' x 4',
      Oil on canvas in lunettes
      Otis Oldfield

53   POWER, 1934
      PWAP
      Coit Tower (outer north wall)
      3' x 3', Fresco
      Fred Olmsted, Jr.

54 POWELL STREET, 1934
PWAP
Coit Tower (stairway to second floor)
Two panels, 6′ x 32′ each, Fresco
Lucien Labaudt

55 COLLEGIATE SPORTS, 1934
PWAP
Coit Tower
(second floor, by staircase)
9′ x 13′, Fresco
Parker Hall

56 SPORTS, 1934
PWAP
Coit Tower
(second floor, by staircase)
9′ x 10′, Fresco
Edward Terada

57 CHILDREN AT PLAY, 1934
PWAP
Coit Tower
(second floor, by staircase)
9′ x 6′, Fresco
Ralph Chesse

58 HUNTING IN CALIFORNIA, 1934
PWAP
Coit Tower
(second floor, elevator wall)
9′ x 12′, Fresco
Edith Hamlin

59 OUTDOOR LIFE, 1934
PWAP
Coit Tower
(second floor, outer wall)
9′ x 22′, Fresco
Ben F. Cunningham

60 HOME LIFE, 1934
PWAP
Coit Tower
(second floor, south alcove)
9′ x 34′, Egg tempera
Jane Berlandina

CHINATOWN

61 BRIDGE OF LOVE, 1988
OCD
On Lok House Senior Citizens' Center
Powell Street near Broadway
18′ x 60′, Novacolor acrylic on concrete
Miranda Bergman

62 THE SEEDS WE PLANT NOW WILL GIVE OUR
CHILDREN SHADE, 1990
OCD; On Lok House
On Lok House Senior Citizens' Center,
Powell near Broadway
10′-2′ x 108′, Acrylic on wood
Miranda Bergman

63 PING YUEN TAI CHI, 1982
OCD
Ping Yuen Housing Project,
795 Pacific Street at Stockton
20′ x 160′, Politec acrylic on concrete
Josie Grant

64 [BOK SEN AND IMMORTALS, THREE WISDOMS, AND
CHINESE ZODIAC], 1979
OCD; NIIP
Ping Yuen Housing Project,
895 Pacific Street at Trenton Alley
Five walls totalling 20′ x 160′, Acrylic on concrete
Josie Grant

65 FISH STRUGGLING UPSTREAM, 1983
MRC; OCD
Ping Yuen Housing Project,
895 Pacific Street at Trenton Alley
35′ x 30′, Various media on asphalt playground
James Dong

66 [CHINESE IN SAN FRANCISCO], 1987
OCD
Building, 950 Washington Street
between Stockton Street and Stone
50′ x 25′, Acrylic on stucco
K. S. Chan

67 HISTORY OF COMMODORE STOCKTON SCHOOL,
1974
Alvarado School Art Workshop
Commodore Stockton School, 950 Clay Street
Approx. 25′ x 70′, Housepaint on concrete
James Dong and the Kearny Street Workshop

68 UNTITLED, 1986
OCD
Wall, Spofford Alley between Washington Street and Clay
8′ x 29′, Liquitex acrylic on masonite
Gail Aratani

69 UNTITLED, 1986
OCD
Chinese Playground wall,
Sacramento Street between Stockton and Waverly
35′ x 45′, Politec acrylic, Liquitex acrylic,
and housepaint on concrete over brick
James Dong

70 [CHINESE-AMERICAN HISTORY], 1988
OCD
YMCA Playground,
855 Sacramento Street at Waverly Alley
8′ x 48′, Pictor acrylic on cement
Victor Fan

71 [PHOENIX], 1988
Private funding
Store wall at Walter U. Lam Place and Clay Street,
Portsmouth Square
12′ x 20′, Acrylic on stucco
K. S. Chan

72 [DRAGON], 1988
Private funding
Store (side wall), Clay and Grant Streets
10′ x 20′, Acrylic on stucco
K. S. Chan

73 *I-HOTEL MURAL, 1975
CETA; NAP
International Hotel, Jackson near Kearny Streets
8′ x 65′, Acrylic on concrete, brick, and wood
James Dong and the Kearny Street Workshop

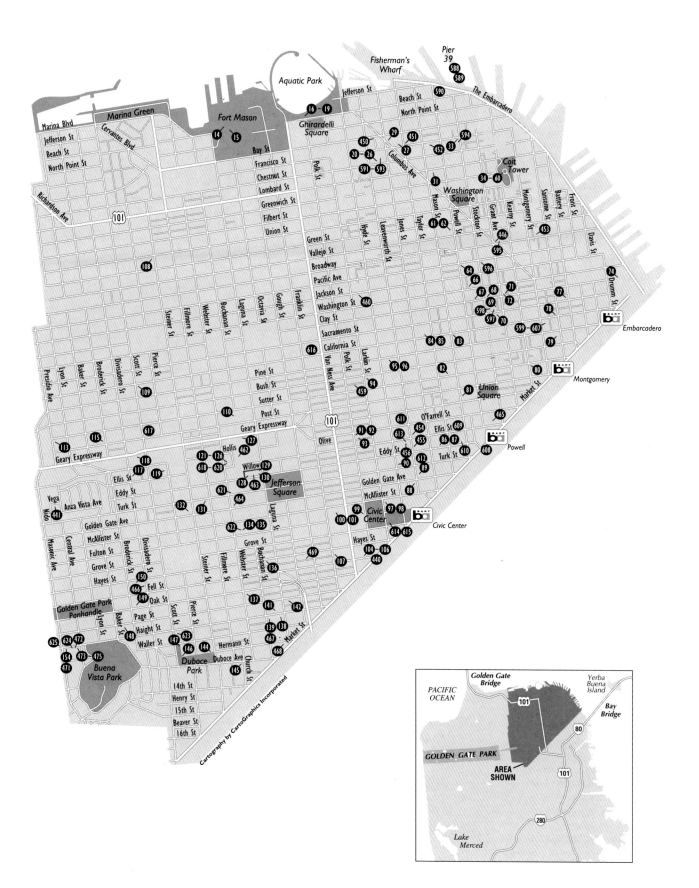

446   NORTH BEACH SCENES, 1988
      Private funding
      Apartment building
      Broadway and Columbus Streets
      Facade of two story building, Kelly-Moore exterior
         housepaint on masonry blocks
      Bill Weber with Tony Klaas

FINANCIAL DISTRICT

74   [FIVE MAPS], 1939
      Golden Gate International Exposition
      World Trade Center,
      Ferry Building (entrance ramp), Market Street
      Various dimensions, Lacquer on wood
      Miguel Covarrubias

75   *MAP, 1962
      Funding unknown
      Ferry Building, Market Street
      5' x 10', Glass mosaic
      Edith Hamlin

76   *[SAN FRANCISCO HISTORY], 1965
      Private funding
      Fidelity Savings and Loan Association,
      260 California Street
      Three panels, Fresco
      Lucienne Bloch and Stephen Dimitroff

77   TRADERS OF THE ADRIATIC, 1922
      Federal Reserve Bank
      Kaplan, McLaughlin, Diaz Company (lobby),
      301 Battery Street at Sacramento
      9' x 40', Oil on canvas
      James Guerin

78   [SAN FRANCISCO SCENES], 1967
      Private funding
      Bank of California, 400 California Street (2nd floor)
      Three panels, 15' wide, Acrylic on canvas
      Don Kingman

79   ALLEGORY OF CALIFORNIA, 1931
      Private funding
      Pacific Stock Exchange Club,
      (stairway and ceiling outside dining room),
      155 Sansome Street near Pine
      142.5 square feet, Fresco
      Diego Rivera

80   [BEACH SCENE], 1984
      Private funding
      Galleria Park Hotel roof,
      Sutter and Kearny Streets
      15' x 20', Acrylic on roof
      Dick Fossleman and Karen Lusebrink

UNION SQUARE

81   LANDSCAPE, 1923
      Spring Valley Water Company
      San Francisco Water Department (north wall),
      425 Mason Street
      8' x 16', Oil on canvas
      Maynard Dixon

82   [WOMEN ROLE MODELS], 1979
      CETA; YWCA
      YWCA Downtown, 620 Sutter Street near Mason
      8' diameter, Politec acrylic on plywood
      Fran Valesco

NOB HILL

83   CALIFORNIA HISTORY AND LEGENDS, 1926
      Private funding
      Mark Hopkins Hotel, Room of the Dons
      999 California Street
      Four panels, 7' x 21',
      One panel, 12' x 7', Oil on canvas
      Maynard Dixon, Frank von Sloun

84   [CHURCH HISTORY], 1949
      Private funding
      Grace Cathedral (north and south interior walls),
      1051 Taylor Street between Sacramento and California
      9' x 105', Wax emulsion on plaster
      Jan Henryk De Rosen

85   ADORATION OF THE VIRGIN, 1946
      Mrs. James L. Flood
      Grace Cathedral (Nativity Chapel),
      1051 Taylor Street between Sacramento and California
      20' x 10', Wax and oil emulsion fresco
      Jan Henryk De Rosen

TENDERLOIN

86   [UNTITLED], 1989
      Parks and Recreation Department; SFAC
      Father Boedekker Park, Jones and Eddy Streets
      11' x 40' free form, Ceramic tiles painted with glazes
      Johanna Poethig and children of the area

87   FLYING DOGS BREATHING FIRE, 1990
      LEF Foundation
      Father Boedekker Park, Jones and Eddy Streets
      15' x 20', Acrylic, tile and wood on plaster
      Johanna Poethig

88   REFLECTIONS OF CULINARY WORKERS' STRUGGLE,
         1988
      Carpenters' Local 22; Local 2 H.E.R.E.
      Leavenworth at Golden Gate Avenue
      12'-1' x 117', Acrylic on concrete
      Ted Abraham, Kim Anno, and Marion Kendrick

89   [THE EARTH], 1979
      Private funding
      Central City Hospitality House (Art Department),
      146 Leavenworth Street
      5' x 8', Liquitex acrylic and oil on concrete
      Mike Mosher, Fell Williams, Claire Davidson, James
         "Spider" Taylor, and the Hospitality House Arts &
         Crafts Program

90   [TROMPE L'OEIL IONIC COLUMNS BEHIND
         DEMOLISHED BRICK WALLS], 1983
      OCD
      Building, Turk and Hyde Streets
      35' x 70', Unknown paint on brick
      John Russell Wullbrandt

POLK GULCH

91   [UNDERWATER SCENE], 1979 (south side restored
         and altered 1990)
      Mitchell Brothers Film Group
      Mitchell Brothers Theater,
      895 O'Farrell Street
      8,000 square feet, Acrylic on concrete
      Gary Graham, Ed Monroe, Todd Stanton, and Lou Silva

92 [FOREST SCENE], 1990
Mitchell Brothers Film Group
Mitchell Brothers Theater,
O'Farrell and Polk
20'-40' x 120', Acrylic on stucco
Lou Silva

93 STRONG ROOTS, HEALTHY TREE, 1989
Private funding; OCD
Center for Southeast Asian Refugee Resettlement,
Olive Alley at Polk Street
40' x 60', Acrylic on stucco
Johanna Poethig

94 TACTILE MURAL, 1976
CETA
Rose Resnick Center for the Blind,
1299 Bush Street
15' x 22', Fabric on plaster
Cynthia Grace

95 [TROPICAL BEASTS], 1977
Private funding
Redding Elementary School,
1421 Pine Street near Larkin
10' x 200', Politec acrylic on concrete
Karen Ezekiel, SFAI students, and elementary school
    children

96 [OUTER SPACE AND ASTRONAUTS], 1978
Private funding
Redding Elementary School,
1421 Pine Street near Larkin
30' x 150', Politec acrylic
and sealer on concrete
Karen Ezekiel, SFAI students, and elementary school
    children

CIVIC CENTER

97 PIONEERS LEAVING THE EAST and PIONEERS
    ARRIVING IN THE WEST, 1914
Panama-Pacific International Exposition
San Francisco Main Library Reference Room
(north wall), Humanities Room (east wall),
Larkin Street at McAllister
Two panels, 12' x 50' each, Oil on canvas
Frank Vincent Dumond

98 THE SEA AND THE LAND, 1931; 1932
Private funding
San Francisco Main Library
(walls flanking main staircase),
Larkin Street at McAllister
Fourteen panels, 11' x 6' each, Oil on canvas
Gottardo F. P. Piazzoni

99 MAP OF SAN FRANCISCO, 1939
WPA
Assessor's office (3rd floor north wall),
City Hall, Civic Center
20' x 50', Oil on canvas
Marion Simpson

100 U.S. SIGNS THE CHARTER OF THE UNITED NATIONS,
    JUNE 26, 1945, 1956
United Nations
Herbst Theater (foyer),
Van Ness Avenue at McAllister
6' x 10', Oil on canvas
Howard Chandler Christy

101 EARTH, AIR, FIRE, AND WATER, 1915
Panama-Pacific International Exposition
Herbst Theater (north and south walls),
Van Ness Avenue at McAllister
Eight panels, 18' x 10 1/2' each, Oil on canvas
Frank Brangwyn

102 *AFRO-AMERICAN HISTORICAL AND CULTURAL
        SOCIETY, 1974
CETA; OCD
Afro-American Historical and Cultural Society,
680 McAllister Street
12' x 25', Politec acrylic on plywood
Arthur Monroe and students from Fillmore-Fell
    Corporation

103 *UNTITLED, 1975
Fillmore-Fell Corporation
Building, 646 Gough Street
10' x 60', Acrylic on plywood
Bob Gayton

104 PRIME TIME/NO TIME, 1980
CAC
New College of California Law School library,
50 Fell Street near Market
Two triangular panels, approx. 8' x 30' each,
Politec acrylic on plaster
Ray Patlan

105 JUST US, 1980
CAC
New College of California Law School, second floor,
50 Fell Street near Market
Approx. 20' x 40', Politec acrylic on concrete
Ray Patlan

440 THE LINEAL DOMINATION OF THE SIXTH AGE, 1988
Funding unknown
New College of California Law School,
second floor, 50 Fell Street near Market
Four panels: two measuring 12' x 50' and two
measuring 12' x 6', Acrylic on sheetrock
Betsie Miller-Kusz and mural students: Liesbeth
    Middelberg, Yung Shin, and Linda Tunner

106 VENCEREMOS, 1981
CAC
New College of California Law School,
Main stairway, 50 Fell Street near Market
1,500 square feet, Politec acrylic on plaster
Ray Patlan

107 LEARNING WALL, 1989
OCD; SFAC
San Francisco Unified School District headquarters,
Rear wall, Franklin and Hayes Streets
45' x 100', Art Guerra acrylic on stucco
Keith Sklar

UNION STREET

108 THE LIFE OF MARY, 1966
Private funding
St. Mary the Virgin Episcopal Church courtyard,
2325 Union Street near Steiner
Five panels, 8' x 4' each, Fresco
Lucienne Bloch and Stephen Dimitroff

UPPER FILLMORE

109 GARDEN, 1982
Learning and Education through the Arts
Cobb School, 2725 California Street near Steiner
3' x 80', House paint on concrete
Patricia Rodriguez and Fran Valesco

JAPANTOWN

110 YWCA-WESTERN ADDITION, 1979
CETA; YWCA
YWCA-Western Addition (interior),
1830 Sutter Street near Buchanan
Two panels, 12' x 50',
Two panels, 12' x 70',
Politec acrylic on plaster
Fran Valesco

111 *UNTITLED, 1981
CAC; MRC; OCD
Building, 1834 Sutter Street
35' x 150', Politec acrylic on wood
James Dong

FILLMORE

112 *WAPAC MURAL, 1975; 1977
OCD
WAPAC building, 1956 Sutter Street
26' x 24', Unknown paint on wood
David Bradford

113 UNTITLED, 1977
Funding unknown
Booker T. Washington Community Center,
800 Presidio Drive
Approx. 15' x 60', Unknown paint on stucco
Bob Gayton

114 *UNTITLED, 1973; 1974; 1975
Private funding
Building, 631 Divisadero Street
6' x 15', Oil on wood
Pyramid-it A. Kaaba

115 UNTITLED, 1977
Private funding
Westside Housing Project,
Post and Broderick Streets
5' x 12', Unknown paint on concrete
Reid

116 *SERGEANT HENDERSON PARK, 1973
Private funding
Building wall next to park,
Divisadero Street between Turk and Eddy
7' x 100', Unknown paint on concrete
Sondra Chirlton, Doug Huntley, Craig Moline, Milton
Schueler, and Mark Soetaert

117 [A SALUTE TO ARTISTS], 1975
NIIP
Beidman Minipark, O'Farrell Street
near Divisadero and Scott
8' x 40', Politec acrylic on wood
Dewey Crumpler and Neighborhood Youth Corps

118 BENJAMIN FRANKLIN, 1985
OCD
Ben Franklin School, 1430 Scott Street
(best viewed from Geary Street near Scott)
30' x 60', Politec and Liquitex acrylics on concrete
Selma Brown

119 [MEDICAL SCIENCE], 1968
SFAC
District Health Center #1 (entrance facade),
1301 Pierce Street
8' x 6', Glazed tiles
Win Ng

120 THE CHILDREN OF SAN FRANCISCO, 1968
SFAC
San Francisco Public Health Center #2,
Steiner and Ellis Streets
8' x 20', Mixed media on masonite
Dewey Crumpler

121 UNTITLED, 1975
FSSA; Private funding
Raphael Weill Elementary School (interior),
1505 O'Farrell Street near Webster
8' x 20', Politec acrylic on plywood
Peretti and Park

122 [MATH GAMES], 1977
Private funding
Raphael Weill Elementary School,
1505 O'Farrell Street near Webster
14' x 60', Politec acrylic on plywood
Peretti and Park

123 THE PEOPLE'S GAME, 1977; 1980
Private funding
Raphael Weill Elementary School,
1505 O'Farrell Street near Webster
14' x 60', Politec acrylic and Roy Anderson
paint on concrete
Peretti and Park

124 [FACES, RAINBOW, BOXES, ANIMALS, AND
FLOWERS], 1980
Private funding
Raphael Weill Elementary School,
1505 O'Farrell Street near Webster
Approx. 6' x 18', Politec acrylic on concrete
Peretti and Park

125 [CAREERS AND LANDSCAPE], 1980; 1982
Private funding
Raphael Weill Elementary School,
1505 O'Farrell Street near Webster
Two panels, approx. 25' x 30' each,
Politec acrylic on concrete
Peretti and Park

126 [THE LIFE OF RAPHAEL WEILL], 1982
OCD; Private funding
Raphael Weill Elementary School,
1505 O'Farrell Street near Webster
Four panels, approx. 20' x 8' each,
Politec acrylic on concrete
Peretti and Park

127 [BLACK HISTORY, AFRICAN MOTIFS, ROLE MODELS,
AND FANTASY], 1975
CETA; OCD; YMCA
YMCA Western Addition,
1530 Buchanan Street near Geary
Two panels, 16' x 60' each,
One panel 16' x 30',
House paint on plaster
Fran Valesco and teenagers from the YMCA

128 AFRICAN MASK, 1976
SFHA
Plaza East Housing Project,
Interior staircases,
1225, 1245, and 1265 Laguna Street near Eddy
Nine panels, 8' x 8' each,
Cal-Western acrylic on concrete
Caleb Williams

129 [AFRICAN SCENES], 1973
Alvarado School Art Workshop; SFHA
Plaza East Housing Project,
Laguna Street and Eddy,
and Buchanan Street and Eddy
Two panels, 8' x 30' each,
Cal-Western acrylic on concrete
Horace Washington and Caleb Williams

130 [AFRICAN SCENES], 1975
CETA; NYC; SFHA
Plaza East Housing Project, west wall,
Turk Street and Laguna
5' x 30', Acrylic on concrete
Caleb Williams and Neighborhood Youth Corps

131 [UNTITLED], 1988
SFAC
Northern Police Station,
Turk Street and Fillmore
3' x 8', Community cast cement
Horace Washington

132 UNTITLED, 1977
CETA
Minipark,
Golden Gate Avenue and Steiner Streets
Two panels, 20' x 30' and 20' x 40',
Acrylic on wood
Dewey Crumpler and Neighborhood Youth Corps

HAYES VALLEY

133 *A TRIBUTE TO BLACK THEATER, 1975
Private funding
Western Addition Cultural Center (interior),
762 Fulton Street between Webster and Buchanan
9' x 45', Acrylic on plaster
Judy Shannon

134 [SAN FRANCISCO BREWING], 1935
Acme Brewery
Western Addition Cultural Center, third floor,
762 Fulton Street between Webster and Buchanan
Two panels, approx. 6' x 18' each,
One panel, 6' x 12', Fresco
Jose Moya del Pino

135 A CELEBRATION OF AFRICAN AND AFRICAN-
AMERICAN ARTISTS, 1984
OCD
Western Addition Cultural Center,
762 Fulton Street between Webster and Buchanan
45' x 131', Politec acrylic on concrete
Dewey Crumpler, with Kemit Amenophis, Bonnie Long,
and Sandra Roberts

136 UNTITLED, 1978
Funding unknown
Hayes Valley Playground,
Hayes Street near Buchanan
Approx. 4' x 120', Acrylic on concrete
Scott Guein

137 ART, NATURE, AND CIVILIZATION, 1934
WPA
John Muir School, auditorium foyer,
Webster Street at Oak
Two panels, 7 1/2' x 15' each, Fresco
David Park

138 A DISSERTATION ON ALCHEMY, 1937
WPA
University of California Extension, Woods Hall,
Laguna Street between Haight and Hermann
10' x 15', Fresco
Reuben Kadish and Urban Neininger

139 [CHILDREN AT PLAY], 1984
Private funding
French American International School schoolyard,
Haight Street and Buchanan
Dimensions unknown, Acrylic on stucco
Marilyn Gaines Gayton

140 *NEIGHBORHOOD ARTS THEATER, 1974
NIIP
Neighborhood Arts Theater,
220 Buchanan Street between Waller and Haight
Approx. 15' x 55', Politec acrylic on concrete
Art Grant, A. Fisher, and neighborhood residents

141 THE WALDEN HOUSE EXTENDED FAMILY UNDER THE
TREE OF ENLIGHTENED WISDOM, 1989
CAC; Private funding
Walden House,
Haight Street between Buchanan and Laguna
23' x 14', Liquitex, Novacolor, and
Politec acrylics on stucco
Michael Rios

142 ODE TO ROUSSEAU, 1976
CETA
Page Street Minipark,
between Laguna Street and Octavia
Approx. 30' x 70', Politec acrylic on wood
Josie Grant

143 *[ATHLETICS], 1976
NIIP
Red Shield Playground,
340 Fillmore Street near Page
8' x 80', Acrylic on plywood
Camille Marvin Breeze

144 MILES DAVIS, 1976
Funding unknown
United Projects (interior),
137 Steiner Street between Herman and Waller
Dimensions unknown,
Cal-Western acrylic on plaster
Caleb Williams

145 UNTITLED, 1979
OCD
Home for Visiting Nurses,
401 Duboce Street at Church
9' x 101', Acrylic on concrete
Caleb Williams

146 HARVEY MILK MEMORIAL MURAL, 1988
OCD
Harvey Milk Recreational Center, Duboce Park,
Duboce Street and Scott
35' x 50', Acrylic on concrete
Johanna Poethig

147 [CAMPFIRE SCENES], 1982
Koret Foundation
Storefront, Scott Street and Haight
20' x 65', Politec acrylic on stucco
Chuy Campusano and youth

148 [CHILDREN'S SILHOUETTES], 1982
Private funding
Florence Martin Children's Center,
1155 Page Street
Two panels, 5' x 85' and 6' x 40',
Politec acrylic on stucco
Elizabeth Greene and P.T. Greene

149 WHALE, 1977
Private funding
San Francisco Fire Department warehouse,
1152 Oak Street
20' x 90', Unknown paint on wood
Kevin McCloskey

150 [STREET SCENE], 1975
Private funding
Church's Fried Chicken,
1309 Hayes Street at Divisadero
Approx. 15' x 25', Acrylic on stucco
Clarkston Peadee

44l THE SPIRIT OF RAOUL WALLENBERG, 1989
San Francisco Education Fund
Raoul Wallenberg High School,
40 Vega Street
12' x 30', Acrylic on stucco
Susan Cervantes and students

151 *OUR HISTORY IS NO MYSTERY, 1976
(replaced by #152 in 1988)
Federal Neighborhood Bicentennial
Beautification Fund; NIIP
Retaining wall at Hayes Street and Masonic
2'-12' x 390', Politec acrylic on concrete
Haight-Ashbury Muralists: Jane Norling, Miranda
   Bergman, Arch Williams, Jo Tucker, Vicky Hamlin, and
   Thomas Kunz

152 EDUCATE TO LIBERATE, 1988
OCD
Retaining wall at Hayes Street and Masonic
2'-12' x 390', Novacolor acrylic on concrete
Miranda Bergman, Jane Norling. Maria Ramos, Vicky
   Hamlin, and Arch Williams

HAIGHT-ASHBURY

153 UNTITLED, 1977
Private funding
Haight-Ashbury Children's Center,
1101 Masonic Street at Page
10' x 17', Acrylic on concrete
Consuelo Mendez

154 CRISPUS ATTUCKS: THE BOSTON MASSACRE,
   MARCH 5, 1770, 1976
SFMMA
William De Avila School (interior),
Haight Street and Masonic
8' x 20', Roy Anderson paint on masonite
Horace Washington and Caleb Williams

155 *TWO HUNDRED YEARS OF RESISTANCE, 1976
SFMMA
Uganda Liquors, Haight Street and Masonic
8' x 20', Politec acrylic on masonite
Haight-Ashbury Muralists: Miranda Bergman, Jane
   Norling, Arch Williams, Jo Tucker, Vicky Hamlin, and
   Miles Stryker

156 *RAINBOW PEOPLE, 1972; 1974
Private funding
Seeds of Life Grocery,
Haight Street near Masonic
8' x 20', Oil on plywood (1972);
Politec acrylic on masonite (1974)
Haight-Ashbury Muralists

157 *UNITY EYE, 1973
Private funding
Building, Haight Street and Ashbury
8' x 15', Politec acrylic on plywood
Miranda Bergman, Andrea Cole, Jane Norling, and Jo
   Tucker

158 EACH COME TOGETHER IN YOUR OWN PERCEIVING
   OF YOURSELF, 1976
Federal Neighborhood Bicentennial
Beautification Fund
Apartment building,
1815 Page Street near Stanyan
44' x 24', Politec acrylic on masonite
Selma Brown and Ruby Newman

159 *THE PHOENIX MURAL, 1974
Private funding
Building,
1818 Haight Street at Shrader
15' x 65', Acrylic on stucco
Eugene Curley

160 EVOLUTION RAINBOW, 1969; 1981; 1983
Private funding
Storefront, Cole Street at Haight
10' x 30', Latex house paints on concrete
Joana Zegri

161 *[NATIVE AMERICAN LANDSCAPE], 1976
Private funding
Storefront apartments
612 Clayton Street near Haight
45' x 7'-10', Acrylic on stucco
Eugene Curley

162 [UNICORN BILLBOARD], c. 1977
Private funding
Billboard on Belvedere Street and Haight
8' x 20', Oil on masonite
Artist unknown

163 THE SPIRIT OF YOUTH IN AMERICA, 1977
Federal Neighborhood Bicentennial
Beautification Fund
Paltenghi Youth Center,
1525 Waller Street near Frederick
2,400 square feet,
Politec acrylic on concrete and plaster
Charles Lobdell, Phil van Dalen, Wendell Jones, and
   Evelyn Messinger

164 [TIGER], 1980
Private funding
Residence,
3579 Frederick Street near Clayton
24' x 35', Unknown paint on wood
Charles Marchiori

165 A PLACE IN THE SUN, 1971
Private funding
Bradley's Corner,
800 Cole Street near Carl
13' x 30', Oil on concrete
Raymond Howells

PARNASSUS HEIGHTS

166 *UNTITLED, 1975
Standard Oil Company
San Francisco Polytechnic High School
Approx. 20' x 350',
Mosaic tiles and acrylic on concrete
Peretti and Park, and students

167 SUPERSTITIOUS MEDICINE, 1935
SERA
UCSF Medical Center,
Health Sciences West,
Classroom HSW 300,
Parnassus Street at 3rd Avenue
7' x 9'7", Fresco
Bernard Baruch Zakheim, Phyllis Wrightson, Leon Bibel,
   and Joseph Kelly

168 RATIONAL MEDICINE, 1935
SERA
UCSF Medical Center,
Health Sciences West,
Classroom HSW 301,
Parnassus Street at 3rd Avenue
7' x 9'7", Fresco
Bernard Baruch Zakheim, Phyllis Wrightson, Leon Bibel,
   and Joseph Kelly

169 HISTORY OF MEDICINE IN CALIFORNIA, 1938
WPA
UCSF Medical Center, UCSF Hospital,
Toland Hall, U142,
Parnassus Street at 3rd Avenue
Six back wall panels, Four front wall panels,
4' 5" x 14'2" each, Fresco
Bernard Baruch Zakheim, with Phyllis Wrightson, and Koi
   Anderson (plasterer)

170 UNIVERSITY OF CALIFORNIA MEDICAL CENTER, 1976
San Francisco Unified School District;
Private funding
UCSF Medical Center,
Parnassus Street at Fourth Avenue
8' x 28', Unknown paint on plaster
Nancy Thompson, Ruth Asawa, Phoebe Brown, and
   students

INNER RICHMOND

171 HARVEST AND LAND, 1934
WPA
Roosevelt Junior High School,
First floor lobby,
Arguello Street and Geary
5' x 20', Oil on canvas
Nelson Pool

172 EDUCATION, 1934
WPA
Roosevelt Junior High School,
Second floor lobby,
Arguello Street and Geary,
5' x 25', Oil on canvas
George Wilson Walker

LAUREL HEIGHTS

173 THE WEDDING CEREMONY, 1933
Private funding
Jewish Community Center courtyard,
3200 California Street
100 square feet, Fresco
Bernard Baruch Zakheim

PRESIDIO

174 PEACETIME ACTIVITIES OF THE ARMY, 1935
SERA
Military Chapel at the Presidio,
Fischer Loop near Infantry Terrace
10' x 35' 8", Fresco
Victor Arnautoff, with Suzanne Scheuer, B. Cunningham,
   Edward Terada, Richard Ayer, M. Hardy, P. Hall, P.
   Vinson, G. Serrano, M. Cohen, P. Zoloth, T. Mead,
   and W. Mannex (plasterer)

OUTER RICHMOND

175 ARGONNE ELEMENTARY SCHOOL MURAL II, 1976
1976
Alvarado School Art Workshop; CETA;
San Francisco Unified School District
Argonne Elementary School,
675 18th Avenue near Anza
Three panels: 16' x 3 1/2',
6 1/2' square, and 3' x 30',
Roy Anderson and Cal-Western paint on wood and metal
Fran Valesco and school children

176 LIFE OF WASHINGTON, 1935
WPA
George Washington High School lobby,
32nd Avenue and Anza
1,600 square feet, Fresco
Victor Arnautoff

177 ADVANCEMENT OF LEARNING THROUGH THE
        PRINTING PRESS, 1936
    WPA
    George Washington High School library,
    32nd Avenue and Anza
    5 1/2' x 27', Fresco
    Lucien Labaudt

178 CONTEMPORARY EDUCATION, 1936
    WPA
    George Washington High School library,
    32nd Avenue and Anza
    5 1/2' x 27', Fresco
    Ralph Stackpole

179 MODERN AND ANCIENT SCIENCE, 1936
    WPA
    George Washington High School library entrance,
    32nd Avenue and Anza
    4' x 10', Fresco
    Gordon Langdon

180 [MULTI-ETHNIC HERITAGE: BLACK, ASIAN,
        NATIVE/LATIN AMERICAN], 1974
    San Francisco Unified School District
    George Washington High School,
    32nd Avenue and Anza
    Three panels: 6' x 15', 12' x 16',
    6' x 15', Politec acrylic on masonite
    Dewey Crumpler

181 PLAYLAND AND THE MOVIE STARS, 1979
    Balboa Merchants Association; CETA
    Balboa Theater (side), 38th Avenue and Anza
    1,600 square feet, Politec acrylic on concrete
    Fran Valesco, Claire Josephson, Dave Warren, CETA
        Summer youth, Playland Research Association,
        Richmond Beautification Project, and Washington High
        School students

182 SAN FRANCISCO SCENES, 1937 (restored 1988)
    WPA
    Beach Chalet main hall,
    Great Highway at Golden Gate Park
    9' high (approx. 1,500 square feet), Fresco
    Lucien Labaudt

SUNSET DISTRICT

183 ELIZABETH MENNIE MEMORIAL MURAL, 1956
    Private funding
    Lawton Elementary School, 1570 31st Avenue
    and Lawton
    6' x 12', Acrylic tempera on canvas
    Edith Hamlin

184 [KITES, THE SUNSET MANDALA, AND LIBRARY
        BOOKS], 1982
    NAP; SFMMA
    Ortega Branch, San Francisco Public Library,
    3223 Ortega at 39th Avenue
    10' x 22', Politec acrylic on stucco
    Joseph Cruz, Paul Kensinger, Henry Sultan, Jennifer
        Badger, and the Sunset Mural Workshop

185 HISTORY OF THE SUNSET, 1980
    CETA
    Retaining wall,
    Ortega between 39th and 40th Avenues
    6'-10' x 2 blocks long,
    Politec acrylic and Triangle
    Varnish on concrete
    Henry Sultan, Fran Valesco, and the Sunset Mural
        Workshop

444 UNTITLED, 1979 (restored 1986)
    Private funding
    Sunset Nursery School, 4245 Lawton at the
    Great Highway
    12' x 50', Acrylic on stucco
    Henry Sultan and the Sunset Mural Workshop

445 UNTITLED, 1979 (restored 1986)
    Private funding
    Sunset Nursery School, 4245 Lawton at
    the Great Highway
    12' x 50', Acrylic on stucco
    Henry Sultan and the Sunset Mural Workshop

186 ST. FRANCIS and CHILDREN AND THEIR ANIMAL
        FRIENDS, 1934
    PWAP
    The Mothers' House entrance,
    Fleishhacker Playfield/Zoo,
    Sloat Boulevard near the Great Highway
    Two panels, 13' x 6' each, Mosaic
    Helen, Margaret, and Ester Bruton

187 NOAH AND HIS ARK, 1938
    WPA
    The Mothers' House (store interior),
    Fleishhacker Playfield/Zoo,
    Sloat Boulevard near the Great Highway
    Two panels: 8' x 30' and 10' x 72', Fresco
    Dorothy Wagner Pucinelli

188 NOAH AND HIS ARK: THE WATERS SUBSIDING AND
        RENEWAL, 1938 (restored 1975)
    WPA
    The Mothers' House (store interior),
    Fleishhacker Playfield/Zoo,
    Sloat Boulevard near the Great Highway
    Two panels: 8' x 30' and 10' x 72', Fresco
    Helen Forbes

189 [SAVANNAH SCENE], 1977
    CETA
    Elephant Yard,
    Fleishhacker Playfield/Zoo,
    Sloat Boulevard near the Great Highway
    20' x 120', Acrylic on concrete
    John Rampley

SAN FRANCISCO STATE UNIVERSITY

190 *[SAN FRANCISCO SKYLINE], 1979 (destroyed 1988)
    SFSU Humanities Department
    San Francisco State University,
    Humanities Building Room 331,
    19th Avenue and Holloway
    9' x 20', Politec acrylic on plaster
    Ray Patlan and university students

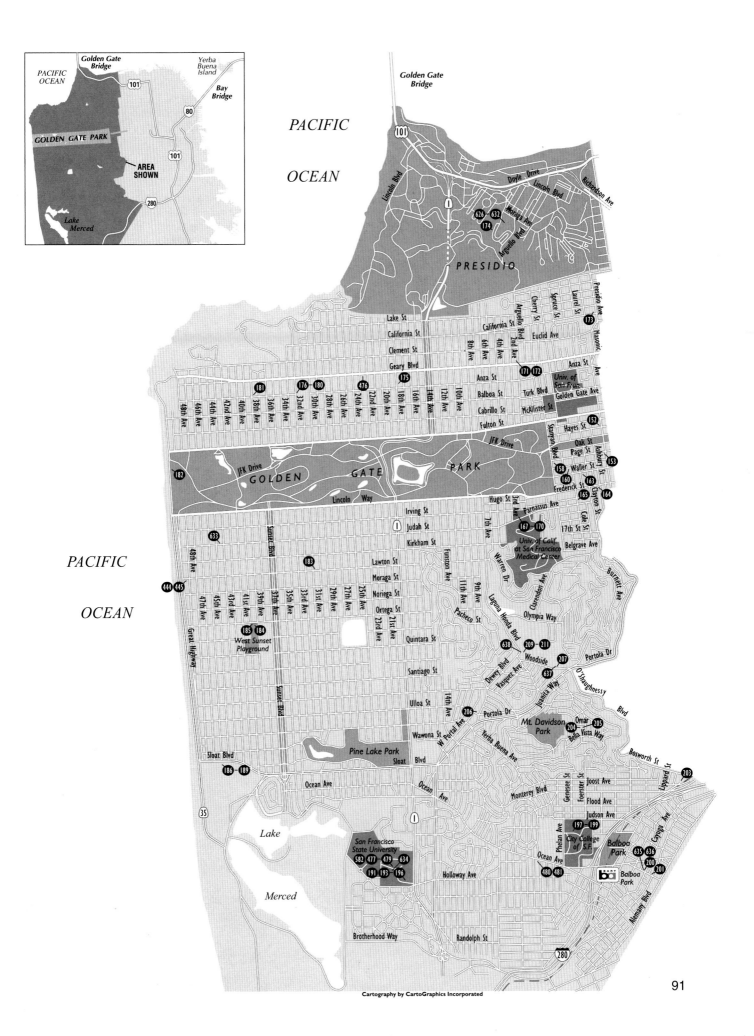

Cartography by CartoGraphics Incorporated

191 [COMPETITIVE AND RECREATIONAL SWIMMING], 1976
SFSU Physical Education,
Recreation and Leisure Studies, School of Health
San Francisco State University gymnasium, (pool),
19th Avenue and Holloway
24' x 28', Acrylic on concrete
Troy Dunham

192 *[UNTITLED], 1977
SFSU Pan African Student Office
San Francisco State University,
Pan African Student Office, B132 Student Union,
19th Avenue and Holloway
6' x 25', Acrylic on canvas
Suzanne de Sandies

193 COMMUNIVERSIDAD, 1977
SFSU Associated Students
San Francisco State University,
Student Union basement,
19th Avenue and Holloway
Two walls, 12' x 30' each,
Politec acrylic on concrete
La Raza Mural Workshop: Ray Patlan, Tony Triqueros,
    with Casper Montemayor, Arla d. Escontrias, Theresa
    L. Guitron, Paco Reyesfahad, Raul Martinez, Betty
    Jones, Virginia Milligan, Jorge Enrique Ocon, Yolanda
    Reyes Fayad, Delia Sanchez, Marciana, Brad Berlin,
    Bill O'Dea, Laura Moral, Tuti Rodriguez, Oswaldo
    Lopez, Carlos Gallardo, Tazaya C. Gonzalez, Angele
    Andino, Roberto Amaraz, Kevin Foutch, David Foutch,
    Patricio Lamorie, Oscar Aviles, Rupert Garcia,
    Angelina Lopez, Zala Nevel, Ivory Walker, and Juan
    Rodriguez

194 CASA BLANCA, 1988
Dr. August Coppola; SFSU School of Creative Arts
San Francisco State University,
School of Creative Arts Building hallway,
19th Avenue and Holloway
Four walls and hallway: 2 walls, 9' x 25',
3 walls, 9' x 17,
Politec acrylic on concrete/plaster
Emmanuel Montoya

195 [FLUTE PLAYER AND CRANES], 1988
SFSU Humanities Department
San Francisco State University,
Humanities Department, HLL 304,
10' x 30', Oil on concrete
Ji Chang-Xiang and Zhang Hong-bin

196 TREGANZA ANTHROPOLOGY MUSEUM, 1990
SFSU Anthropology and Museum Studies Departments
San Francisco State University,
Science Building, third floor (interior)
8' x 60', Acrylic on concrete
Eduardo Pineda

INGLESIDE-CITY COLLEGE OF SAN FRANCISCO

197 PAN-AMERICAN UNITY (MARRIAGE OF THE ARTISTIC
    EXPRESSION OF THE NORTH AND SOUTH OF THIS
    CONTINENT), 1940
Golden Gate International Exposition; Timothy Pflueger
City College of San Francisco, Little Theater lobby,
Ocean and Phelan Avenues
22' x 73', Fresco on movable steel frames
Diego Rivera

198 EDUCATION, 1940
WPA
City College of San Francisco,
Science Hall, north and south porticos,
Ocean and Phelan Avenues
Two panels, 50' x 45' each, Mosaic
Herman Volz

199 EDUCATION, 1940
WPA
City College of San Francisco,
Science Hall, main entrance,
Ocean and Phelan Avenues
Two panels, 12' x 8' each, Fresco
Fred Olmsted, Jr.

CAYUGA

200 IN GOD WE TRUST, 1982
OCD
Balboa High School,
1000 Cayuga Street at Onondaga
45' x 10', Politec acrylic on plaster
Pasto Medina

201 COMMUNITY SPIRIT, 1935
SERA
Alemany Day Treatment Center waiting room,
45 Onondaga Street at Alemany
Approx. 8 1/2' x 5', Fresco
Bernard Baruch Zakheim, Phyllis Wrightson, and Joseph
    Kelly (plasterer)

MISSION TERRACE

202 *A PORTRAIT OF THE SAN FRANCISCO ARTS
    FESTIVAL, 1981
American Express for the San Francisco Arts Festival
Excelsior branch, San Francisco Public Library
Conference room, 4440 Mission Street near Cotter
8' x 16', Politec acrylic on canvas
Precita Eyes Muralists: Susan Cervantes, Margo Bors,
    Tony Parrinello, Judy Jamerson, and Patricia Rose

GLEN PARK

203 THE BICENTENNIAL, 1976
Glen Park Association
Glen Park School, 151 Lippard Avenue
15' x 30', Cal-Western paints on concrete
Fran Valesco and school children

SHERWOOD HEIGHTS

204 [KINDERGARTEN, ALPHABET, AND LANDSCAPE],1980
CETA
Mira Loma School Parents Association
Mira Loma School, 175 Omar Way near Myra
One panel, 4' x 5', and two panels, 6' x 15',
Roy Anderson paint on two wood walls
and one concrete wall
Fran Valesco

205 [CHILDREN'S FANTASY ANIMALS IN A FANTASY
    LANDSCAPE], 1979
CETA
Mira Loma Park, Omar Way and Sequoia
12' x 50', Politec acrylic on concrete
Cynthia Grace

WEST PORTAL

206 [HISTORY OF WEST PORTAL], 1978
Greater West Portal Neighborhood Association; NIIP
West Portal branch, San Francisco Public Library,
190 Lenox Way at Ulloa
30′ x 13′, Politec acrylic on stucco
Nancy Thompson and residents

LAGUNA HONDA

207 UNTITLED, 1977
CETA
San Francisco Youth Guidance Center,
(cell doors in the maximum security section),
375 Woodside Avenue
8′ x 4′ each, Politec acrylic on metal
Miranda Bergman and detainees in Youth Guidance
Center

208 *HISTORY OF SAN FRANCISCO, 1976
CETA; San Francisco Department of Electricity
Twin Peaks Communication Tower,
Twin Peaks Boulevard
Three panels, 15′ x 30′; three panels, 15′ x 4′,
Politec acrylic on concrete
Fran Valesco, Jean Gindreau, Carol Nast, and Beatrice
Spiegel

209 FIRE, EARTH, WATER, AIR [STEEL, FARMING,
FISHING, FLIGHT], 1934
PWAP
Laguna Honda Hospital main lobby,
375 Laguna Honda Boulevard
8′ x 6′, Oil on canvas
Glen Wessels

210 [ECUMENICAL SPIRIT], 1976
CETA
Laguna Honda Hospital (interior),
375 Laguna Honda Boulevard
500 square feet,
Politec acrylic on plaster or stucco
Karen Ezekiel, Lee Hastings, and Jill Light

211 THE CITY'S MUSIC, 1990
Private funding
Laguna Honda Hospital, 8th floor east interior,
375 Laguna Honda Boulevard
Eight shaped panels, approx. 3′ x 4′ each,
Acrylic on plywood
Mike Mosher

212 [WILDLIFE AND INDIAN TRIBES OF THE SAN
FRANCISCO PENINSULA], 1981
CETA; MRC
Josephine Randall Junior Museum lobby,
199 Museum Way
12′ x 30′, Politec acrylic on concrete
Mike Mosher

213 UNTITLED, 1983
CAC; Eureka Valley Trails and Art Network
Retaining wall, Market and 19th Street
Approx. 15′-20′ x 254′,
Politec acrylic on concrete
Betsie Miller-Kusz and 135 contributors

214 BEAVER MOUNTAIN, 1975
Private funding
Residence, 4550 18th Street,
Exterior of two-story house,
Politec acrylic on stucco and wood
Timothy Jencks

EUREKA VALLEY

215 EUREKA VALLEY RECREATION CENTER, 1977
CETA
Eureka Valley Recreation Center,
Collingwood between 18th and 19th Streets
Approx. 12′ x 200′, Politec acrylic on concrete
Cynthia Grace

NOE VALLEY

216 ALVARADO ELEMENTARY SCHOOL MURAL, 1972
Zellerbach Family Fund
Alvarado Elementary School schoolyard,
625 Douglass Street
2,770 square feet, Mosaic
Nancy Thompson

217 THE ALPHABET, 1975
Alvarado School Art Workshop; CETA
Alvarado Elementary School,
625 Douglass Street
3′ x 117′, Acrylic with sealer on concrete
Fran Valesco

218 *NOCHE VERACRUZANO, 1983
Private funding
Pablo's Restaurant (interior),
4166 24th Street between Castro and Diamond
8′ x 25′, Politec acrylic on stucco,
sealed with Danacolors plastic sealer
Juana Alicia

219 *LA OAXAQUENA, 1983
Private funding
Pablo's Restaurant (interior),
4166 24th Street between Castro and Diamond
8′ x 25′, Politec acrylic on stucco,
sealed with Danacolors plastic sealer
Juana Alicia

SOUTH OF MARKET

220 I.L.W.U. MURAL-SCULPTURE, 1986
I.L.W.U. and other unions; OCD
Free-standing sculpture, Mission and Steuart Streets
18′ x 24′, AwL Grip polyurethane epoxy
on 3/8″ structural steel
M.E.T.A.L.
(Mural Environmentalists Together in Art Labor): Miranda
Bergman, Tim Drescher, Nicole Emanuel, Lari Kilolani,
James Morgan, Ray Patlan, Eduardo Pineda, James
Prigoff, O'Brien Thiele, and Horace Washington

221 HISTORY OF SAN FRANCISCO, 1948
Treasury Department Section of Painting
Rincon Center lobby, Spear and Mission Streets
Twenty-one panels totaling 8′ x 460′,
Casein paint on prepared walls
Anton Refregier

222 [LABOR HISTORY AND PRINTING TECHNOLOGY], 1983
Bay Area Typographical Union
Bay Area Typographical Union second floor,
433 Natoma Street
4' x 16', Acrylics and collage on masonite
Jenny McClure, Mike Mosher, Evelyn Nizberg, Lynette
Neidhardt, and Fred Nizberg

223 [PHOENIX DINING ROOM], 1967
Standard Oil Company
Standard Oil Company building, 555 Market
12' x 110', Oil and acrylic tempera on canvas
Edith Hamlin

224 DANCE OF LIFE, 1978
Private funding
Storefront, 693 Mission Street
8' x 12', Politec acrylic on masonite
Claire Josephson

225 DESCENDANTS OF LAPU-LAPU/ANG LIPI NI LAPU-
LAPU, 1984
OCD
Dimasalang House, 50 Rizal Street
90' x 25', Politec acrylic on concrete
Johanna Poethig, Vic Clemente, and Presco Tabios

226 UNCLE SAM, 1988
Chevrolet Automobiles
Wall, 660 3rd Street near Townsend
35' x 50', Oil on brick
Artist unknown

227 [RAINBOW], 1982
NIIP; OCD
Filipino Education Center,
824 Harrison Street near 4th Street
Approx. 20' x 65', Politec acrylic on concrete
Judy Jamerson

228 MY JOURNEY, 1986
AT&T; CAC; FSSA; Pacific Bell
Filipino Education Center,
824 Harrison Street near 4th Street
15' x 100', Politec acrylic on concrete
Johanna Poethig and Southeast Asian children

229 WONDERS OF THE WORLD, 1987
AT&T; CAC; Pacific Bell
Filipino Education Center,
824 Harrison Street
26' x 80', Acrylic on concrete
Johanna Poethig

230 [WORKERS AND TRACTORS], 1948
Private funding
Caterpillar Tractor Company
943 Harrison Street at Oak Grove
15' x 39', Oil on concrete
Don Clever

231 *CENTRAL CITY HEAD START, 1976
CETA
Storefront, 360 5th Street
9' x 15', Politec acrylic on plaster
Cynthia Grace

232 SUN MOSAIC, 1986
CAC; Ursula McGuire
Creatice Polite Apartments,
321 Clementina Street
5' x 5', Venetian glass mosaic
Johanna Poethig and Ursula McGuire

233 ELEMENTS OF INFINITY, 1982
OCD
St. Patrick's Day Care Center (side),
366 Clementina Street near Gallagher
32' x 80', Politec acrylic on concrete
Selma Brown, Johanna Poethig, and Claire Josephson

234 REFLECTIONS, 1984
Bank of America; OCD
Wall facing parking lot, 260 5th Street
30' x 100', Politec acrylic on concrete aggregate
John Wehrle, with Dan Fontes and Jim Petrillo

235 LAND AND FOODSCAPE, 1978
City and County of San Francisco
San Francisco Community College Downtown Center
Cafeteria, 4th and Mission Streets
6' x 60', Politec acrylic on canvas
Cynthia Grace

236 *SISTERSONGS OF LIBERATION, 1975
Rhine and Morgan
San Francisco Neighborhood Legal Assistance
Foundation, third floor, 109 Market Street
8' x 22', Politec acrylic on canvas
Jane Norling

237 PEOPLE'S PARK, 1979
CETA
Park, 6th Street between Mission Street and Minna
15' x 60', Acrylic on concrete
Bob Gayton and CCSF Center Crew

238 [ABSTRACT], 1976
NIIP
South of Market Health Center,
551 Minna Street
40' x 88', Colony acrylics on concrete
Jane P. Speiser assisted by B. Marchal

239 PHIL-AM FRIENDSHIP, 1983
OCD; Philippine-American Friendship Association
Building, Howard and Langton Streets
32' x 100', Politec acrylic on concrete
Peretti and Park

240 TWO HUNDRED YEARS OF CHILDREN'S TOYS AND
GAMES, 1976
NEA; SFMMA
Bessie Carmichael Prekindergarten Center,
55 Sherman Street
8' x 20', Politec acrylic on masonite
Shoshana Dubiner and twenty-nine fourth grade children

241 *[JAIL/STREET SCENE], 1982
San Francisco Sheriff's Department
County Jail #2, seventh floor lobby,
850 Bryant Street
Two walls, 12' x 12' each,
Two walls, 12' x 24' each,
Politec acrylic on concrete
Mike Mosher

242 [UNTITLED], 1979
San Francisco Sheriff's Department
San Francisco Hall of Justice, sixth floor,
Women's section, 850 Bryant Street
3 1/2' x 35', Acrylic on concrete wall
Emmanuel Montoya

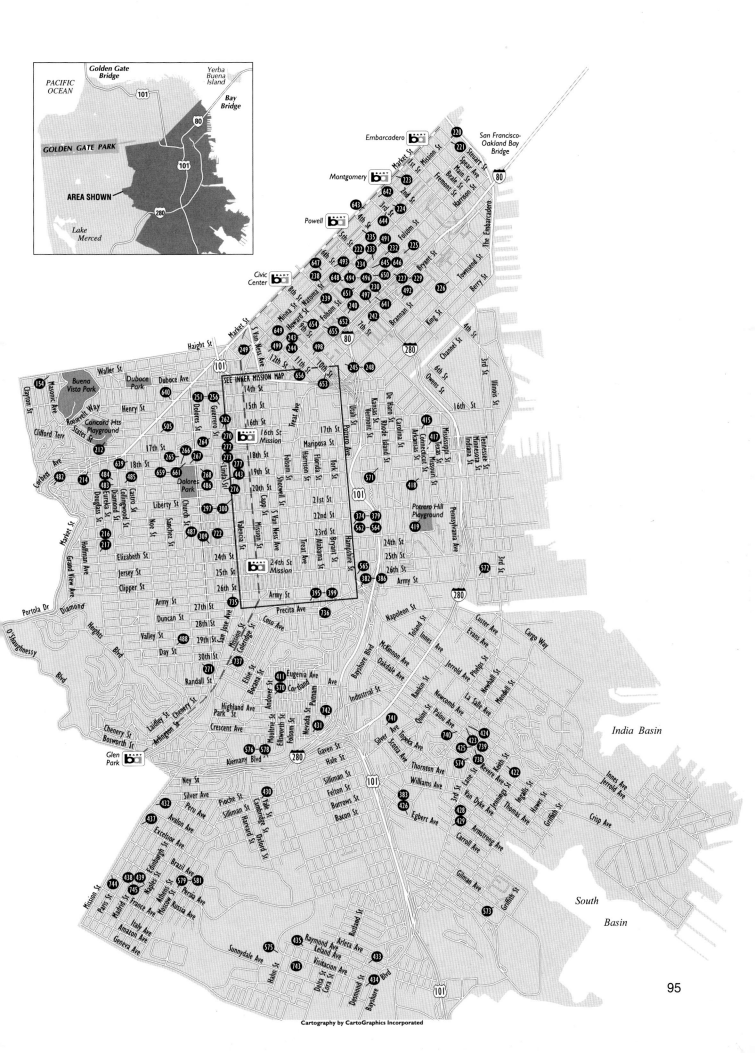

PACIFIC
OCEAN

Golden Gate
Bridge

Yerba
Buena
Island

Bay
Bridge

GOLDEN GATE PARK

AREA SHOWN

Lake
Merced

Embarcadero

Montgomery

Powell

Civic
Center

Haight St

SEE INNER MISSION MAP

16th St
Mission

24th St
Mission

Glen
Park

San Francisco-
Oakland Bay
Bridge

India Basin

South

Basin

95

Cartography by CartoGraphics Incorporated

243 TRANSFORMATION AND HEALING, 1987
CAC; Private funding
Northeast Lodge
272 9th Street near Folsom
18′ x 40′, Acrylic on concrete
Johanna Poethig and clients of Northeast Lodge

244 LOST CITY, 1987
CAC; Private funding
Northeast Lodge
272 9th Street near Folsom
Several panels, Acrylics on walls and stairs
Johanna Poethig and clients of Northeast Lodge

245 UNTITLED, 1978
CETA; NAP; SFAC
South of Market Cultural Center, back of garden,
934 Brannan Street
Two portable panels painted on both sides,
4′ x 8′ each, Politec acrylic on plywood
Fran Valesco

246 SAN FRANCISCASTROLOGY, 1980
CETA; MRC
South of Market Cultural Center, back of garden,
934 Brannan Street
8′ x 24′, Politec acrylic on plywood
Mike Mosher, Leo Hennessey, and Laralyn Lambert

247 BUFFALO SKY, 1982
NIIP
South of Market Cultural Center,
934 Brannan Street
30′ x 50′, Politec acrylic on concrete
with Triangle Sealer
Fran Valesco, CETA Summer Youth, and volunteers from
   the Sunset Mural Workshop

248 ARTIFACT, 1990
FSSA; MRC; OCD
South of Market Cultural Center, west wall,
934 Brannan Street
40′ x 80′, Acrylic on concrete
Johanna Poethig

249 MANPOWER, 1977
CETA
Office building, interior, 1453 Mission Street
8′ x 22′, Politec acrylic on masonite
Cynthia Grace and Carol Nast

MISSION DISTRICT

250 *WHEN THE BUFFALO WERE ON THE MOUNTAINS,
   1976
CETA; SFAC
American Indian Center,
225 Valencia Street near Duboce
Two panels, 16′ x 30′ and 12′ x 22′,
Unknown paint on concrete
Gary McGill

251 [HOT AIR BALLOONS ABOVE BRYCE CANYON], 1975
CETA
Valencia Gardens,
Guerrero Street between 14th and 15th Streets
Approx. 20′ x 10′, Politec acrylic on concrete
Jack Frost

252 REDWOOD CREEK, 1979
CETA
Valencia Gardens,
Guerrero Street between 14th and 15th Streets
Dimensions unknown, Politec acrylic on concrete
R.D. James

253 GARDEN VEGETABLES, 1976
CETA
Valencia Gardens,
Guerrero Street between 14th and 15th Streets
Dimensions unknown, Politec acrylic on concrete
Shoshana Dubiner

254 [SILHOUETTE MANDALA], 1976
CETA
Valencia Gardens,
Guerrero Street between 14th and 15th Streets
Approx. 30′ x 15′, Politec acrylic on concrete
George Mead

255 [WORLDVIEW], 1976
CETA
Valencia Gardens,
Guerrero Street between 14th and 15th Streets
30′ x 15′, Politec acrylic on concrete
George Mead

256 PLANET EARTH, 1975
CETA
Valencia Gardens,
Guerrero Street between 14th and 15th Streets
Dimensions unknown, Acrylic on concrete
Guillermo Pulido

257 OUR PRESIDENT RICHARD NIXON AND DAUGHTERS
   JULIE AND TRICIA VISIT PAT NIXON IN THE
   HOSPITAL, 1978, 1988
Private funding
Storefront studio, 14th Street and Natoma
12′ x 18′, Latex on wood
Bill Wolf

258 LILLI ANN, 1986
OCD
Lilli Ann Building, 17th Street and Harrison
48′ x 46′, Oil on concrete
Chuy Campusano, Elias Rocha, Samuel Duenas, Roger
   Rocha, Carlos Anaya, and members of Signpainters
   Local 510

259 MISSION NEIGHBORHOOD HEALTH CENTER, 1976
CETA
Mission Neighborhood Health Center,
240 Shotwell Street near 16th Street
25′ x 20′, Politec acrylic on stucco or
plaster over concrete
Michael Rios

260 HUMANIDAD, 1976
CETA
Mission Neighborhood Health Center,
240 Shotwell Street near 16th Street
25′ x 20′, Politec acrylic on concrete
Graciela Carrillo

261 DREAMER'S GAZE, 1982
OCD
Victoria Theater,
2961 16th Street near Capp Street
45′ x 90′, Politec acrylic on brick
cleaned with water blaster
Claire Josephson and Monica Armstrong

262 16TH STREET, 1983
OCD
Storefront,
3166 16th Street between Valencia and Guerrero
8' x 60', Politec acrylic on masonite
Cynthia Grace

263 *THE MISSION REDS AT WOODWARD'S GARDENS,
1982
NIIP
Andy's Ice Cream,
Albion Street at 16th Street between Valencia and
Guerrero
8' x 25', Politec acrylic on wood
Mike Mosher

264 BOYS AT PLAY, 1956
Private funding
Columbia Park Boys' Club, second floor,
450 Guerrero Street
14' x 22', Unknown paint on plaster
David Russo

265 [STUDENTS WITH LAMP OF KNOWLEDGE], 1981
CETA; Summer Youth Employment Program
Fence on Church Street near 18th Street
21' x 45', Politec on wood and concrete
Judy Jamerson and Mission High School students

266 [MISSION DISTRICT SILHOUETTES], 1981
CETA; Summer Youth Employment Program
Retaining wall, Church Street at 18th Street
5' x 60', Acrylic on concrete
Judy Jamerson and students

267 THE MISSIONS (CIVILIZATION AND MISSION SAN
FRANCISCO DE ASIS), 1937
WPA
Mission High School library,
18th Street and Dolores
Two panels, 6' x 24' each, Egg tempera on canvas
Edith Hamlin

268 SAN FRANCISCO COMMUNITY LAW COLLECTIVE,
1977
CETA
Building,
503 Dolores Street near 18th Street
16' x 8', Politec acrylic on stucco
Michael Rios

269 *LET THERE BE LIGHT, 1977
Private funding
U.S. Army Recruiting Center,
2300 Mission Street at 19th Street
10' x 80', Unknown paint on stucco
Scarlet Manning

270 OUT OF THE CLOSET, 1981
Private funding
Women's Building, interior,
3543 18th Street near Valencia
Four panels, 5' x 10' each,
Politec acrylic on plaster
Johanna Poethig, Selma Brown, Claire Josephson, K.
Bucklew, Ariella Seidenberg, and Deborah Greene

271 A VISION OF AMERICA AT PEACE, 1984
Capp Street Foundation
Fairmount Elementary School,
30th Street between Chenery and San Jose Avenue
8' x 20', Politec acrylic on exterior plywood
Precita Eyes Muralists: Susan Cervantes, Kit Davenport,
Tony Parrinello, and Patricia Rose

272 WOMEN'S CONTRIBUTION, 1982
Private funding
Women's Building,
3543 18th Street near Valencia
Approx. 15' x 90', Oil on plaster and stucco
Patricia Rodriguez, Francis Stevens, Miranda Bergman,
Nicole Emanuel, and Celeste Snealand

273 *DESIRE, WHAT IT IS, WHAT IT AIN'T. . . WILL YOU
DANCE WITH ME? 1981
Private funding
Women's Building, third floor bathroom,
3543 18th Street near Valencia
4' x 5', Enamel on plaster
Sefa

274 MISSION NEIGHBORHOOD ADULT CENTER, 1976
CETA; Private funding
Mission Neighborhood Adult Center interior,
302 Capp Street
5' x 2 1/2', Politec acrylic and sealer on plaster
Fran Valesco, MNAC staff, and clients

275 *MISSION REBELS, 1973
STEP
Missions Rebels headquarters building
18th Street and South Van Ness
8' x 10', Outdoor enamel on stucco and plywood
Bob Caff, Chuy Campusano, Gerald Concha, Robert
Crumb, and Ruben Guzman

276 BALANCE OF POWER, 1985
OCD; San Francisco Mayor's Youth Fund
Mission Playground and Pool,
Linda Street at 19th Street
Approx. 15' x 150', Politec acrylic on stucco
Juana Alicia, Susan Cervantes, Raul Martinez, Emmanuel
Montoya, with the assistance of Robert Chavarria,
Daniel Socarras, Frank Cortez, Roberto Mendez, Irma
Campos, Scott Brown, Damien Contrerras, Filberto
Fuentes, Cathy Ross, Linda Fields, and Mike Mosher

277 NEW WORLD TREE, 1987
OCD
Mission Pool
19th Street between Valencia and Guerrero Streets
Approx. 25' x 75',
Politec acrylic and Novacolor on stucco
Juana Alicia, Susan Cervantes, and Raul Martinez

443 STOP POLLUTION AND MAKE SOLUTIONS, 1990
Northern California Grantmakers;
California Department of Conservation,
Division of Recycling
Mission Playground,
Valencia Street at 19th Street
Twelve panels, totalling 8' x 48',
Novacolor on wood
Susan Cervantes, Kim Anno, and youth from the San
Francisco Conservation Corps Youth Action Program

278 *REAL ALTERNATIVES PROGRAM, 1981
RAP
Storefront, 16th and Mission Streets
Four panels, 4′ x 8′ each,
Politec acrylic on masonite
Chuy Campusano and RAP Youth

279 *[UNTITLED], 1981
RAP
Storefront, 16th and Mission Streets
8′ x 32′, Acrylics on plywood
Raul Martinez, Carlos Gonzalez, and area youth

280 EL FARO SAN FRANCISCO Y LA MISSION, 1987; 1988
Private funding
El Faro Restaurant, 20th Street and Folsom
12′ x 90′, Politec acrylic on wood
Michael Rios

281 NEW VISIONS BY DISABLED ARTISTS, 1986
Columbia Foundation; OCD; Zellerbach Family Fund
Apartment building, 20th Street and Folsom
24′ x 37′, Politec acrylic on plywood
Susan Greene, Jane Norling, Eduardo Pineda, Eddie
    Hippley, Vincent Jackson, Melody Lima, Michael
    Bernard Loggins, and Cam Quach

282 REFLECTIONS, 1982
OCD
Las Americas Children's Center,
3200 20th Street between Folsom and Harrison
8′ x 16′, Politec acrylic on plywood
Precita Eyes Muralists: Kit Davenport, Karin Schlesinger,
    and Judy Jamerson

283 CELESTIAL CYCLES, 1982
OCD
Las Americas Children's Center,
3200 20th Street between Folsom and Harrison
8′ x 16′, Politec acrylic on plywood
Precita Eyes Muralists: Luis Cervantes and Susan
    Cervantes

284 THE UNICORN'S DREAM, 1982
OCD
Las Americas Children's Center,
3200 20th Street between Folsom and Harrison
8′ x 16′, Politec acrylic on plywood
Precita Eyes Muralists: Patricia Rose, Beatrice Spiegel,
    Carlos del Valle, Margo Bors, and Luis Cervantes

285 EVERY CHILD IS BORN TO BE A FLOWER, 1979
OCD
Las Americas Children's Center,
3200 20th Street between Folsom and Harrison
8′ x 16′, Politec acrylic on plywood
Precita Eyes Muralists: Kit Davenport, Pat Stallings,
    Denise Mehan, Judy Jamerson, Susan Cervantes,
    Barbara Kosman, Greg Edwards, Thomas Gaviola, and
    Star Carroll-Smith

286 SUARO'S DREAM, 1979
OCD
Las Americas Children's Center
3200 20th Street between Folsom and Harrison
8′ x 16′, Politec acrylic on plywood
Precita Eyes Muralists: Tony Parrinello, Margo Bors, Basil
    Brummel, Jeanne Babette, Karin Schlesinger, Beatrice
    Spiegel, Luis Cervantes, and Joe Gomez

287 MASKS OF GOD/SOUL OF MAN, 1978
CETA
Las Americas Children's Center,
3200 20th Street between Folsom and Harrison
8′ x 16′, Politec acrylic on plywood
Precita Eyes Muralists: Susan Cervantes, Tony Parrinello,
    Judy Jamerson, Margo Bors, Karen Magnusen, Star
    Carroll-Smith, Thomas Gaviola, Beatrice Spiegel, Joe
    Gomez, Pete Anoa'i, and Denise Mehan

288 WONDER WELDERS, 1982
Private funding
John O'Connell School interior,
Harrison Street and 21st Street
9′ x 20′, Acrylic on plaster
Vicky Hamlin and students

289 PEOPLE'S RESTAURANT MURAL, 1977
Private funding
San Francisco Mime Troupe back lot,
855 Treat Street between 21st and 22nd Streets
4′ x 30′, Acrylic on plywood
Vicky Hamlin and Dan Macciarini

290 FOR THE ROSES/PA' LAS ROSAS, 1985
OCD; Pacific Bell
San Francisco Mime Troupe studio,
855 Treat Street between 21st and 22nd Streets
30′ x 50′, Politec acrylic,
Danacolors, and plastic sealer on concrete
Juana Alicia

442 UNTITLED, 1989
Parks and Recreation Department
Mission Recreation Center interior,
Treat Street between 20th and 21st Streets
Two walls totalling 12′ x 30′,
Acrylic on plaster
Betsie Miller-Kusz

291 BARRIO FOLSOM, 1982
OCD; Zellerbach Family Fund;
Youth Environment Study
Playground, 21st and Folsom Streets
5′ x 200′, Politec acrylic on concrete
Ray Patlan and playground youth

292 DESERT, 1982
NIIP
St. John's School,
1050 South Van Ness near 21st Street
11′ x 86′, Politec acrylic on concrete
Fran Valesco

447 [TROPICAL SCENE], 1983
Private funding
Cafeteria, Day Treatment Center, Mission Mental Health
    Center
365 South Van Ness
8′ x 20′, Politec on concrete
Patricia Rodriguez and clients

293 *[UNTITLED], 1976
Private funding
Building at 20th Street and South Van Ness
18′ x 20′, Acrylic on plaster
City Muralists

294 [HOMAGE TO SIQUEIROS], 1974
Bank of America Community Outreach
Bank of America, 22nd and Mission Streets
10′ x 90′, Liquitex on Japanese birchwood
Chuy Campusano

295 ALTO AL FUEGO/CEASEFIRE, 1988
Private funding
Cafe Nidal, 21st and Mission Streets
9' x 13', Politec and Novacolor acrylics on stucco
Juana Alicia

296 EVERYONE DESERVES A HOME, 1990
Private funding
Storefront, 21st and Mission Streets,
14' x 29', Acrylic on stucco and wood
Break the Silence Mural Project: Miranda Bergman,
    Susan Greene, and Marlene Tobias

297 UNTITLED, 1986
CAC; La Raza Graphics;
Walter and Elise Haas Foundation
La Raza Graphics Center,
938 Valencia Street at Liberty
Three panels, 40" x 60", Politec acrylic on wood
Sylvia Soriano

298 UNTITLED,1986
CAC; La Raza Graphics;
Walter and Elise Haas Foundation
La Raza Graphics Center,
938 Valencia Street at Liberty
40" x 60", Politec acrylic on wood
Juana Alicia

299 UNTITLED, 1986
CAC; La Raza Graphics;
Walter and Elise Haas Foundation
La Raza Graphics Center,
938 Valencia Street at Liberty
40" x 60", Politec acrylic on wood
Juan Antonio Aviles

300 UNTITLED, 1986
CAC; La Raza Graphics;
Walter and Elise Haas Foundation
La Raza Graphics Center,
938 Valencia Street at Liberty
40" x 60", Politec acrylic on wood
Bob Thawley

301 INSPIRE TO ASPIRE: TRIBUTE TO CARLOS SANTANA,
    1987
OCD
Apartment house, 22nd Street and South Van Ness
35' x 95',
Novacolor, Politec, and Golden colors on wood
Michael Rios, Carlos Gonzalez, and Johnny Mayorga

302 EL LENGUAJE MUDO DEL ALMA/THE SILENT
    LANGUAGE OF THE SOUL, 1990
Columbia Foundation; LEF Foundation; OCD;
Zellerbach Family Fund
Hawthorne School,
Shotwell between 22nd and 23rd Streets
32' x 300', Acrylic on stucco
Juana Alicia and Susan Cervantes

303 IMAGINATION, 1986
San Francisco Educational Fund;
Parents Club; NYC
Hawthorne School, east wall,
Shotwell between 22nd and 23rd Streets
6' x 200', Acrylic on concrete
Scott Brown, Juana Alicia, Susan Cervantes, and Enrique
    Rodriguez

304 *HORIZONS UNLIMITED, 1972
NAP; STEP
Horizons office interior and exterior,
22nd and Folsom Streets
6' x 15' (exterior only),
Outdoor enamel on stucco
Bob Caff, Chuy Campusano, Ruben Guzman, and Spain

305 *MCO, 1972
Galeria de la Raza; STEP
Mission Coalition Organization legal office,
23rd Street and Folsom
15' x 80', Politec acrylic on wood
Michael Rios

306 PEOPLE WE KNEW, THE BEAUTY OF LIFE, and
    DREAMS AND FANTASIES, 1983
CAC
Mission Mental Health Center,
810 Capp at 23rd Street
8' x 20', Politec acrylic on plywood
Patricia Rodriguez and MHC clients

307 SOCIALIST BOOKSTORE, 1985
Private funding
Socialist Bookstore,
3284 23rd Street at Mission
15' x 30',
Politec and Liquitex acrylics on concrete
Susan Greene and Pedro Oliveri

308 THE SCARLATA MURAL, 1977
Private funding
Dr. Scarlata's dental office waiting room,
2639 Mission Street
12' x 45', Liquitex on birchwood
Chuy Campusano

309 [JAMESTOWN MURAL], 1973
STEP
Jamestown Community Center,
Second floor hallway,
180 Fair Oaks Street at 23rd Street
5' x 10', Indoor enamel on plaster
Patricia Rodriguez, Chuy Campusano, Ruben Guzman,
    Consuelo Mendez, Jerome Pasias, Elizabeth Raz, and
    Tom Rios

310 [AZTEC, EARLY CALIFORNIA, AND COSMIC HISTORY],
    1988
Private funding
Garage doors, Bartlett Street at 24th Street
7' x 25', Acrylic on wood
M. Paredes

311 UNTITLED, 1979
Private funding
Building, Bartlett Street and 24th Street
Approx. 12' x 30', Unknown paint on stucco
Anodea Judith

312 BART, 1975
CETA; NEH
BART Station,
Mission Street and 24th Street
Approx. 12' x 100', Politec acrylic on concrete
Michael Rios, Anthony Machado, and Richard Montez

313 *PARA EL MERCADO, 1974 (partially saved)
Mr. Bonilla
Paco's Tacos fence,
South Van Ness and 24th Streets
24' x 76',
Politec and Cal-Western acrylics on wood
Mujeres Muralistas: Graciela Carrillo, Consuelo Mendez,
Susan Cervantes, and Miriam Olivas

314 CARNAVAL, 1983
MRC
Apartment above House of Brakes,
South Van Ness and 24th Streets
24' x 76',
Primer, oil enamel, and plastic shield on wood
Daniel Galvez, with Dan Fontes, James Morgan, Jan
Shield, and Keith Sklar

315 *CASA SANDINO, 1979 (replaced by #316)
Private funding
Wall, 24th Street at Balmy Alley
9'-12' x 75', Oil enamel on wood
Brigada Orlando Letelier

316 *CULTURE OF NICARAGUA, 1983 (replaced by #352)
Casa Cultural Nicaraguense; UNE
Wall, 24th Street at Balmy Alley
9'-12' x 75', Acrylic on wood
Nicole Emanuel, Nicole George, and Patricia Rodriguez

BALMY ALLEY

Murals are listed beginning on the west side of the alley at 24th
Street and continuing toward 25th Street. Murals are located on
fences, walls, and garage doors. Dimensions of most murals are
approximately 6'-10' x 25'. Restoration of Balmy Alley murals
began in 1990.

317 *UNTITLED, 1973
Private funding
Balmy Alley between 24th and 25th Streets
Politec acrylic on wood
Susan Cervantes, Carlos Loarca and children

318 *REGENERATION/REGENERACION, 1984
PLACA
Balmy Alley between 24th and 25th Streets
Politec acrylic and spray can on wood
PLACA: Osha Neumann

319 [AZTEC MYTHOLOGY], 1990
PLACA
Balmy Alley between 24th and 25th Streets
Acrylic on wood
PLACA: Antonio Chavez and Guillermo Galicia

320 WOVEN MASKS/MASCARAS TEJIDAS, 1984
PLACA
Balmy Alley between 24th and 25th Streets
Politec acrylic on wood
PLACA: Susan Greene

321 YOUTH OF THE WORLD, LET'S CREATE A BETTER
WORLD/JUVENTUD DEL MUNDO VAMOS A CREER
UN MUNDO MEJOR, 1984
PLACA
Balmy Alley between 24th and 25th Streets
Politec acrylic on wood
PLACA: Crystal Nevel and Xochitl Nevel-Guerrero

322 UNITED IN THE STRUGGLE/UNIDOS EN LA LUCHA,
1984
PLACA
Balmy Alley between 24th and 25th Streets
Politec acrylic on wood
PLACA: Jose Mesa

323 GUERRA, INCORPORATED, 1984
PLACA
Balmy Alley between 24th and 25th Streets
Politec acrylic on wood
PLACA: Roberto Guerrero

324 *THE RESURRECTION OF THE CONQUEST/
LA RESURRECCION DE LA CONQUISTA, 1984
PLACA
Balmy Alley between 24th and 25th Streets
Politec acrylic on wood
PLACA: Patricia Rodriguez

325 GIRLS' FUTURE CAREERS, 1990
PLACA; YWCA
Balmy Alley between 24th and 25th Streets
Acrylic on wood
PLACA: Patricia Rodriguez, Sandra Fottin, Alicia Gomez,
Ruby Hernandez, Maribel Martinez, Sally Mendez,
Carolina Nunez, Laura Ordonez, and Karina Segura

326 *TO THREE NUNS AND A LAYPERSON/A UNA MUJER
SECULAR Y TRES MONJAS, 1984
PLACA
Balmy Alley between 24th and 25th Streets
Politec acrylic on wood
PLACA: Randall Bronner and Jim Lewis

327 *INDIGENOUS BEAUTY/BELLEZA INDIGENA, 1984
PLACA
Balmy Alley between 24th and 25th Streets
Politec acrylic on wood
PLACA: Nicole Emanuel

328 INDIGENOUS EYES, 1990
PLACA
Balmy Alley between 24th and 25th Streets
Politec and Novacolor acrylics on wood
PLACA: Susan Cervantes

329 ON THE WAY TO THE MARKET/CAMINO AL
MERCADO, 1984
PLACA
Balmy Alley between 24th and 25th Streets
Politec acrylic on wood
PLACA: Ray Patlan and Francisco Camplis

330 KEEPING THE PEACE (IN CENTRAL AMERICA)/
PRESERVANDO LA PAZ (EN CENTRO AMERICA),
1984
PLACA
Balmy Alley between 24th and 25th Streets
Politec acrylic on wood
PLACA: Carlos "Cookie" Gonzalez and Julian "Jueboy"
Torres

331 AFTER THE TRIUMPH/DESPUES DEL TRIUNFO, 1984
PLACA
Balmy Alley between 24th and 25th Streets
Politec acrylic on wood
PLACA: Herbert Siguenza

332 WAVES/ONDAS, 1984
PLACA
Balmy Alley between 24th and 25th Streets
Enamel on wood
PLACA: Kriska Boiral

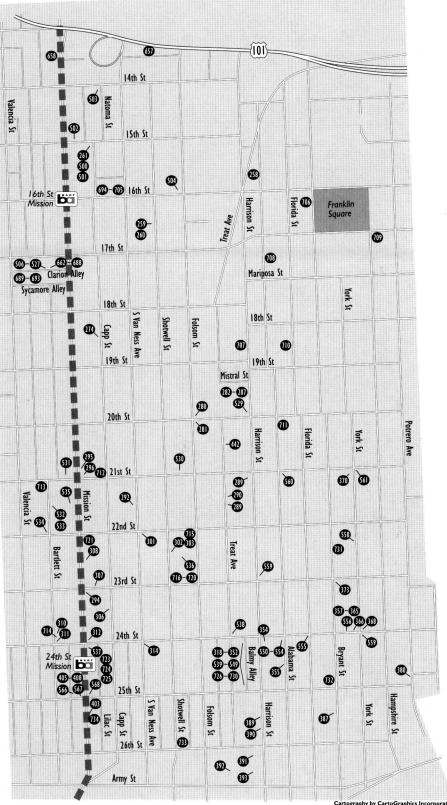

14th St

Valencia St

658

657

101

503

Natoma St

502

15th St

261
500
501

504

258

706

Florida St

Franklin
Square

694 705   16th St

16th St
Mission

259
260

17th St

Harrison St

Treat Ave

709

708

Mariposa St

York St

506 527   662 ═ 688

689 693   Clarion Alley

Sycamore Alley

18th St

274

Capp St

S Van Ness Ave

Shotwell St

Folsom St

18th St

707

710

19th St

19th St

Mistral St

282 ─ 287
529

280

20th St

281

442

Harrison St

711

Florida St

York St

Potrero Ave

530

531   295
296   712   21st St

713   535

Valencia St   Mission St

532
534   533

292

22nd St

289

290
289

560

370   561

301

721
308

715
302 303

Treat Ave

558

731

307

23rd St

536

716 720

559

294

373

306

538

354

357 365
556 366 368

559

310
311

714   312

24th St

314

318 ─ 352
539   549
726   730

550
554

Balmy Alley

Alabama St

555

355

Bryant St

380

Bartlett St

537
723
724
725
568

24th St
Mission

405 408
566 567

732

403

734

Lilac St

Capp St

25th St

S Van Ness Ave

Shotwell St

Folsom St

389
390

Harrison St

387

York St

Hampshire St

26th St

733

392

391
393

Army St

PACIFIC
OCEAN

Golden Gate
Bridge

Yerba
Buena
Island

Bay
Bridge

101

80

GOLDEN GATE PARK

101

AREA SHOWN

280

Lake
Merced

Cartography by CartoGraphics Incorporated

101

333 FOR CENTRAL AMERICA/PARA CENTRO AMERICA, 1984
PLACA
Balmy Alley between 24th and 25th Streets
Enamel on wood
PLACA: Keith Sklar

334 [UNTITLED], 1990
PLACA
Balmy Alley between 24th and 25th Streets
Acrylic on wood
PLACA: Codices

Murals on the east side of the alley are listed beginning at 25th Street and continuing toward 24th Street.

335 UNTITLED, 1973
Private funding
Above garage doors,
Balmy Alley between 24th and 25th Streets
Politec acrylic on wood
Irene Perez

336 MY CHILD HAS NEVER SEEN HIS FATHER/VOLAN LEJOS LOS SENTIMENTOS CUANDO LOS AMADOS HAN MUERTOS TODOS, 1984
PLACA
Balmy Alley between 24th and 25th Streets
Enamel on wood
PLACA: Brooke Fancher

337 *WE HEAR YOU GUATEMALA/TE OIMOS GUATEMALA, 1984
PLACA
Balmy Alley between 24th and 25th Streets
Politec acrylic on wood
PLACA: Juana Alicia

338 UNA LEY INMORAL, NADIE TIENE QUE CUMPLIRLA/NO ONE SHOULD COMPLY WITH AN IMMORAL LAW, 1990
PLACA
Balmy Alley between 24th and 25th Streets
Acrylic on wood
PLACA: Juana Alicia

339 *POWER PLAY/JUEGOS DE PODER, 1984
PLACA
Balmy Alley between 24th and 25th Streets
Politec acrylic on wood
PLACA: Eduardo Pineda

340 [UNTITLED], 1990
PLACA
Balmy Alley between 24th and 25th Streets
Acrylic on wood
PLACA: Edythe Boone, Bosmi Arens, Regina Davis, and Zigi Lowenberg

341 NEW UN-IMPROVED WASH 'N' WAR/NUEVECITO SIN MEJORAMIENTO LA ROPA DE GUERRA, 1984
PLACA
Balmy Alley between 24th and 25th Streets
Politec acrylic on wood
PLACA: Wendy Miller, Marsha Ercegovic, Michele Tavernite, and Janet Storm

342 A DREAM OF DEATH FALLING, SPIRIT RISING: PEACE TO CENTRAL AMERICA/UN SUENO DE LA MUERTE CALLENDO Y EL ESPIRITU LEVANTANDOSE: PAZ PARA CENTRO AMERICA, 1984
PLACA
Balmy Alley between 24th and 25th Streets
Politec acrylic on wood
PLACA: Susan Cervantes

343 THE VOICE OF MUSIC/LA VOZ DE LA MUSICA, 1984
PLACA
Balmy Alley between 24th and 25th Streets
Politec acrylic on wood
PLACA: Carl Araiza

344 THE CONTEST BETWEEN THE SUN AND THE WIND/ EL TORNEO ENTRE EL SOL Y EL VIENTO, 1984
PLACA
Balmy Alley between 24th and 25th Streets
Politec acrylic on wood
PLACA: Fran Valesco

345 UNTITLED, 1972
Private funding
Balmy Alley between 24th and 25th Streets
Politec acrylic on wood
Patricia Rodriguez and Graciela Carrillo

346 GIVE THEM ARMS AND ALSO TEACH THEM HOW TO READ/DARLES ARMAS Y TAMBIEN ENSENARLES A LEER, 1984
PLACA
Balmy Alley between 24th and 25th Streets
Politec acrylic on wood
PLACA: Jane Norling

347 CULTURE CONTAINS THE SEED OF RESISTANCE WHICH BLOSSOMS INTO THE FLOWER OF LIBERATION/ LA CULTURA CONTIENE LA SEMILLA DE LA RESISTENCIA QUE RETORNA EN LA FLOR DE LA LIBERACION, 1984
PLACA
Balmy Alley between 24th and 25th Streets
Politec acrylic on wood
PLACA: Miranda Bergman and O'Brien Thiele

348 UNTITLED, 1984
PLACA
Balmy Alley between 24th and 25th Streets
Politec acrylic on wood
PLACA: Terry Brackenbury, Gary Crittendon, and Marsha Poole

349 HONOR THE AMERICAN INDIANS/HONOR A TODOS LOS INDIOS DE AMERICA, 1984
PLACA
Balmy Alley between 24th and 25th Streets
Politec acrylic on wood
PLACA: Zala Nevel

350 TRIBUTE TO ARCHBISHOP OSCAR ROMERO/ HOMENAJE A ARZOBISPO OSCAR ROMERO, 1984
PLACA
Balmy Alley between 24th and 25th Streets
Politec acrylic on wood
PLACA: James Morgan and Karen Bennett (thanks to Mike Mosher)

351 TINY THUMB/EL PULGARCITO, 1984
   PLACA
   Balmy Alley between 24th and 25th Streets
   Politec acrylic on wood
   PLACA: Anne Fitzpatrick, Anthony Senna, Jose Antonio
      Ochoa, Jo Tucker, and Arch Williams

352 [INTERGENERATIONAL MURAL], 1990
   Festival 2000
   Balmy Alley at 24th Street
   Acrylic and multimedia on plywood
   PLACA: Susan Cervantes, Mia Gonzalez, and local
      residents

353 *UNTITLED, 1976; 1977; 1978
   CETA
   Mission Family Center,
   3013 24th Street
   Block long series of panels, windows, and doors,
   Measuring 2' x 2' - 4' x 8',
   Politec acrylic with varnish sealer on stucco and wood
   Susan Cervantes

354 A BOUNTIFUL HARVEST, 1978
   Private funding
   China Books,
   2929 24th Street between Florida and Alabama
   Approx. 20' x 25', plus top area, 4' x 6',
   Politec acrylic on stucco
   Precita Eyes Muralists: Denise Mehan, Susan Cervantes,
      Tony Parrinello, Margo Bors, Jose Gomez. Assistants:
      Kathryn Brousse, Thomas Gaviola, S. McViker, Pete
      Anoa'i, and China Books staff

355 CLUB LATINO, 1981
   Fuller O'Brien
   St.Peter's School, Florida Street and 24th Street
   8' x 29', Enamel on wood
   Mike Mosher, Laura Parks, and members of the Club
      Latino (mostly eighth grade girls)

356 *VIETNAMESE, 1975
   CETA
   Punjab restaurant, 24th Street and Bryant
   40' x 80', Politec acrylic on un-prepared wood
   Michael Rios

MINIPARK

Murals were restored in 1990.

357 [QUETZALCOATL], 1974
   CETA
   Minipark, 24th Street near Bryant (east side)
   8' x 32', Politec acrylic on wood
   Michael Rios, Anthony Machado, and Richard Montez

358 [CHILDREN DANCE AROUND THE WORLD], 1982
   CETA
   Minipark, 24th Street near Bryant (east side)
   15' x 30', Politec acrylic on wood
   Michael Rios

359 UNTITLED, 1975
   CETA
   Minipark, 24th Street near Bryant
   Approx. 15' x 20', Politec acrylic on wood
   Michael Rios, Anthony Machado, and Richard Montez

360 *NO SOMOS HIPPOS PLASTICOS, 1975
   Private funding
   Minipark, 24th Street near Bryant
   8' x 12', Acrylic paint on a wooden fence
   Gerald Concha

361 UNTITLED, 1983 (partially destroyed in 1990)
   OCD
   Minipark,
   24th Street near Bryant (back and west side)
   20' x 20', Danacolor on wood
   Emmanuel Montoya, Ben Morales, and Noel Santiago

362 HOMENAJE A RALPH MARADIAGA, 1990
   OCD
   Minipark, 24th Street near Bryant
   10'-30' x 40', Acrylic on wood
   Tirso Gonzalez and Ricardo Anguio

363 FANTASY WORLD FOR CHILDREN, 1975
   CETA; NAP
   Minipark, 24th Street near Bryant
   40' x 20', Politec acrylic on wood
   Mujeres Muralistas: Graciela Carrillo, Irene Perez, and
      Patricia Rodriguez

364 *PSYCHO-CYBERNETICS, 1975
   (replaced in 1982 by #365)
   CETA; NAP
   Minipark, 24th Street near Bryant Street
   40' x 20', Acrylic on wood
   Domingo Rivera

365 ABC, 1982
   OCD
   Minipark, 24th Street near Bryant
   40' x 20', Politec acrylic on wood
   Michael Rios

366 UNTITLED, 1977
   Private funding
   Madero Realty, 24th Street at York
   5' x 5', Acrylics on stucco
   Graciela Carrillo

367 Y TU Y YO Y QUE, 1984
   24th Street Merchants Association; OCD
   Storefront, 24th Street and York
   12' x 60', Politec acrylic on stucco
   Ray Patlan and Carlos Gonzalez

368 THE WOMEN LETTUCE WORKERS/LAS
      LECHUGUERAS, 1985
   OCD
   Market, York and 24th Streets
   30' x 50', Politec acrylic, Danacolors, and
   plastic sealer on stucco and wood
   Juana Alicia

369 EVERY CHILD IS A FLOWER, 1989
   Precita Eyes Workshop,
   Bryant School, 1050 York at 23rd Street
   Eight sections, 9' x 27', Nova acrylic on concrete
   Vicky Rega, Susan Greene, Margo Bors, Marta Estrella
      and Susan Cervantes

370 [FANTASY SCENE], date unknown
   Funding unknown
   Bryant School cafeteria,
   1050 York Street
   8' x 200', Politec acrylic on plasterboard
   Peretti and Park, and students

371 *UNTITLED, 1970
   NYC
   Martin de Porres House, 23rd Street near Bryant
   Approx. 15' x 50', Unknown paint on plaster
   The Brothers of Martin de Porres and Neighborhood
      Youth Corps

372 *PRISM, 1983
Private funding
Fairway Produce, Bryant and 22nd Streets
16' x 80', Politec acrylic on stucco
Johanna Poethig and Charlie de Limur

373 THE CIRCUS, 1974
Private funding
Building, Bilbao Iron Works, 2509 Bryant Street
20' x 50', Housepaint on brick
No Moral Muralists

374 UNTITLED, 1974
Private funding
San Francisco General Hospital,
Mechanical Building courtyard,
1001 Potrero at 23rd Street
8' x 20', Mosaic
Gerald Concha

375 UNTITLED, 1974
Private funding
San Francisco General Hospital,
Mechanical Building courtyard,
1001 Potrero at 23rd Street
8' x 20', Mosaic
Carlos Loarca

376 UNTITLED, 1974
Private funding
San Francisco General Hospital,
Mechanical Building courtyard,
1001 Potrero at 23rd Street
8' x 20', Mosaic
Michael Rios

377 UNTITLED, 1974
Private funding
San Francisco General Hospital,
Mechanical Building courtyard,
1001 Potrero at 23rd Street
8' x 20', Mosaic
Manuel Villamor

378 CHILDREN'S MURAL, 1977
San Francisco Hotel Tax Fund
San Francisco General Hospital,
Sixth floor waiting room,
1001 Potrero at 23rd Street
4' x 10', Politec acrylic on plywood
Selma Brown and Ruby Newman

379 GARDENS OF HEALING, 1986
Volunteers of San Francisco General Hospital
San Francisco General Hospital,
Child and Adolescent Sexual Abuse Resource Center,
1001 Potrero at 23rd Street
8' x 18', Acrylic on canvas
Jo Tucker

380 A LETTER TO THE FUTURE/UNA CARTA AL FUTURO,
1986
CAC; La Raza Graphics;
Walter and Elise Haas Foundation
Good Samaritan Community Center interior,
1294 Potrero at 24th Street
Two panels, 9 1/2' x 18', and 9 1/2' x 9 1/2',
Politec acrylic on sheetrock
Juana Alicia, Mauricio Aviles, Corrano, Kathy D'Onofrio,
Carol Fadeff, Guillermo Galicia, Carmen Matthew,
Maria Theresa Ramos, Sylvia Soriano, and Bob
Thawley

381 *MY TIS OF THEE. . . , 1974
Funding unknown
San Francisco Department of Social Services,
Potrero at 24th Street
10' x 20', Enamel on brick
Tomas Belsky, Bob Primus, and others

382 OUR CHILDREN ARE OUR ONLY REINCARNATION,
1985
Precita Eyes Workshop; Susan Cervantes
The Farm, 1499 Potrero at Army
8' x 8', Politec acrylic on exterior plywood
Susan Cervantes

383 HARVEST, 1985
Precita Eyes Workshop; Patricia Rose
The Farm, 1499 Potrero at Army
8' x 8', Politec acrylic on exterior plywood
Patricia Rose

384 UNTITLED, 1985
Precita Eyes Workshop; Henry Sultan
The Farm, 1499 Potrero at Army
8' x 8', Politec acrylic on exterior plywood
Henry Sultan

385 UNTITLED, 1985
Precita Eyes Workshop; Karl Lorenzin
The Farm, 1499 Potrero at Army
8' x 8', Politec acrylic on exterior plywood
Karl Lorenzin

386 UNTITLED, 1985
Precita Eyes Workshop; Michelle Irwin;
Rita Luisa Bairley
The Farm, 1499 Potrero at Army
8' x 8', Politec acrylic on exterior plywood
Michelle Irwin and Rita Luisa Bairley

387 RETABLO OF PARENTS/RETABLO DE LOS PADRES,
1988
OCD
Family Development Center,
25th Street and Bryant
28' x 60', Novacolor acrylic on concrete
Eduardo Pineda

388 *[CIA DIARY], 1975
CETA
Garfield Park Pool, north side,
Harrison and 25th Streets
Approx. 20' x 100', Politec acrylic on stucco
Domingo Rivera

389 [AZTEC SPACE SHIP], 1975
CETA
Garfield Park Pool, east side,
Harrison and 25th Streets
Approx. 12' x 36', Politec acrylic on stucco
Domingo Rivera

390 THE PRIMAL SEA, 1980; 1989
CAC; CETA; NYC; Parks and Recreation Department
Garfield Park Pool, Harrison and 25th Streets
Approx. 12' x 90', Politec acrylic on stucco
Precita Eyes Muralists: Susan Cervantes, Denise Mehan,
Pete Anoa'i, Star Carroll-Smith, Tony Parrinello, Nina
Eliasoph, and Joe Gomez

391 UNTITLED, 1976
CETA
Bernal Dwellings (facing Garfield Park),
Harrison and 26th Streets
29' x 36', Politec acrylic on stucco
Michael Rios, Graciela Carrillo, Sekio Fuapopo, Patricia
Rodriguez, Fran Valesco, and the Neighborhood Youth
Corps

392 UNTITLED, 1975
CETA
Bernal Dwellings (facing Garfield Park),
Harrison and 26th Streets
Approx. 29' x 36', Politec acrylic on concrete
Graciela Carrillo, Patricia Rodriguez, and the
Neighborhood Youth Corps

393 KOOL BLUE, 1975
CETA
Bernal Dwellings,
Army Street near Harrison
29' x 36', Politec acrylic on concrete
Susan Cervantes, Patricia Rodriguez, Fran Valesco and
the Neighborhood Youth Corps

394 *LULAC MURAL, 1975 (destroyed 1984)
Private funding
League for United Latin American Citizens
26th Street and Folsom
30' x 60', Unknown paint on concrete
Gilberto Ramirez

395 WE LEARN FROM EACH OTHER, 1989
OCD
Leonard R. Flynn Elementary School, east wall,
Army Street at Harrison
24' x 40', Novacolor acrylic on stucco
Ray Patlan, Eduardo Pineda, Mauricio Aviles, and
Guillermo Galicia

396 TARGET, 1975
CETA; Alvarado School Arts Program
Leonard R. Flynn Elementary School handball court,
Precita Avenue at Harrison
12' x 30', Politec acrylic on concrete
Susan Cervantes and children

397 FAMILY LIFE and THE SPIRIT OF MANKIND, 1977
CETA; NIIP
Leonard R. Flynn Elementary School, south side,
Precita Avenue at Harrison
Two panels, 30' x 26', Politec acrylic on stucco
Susan Cervantes, Judy Jamerson, Tony Parrinello,
Maurice Lacy, Robert Junti, and mural workshop
volunteers

398 EARTH, FIRE, WATER, AIR, 1976
CETA; Alvarado School Arts Workshop
Leonard R. Flynn Elementary School,
Precita Avenue at Harrison
4'-12' x 120', Acrylic on concrete
Susan Cervantes and students

399 FOUR SEASONS OF LIFE, 1977
CETA; NIIP
Leonard R. Flynn Elementary School,
Precita Avenue at Harrison
12' x 7', Politec acrylic on stucco
Susan Cervantes, Judy Jamerson, and mural workshop
volunteers

400 A DAY IN THE LIFE OF PRECITA VALLEY, 1974; 1984
NAP
Precita Valley Community Center
Precita Avenue
Two panels, 8' x 20', and 8' x 6',
Designers acrylics on plywood
Patricia Rodriguez, with Susan Cervantes, Ray Rios,
Maria Brecker, Maria Juarequi, Dialo Seitu, Judy
Jamerson, and Edith Jeffries

401 THE BEATLES, 1977; 1984
Private funding
Residence, 189 Precita Avenue
House facade, Enamel housepaint on stucco
Jane Weems

402 *LATINOAMERICA, 1974
Private funding
Mission Model Cities Building,
Mission Street between 25th and 26th Streets
20' x 76', Roy Anderson paints on concrete
Mujeres Muralistas: Patricia Rodriguez, Graciela Carrillo,
Consuelo Mendez, Irene Perez, Tuti Rodriguez, Miriam
Olivas, Esther Hernandez, and Xochitl Nevel-Guerrero

403 [TREE WITH ANIMALS], 1973
Mission Model Cities
Childcare Consortium interior,
Mission Street and 25th Streets
26' x 20',
Roy Anderson acrylic housepaint on concrete
Graciela Carrillo and Patricia Rodriguez

404 SIERRA QUEEN, 1983
Private funding
Retlaw Camera, Mission Street near 26th Street
Approx. 16' x 28', Politec acrylic on stucco
Susan Cervantes and the Precita Eyes Workshop

405 [NATIVE AMERICAN MEXICANS], 1982
CETA
Mission Cultural Center,
2868 Mission Street at 25th Street
30' x 160', Politec acrylic on concrete
Carlos Loarca, Manuel Villamor, and Betsie Miller-Kusz

406 THE STRUGGLE FOR LOW INCOME HOUSING, 1976
SFMMA
Mission Cultural Center,
2868 Mission Street at 25th Street
14' x 24', Acrylic on plywood
James Dong and Nancy Hom

407 HOMAGE TO WOMAN, 1978
CETA
Mission Cultural Center, second floor,
2868 Mission Street at 25th Street
12' x 36', Enamel on plaster
Carlos Loarca, Alvarado School Arts Program, Juanita
Brand, Jaime Gomez, Jose Gutierrez, Maria Gomez,
Dolores Miazzo, and Fernando Picazo

408 ESTA GRAN HUMANIDAD HA DICHO BASTA!/THIS
GREAT PEOPLE HAS SAID ENOUGH!, 1976
SFMMA
Mission Cultural Center,
2868 Mission Street at 25th Street
8' x 12', Politec acrylic on masonite
Michael Rios and Anthony Machado

BERNAL HEIGHTS

409 TOOLS FOR PEACE, 1984
OCD
Building, Fair Street between Valencia and Mission
Approx. 15′ x 45′, Politec acrylic on cinderblock
Arch Williams, Jose Antonio Ochoa, Anne Fitzpatrick,
Anthony Senna, and Jo Tucker

410 *PUERTO RICAN MURAL, 1977
CETA; Puerto Rican Club
Puerto Rican Center, north wall,
3249A Mission Street
36′ x 60′, Politec acrylic and sealer on wood
Fran Valesco, Theresa Baca, Gary Rees, Puerto Rican
Club members, and volunteers

411 UNTITLED, 1982
OCD; Private funding
Bernal branch, San Francisco Public Library,
500 Cortland Avenue
1,100 square feet, Politec acrylic on stucco
Arch Williams, Carlos Alcala, Jo Tucker, and volunteers

412 *THE HOLLY COURTS HOUSING PROJECT, 1976
CETA; NIIP
Holly Courts Housing Project,
100 Appleton Street
30′ x 40′, Politec acrylic and sealer on concrete
Fran Valesco and tenants

413 *[MULTICOLORED FACES], 1980
OCD
Holly Courts Housing Project,
100 Appleton Street
Two panels, 6′ x 16′ and 8′ x 24′,
Acrylic on concrete
Mike Mosher

414 *UNTITLED, 1980
CETA; NIIP
Holly Courts Housing Project,
100 Appleton Street
Two panels, 8′ x 26′ and 28′ x 8′,
Acrylic on concrete and cinder block
Claire Josephson

POTRERO HILL

415 REFLECTIONS OF POTRERO HILL, 1987
Private funding; San Francisco Hotel Tax Fund;
New Lambda Foundation; OCD; Zellerbach Family Fund
Building, 1345 17th Street at Connecticut
20′ x 100′, Politec acrylic on concrete
Nicole Emanuel, Scott Branham, Brooke Fancher, Dan
Fontes, Stormey Weber, and Luke McGlynn

416 *IRISES, 1979
Private funding
Mary Price Flowers, 1419 18th Street
10′ x 6′, Politec acrylic on plaster
Margo Bors

417 [FLYING CRANE], 1976
Private funding
Storefront,
247 Missouri Street near 18th Street
25′ x 30′, Politec acrylic and sealer on stucco
Karen Ezekiel and Lee Hastings

418 POTRERO HILL PAST AND PRESENT, 1982
Funding unknown
Potrero branch, San Francisco Public Library,
1616 20th Street
8′ x 8′, Politec acrylic on masonite
Margo Bors

419 [ATHLETES], 1977
Private funding
Potrero Hill Recreation Center,
Arkansas and Madera Streets
Approx. 8 1/2′ x 80′, Politec acrylic on stucco
Pamela Dickens

420 *BLACK HISTORY, 1976
CETA
Potrero Hill Legal Community Center,
Wisconsin and 23rd Streets
6′ x 100′, Politec acrylic and sealer on wooden fence
Graciela Carrillo, Patricia Rodriguez, and Fran Valesco

421 *MASTERS OF METAL, 1978
Private funding
Diamont Tool and Die Company, 1810 Army Street
8′ x 12′, Politec acrylic on masonite
Selma Brown

HUNTER'S POINT-BAYVIEW

422 SUNFLOWERS OF NATURE, 1985
OCD
Hunter's Point Housing, east wall,
1033 Oakdale
23′ x 23′, Acrylic on concrete
James Phillips, with Sara Williams and Todd Duncan

423 THE FIRE NEXT TIME I, 1977
CETA; NAP
Joseph P. Lee Recreation Center,
3rd and Oakdale Streets
35′ x 45′, Politec acrylic on concrete
Dewey Crumpler, assisted by Tim Drescher

424 THE FIRE NEXT TIME II, 1984
Dewey Crumpler's Uncle; OCD
Joseph P. Lee Recreation Center,
3rd and Newcomb Streets
5,500 square feet,
Politec acrylic on concrete
Dewey Crumpler

425 TUZURI WATU/WE ARE A BEAUTIFUL PEOPLE, 1987
OCD
Building, 4900 3rd Street at Palou
35′ x 60′, Liquitex on stucco
Brooke Fancher

426 FOOD FOR THE PEOPLE, 1989
S.H.A.R.E.; OCD;
SLUG (SF League of Urban Gardeners)
SLUG building, Newhall and Carroll Streets
21′ x 180′, Acrylic on concrete
Susan Cervantes

427 *EDUCATION IS TRUTH, 1971
SFMMA MIX Program
Hunter's Point II Elementary School,
Kiska Road
18′ x 35′, Latex acrylic housepaint on stucco
Dewey Crumpler

428 [AMERICAN BLACK HISTORY], 1984
OCD
Martin Luther King Jr. Swimming Pool,
3rd and Carroll Streets
Six panels, 6′ x 5′ each, Ceramic tiles
Painted with Roy Anderson and Liquitex acrylics
Horace Washington, Seitu Din, and Kate Singleton

429 UNTITLED, n.d.
Funding unknown
Martin Luther King, Jr. Swimming Pool,
3rd and Carroll Streets
8′ x 16′, Florentine glass mosaic
Anthony Stellon

UNIVERSITY MOUND

430 UNTITLED, 1956
Funding unknown
Hillcrest Elementary School library,
810 Silver Avenue
Seven panels, approx. 5′ x 3′ each, Mosaic
Emmy Lou Packard and Hillcrest School children

431 LAKAS SAMBAYANAN/PEOPLE'S POWER, 1986
OCD
Market,
300 Alemany Boulevard at Highway 101
35′ x 80′, Acrylic on stucco
Johanna Poethig, Vicente Clemente, and Presco Tabios

432 PROMISED LAND, 1939
Funding unknown
Jewish Home for the Aged, near main lobby,
302 Silver Avenue
10′ x 6′, Oil on canvas
Angelina Minultoli

433 SHARE OUR PAST, BUILD OUR FUTURE, 1988
CAC; OCD; San Francisco Conservation Corps
Visitacion Valley Recreation Center,
50 Raymond Street at Alpha
15′ x 200′, Acrylic on stucco
Jo Tucker and others

434 VALLEY VISION, 1987
OCD
Visitacion Valley branch,
San Francisco Public Library,
45 Leland Avenue at Desmond Street
25′ x 80′, Acrylic on stucco
Jo Tucker, Dick Fong, Maureen Kane, and others

435 TREASURE OUR EARTH, 1989
CAC; OCD;
California Department of Conservation,
Division of Recycling
San Francisco Conservation Corps
325 Leland Street near Schwerin
Five walls, 2,000 square feet
Acrylic on concrete and wood
Jo Tucker, Dick Fong, Maureen Kane, and others

SUNNYDALE

436 *SUNNYDALE COMMUNITY CENTER, 1975
NIIP
Sunnydale Community Center,
1654 Sunnydale Avenue
40′ x 30′, Acrylic on concrete
Bill Boseman and Ronnie Jacobson

EXCELSIOR

437 WAITING FOR THE 52, 1985
Excelsior Youth Club; Private funding
Storefront, Mission Street and Excelsior
25′ x 75′, Acrylic on stucco
Ron J. Mares, Jose Aguirre, Jr., Kim Hallinan (design),
and Pasto Medina, consultant

438 [DESIGNS], 1977
CETA; NAP
Excelsior Playground retaining wall,
Madrid Street at Russia
12′ x 180′; Acrylic on concrete
Sekio Fuapopo

439 *BARRIO GRANDE, EXCELSIOR, SAN PANCHO, 1980
Local Merchants; OCD
Excelsior Playground retaining wall,
Madrid Street at Russia
12′ x 180′, Acrylic on concrete
Excelsior Youth Club

NOTE: The following additional murals, grouped by neighborhood, and listed on the appropriate maps, are provided in this expanded edition. The mural numbers have been retained from the previous editions and new murals, beginning with #582, have been added to their correct geographic location in the listing and on the maps.

NORTH BEACH

450 REFLECTIONS, 1991
Private funding
641–43 Bay Street, near Columbus
46′ x 30′, acrylic on wood and stucco
Bill Weber

451 MULTICULTURAL CABLE CAR, 1994 (replaces #28)
JAM
590 Francisco St. at Taylor
30′ x 12′, acrylic on concrete
Jason Leong, Dennis Taniguchi

452 [TELEGRAPH HILL NEIGHBORHOOD CENTER], 1975
NEA
500 Chestnut Street near Mason
30′ x 40′, acrylic on wood
Karen Ezekiel

588 SHARKS OF THE BAY AREA, 1997
Pier 39 Underwater World
Pier 39
9′ x 50′, acrylic on sheetrock
Gary Graham, Manuel Valdivia, Tyrone Skelton, Jorge
Rios and others

589 SPYHOPPING GRAY WHALES, 1994
Private funding
Pier 39, east side
20′ x 68′, acrylic on stucco
Wyland

590 GRAYS OFF SAN FRANCISCO COAST, 1994
Private funding
Pier 39 Parking Structure
58′ x 52′, acrylic on concrete
Wyland

591 [DRAWING CLASS], c.1937
California School of Fine Arts (now San Francisco Art
    Institute)
SFAI, 800 Chestnut Street
6′ x 9′, fresco
Bates

592 [PICNIC IN FRONT OF GOLDEN GATE], c.1936
California School of Fine Arts (now SFAI)
SFAI, 800 Chestnut Street
10′ x 5′, fresco
Eakin

593 [FARM SCENE], 1937–8
California School of Fine Arts (now SFAI),
Phelan Scholarship Fund
Room 26 (now covered by false wall),SFAI, 800
    Chestnut
6′ x 20′, fresco
Una McCann

594 MAGIC CARPET, 1996
NBF, Levi Strauss and Company, SF Beautiful
Francisco Middle School, 2190 Powell at Francisco
12′ x 18′, acrylic on concrete
Fran Valesco and students

CHINATOWN

595 GOLD MOUNTAIN, 1994
MOCD, private donations, businesses
Romolo between Broadway and Vallejo
15′ x 115′, acrylic, wood, stucco, concrete
Ann Sherry

596 IN MEMORY OF SING KAN MAH AND THOSE WHO
    HAVE STRUGGLED TO MAKE AMERICA THEIR
    HOME, 1995
MOCD, MRC
795 Stockton at Pacific
20′ x 60′, acrylic, painted concrete
Daryl Mar, assisted by Darren Acoba, Joyce Lu, Ronia
    Chen

453 THE SEEDS THAT WE PLANT NOW WILL GIVE OUR
    CHILDREN SHADE, 1991
MOCD
Bartol Street off Broadway near Montgomery
6′–10′ x 97′, acrylic on concrete and plywood
Miranda Bergman, assisted by Selma Brown, Sylvia
    Soriano, Suzie Rivo, Gayle Markow, Marlene Tobias,
    mica Meri Furnari, Steve Lew,
    Rafael Chang

597 CHINESE PLAYGROUND, 1997
MOCD
Sacramento between Grant and Stockton Streets
8′ x 24′, acrylic on concrete
Kendal Wooden-Aw

598 MUSIC OF THE SPHERES, 1994
Private funding
Clarion Music Center,Sacramento and Waverly
12′x 40′, acrylic on stucco
Dmitri Stravinsky, assisted by Dmitri Grudsky and
    Michael Lubka

FINANCIAL DISTRICT

599 [INDIANS, FRIARS, SAILING SHIPS OFF THE
    MARINA], c. 1933
Merchants' Exchange Club
Basement, Merchants' Exchange Club, 465 California at
    Leidesdorff
7′ x 24′, oil on canvas
Jose Moya del Pino

600 [WORKING CARGO IN YERBA BUENA COVE], c.1933
Merchants' Exchange Club
Basement, Merchants' Exchange Club, 465 California at
    Leidesdorff
7′ x 24′, oil on canvas
Jose Moya del Pino

601 [FINANCIAL DISTRICT, YERBA BUENA ISLAND, AND
    BAY BRIDGE], c.1936
Merchants' Exchange Club
Basement, Merchants' Exchange Club, 465 California at
    Leidesdorff
7′ x 24′, oil on canvas
Jose Moya del Pino

602–6 PORT COSTA,1910; HONOLULU HARBOR,1911;
    ARRIVED "ALL WELL",1909; "FULL AND BY",1909;
    WAR TIME,1920
Merchants' Exchange Club
Assembly Room, Merchants' Exchange Club, 465
    California at Leidesdorff
Five lunettes, each 16′ x 18′, oil on canvas
William A. Coulter

607 NORTHWEST PASSAGE, 1903–6
Private funding
Assembly Room, Merchants' Exchange Club, 465
    California at Leidesdorff
15′ x 12′, oil on canvas
Nils Hagerup

NOTE; For #75, listed in this neighborhood previously, see San
Bruno in the Peninsula list.

UNION SQUARE

465 ALPINE MOTORCYCLE RALLY, 1994
S. F. City Earthquake Retrofit funds
Parking lot interior on Ellis near O'Farrell
9′ x 35′, acrylic on concrete
Peter Collins, Catalina Gonzalez

608 PUTTING THE PIECES TOGETHER, 1996
Larkin Street Youth Center
Powell Street BART Station
96 panels, each 2′ x 4′, mosaic tile
Peter Carpou and 309 youths

TENDERLOIN

454 ESCAPE INTO GRACE, 1992
509 Cultural Center, NBAGCF
Leavenworth at Ellis
18′–15′ x 100′, acrylic on brick and plywood
Johanna Poethig, Gia Hy Chung, Sokly Ny, Glades
    Perreras, Pathara Chuop, and the Vietnamese Youth
    Development Center

FILLMORE

HAYES VALLEY

GOLDEN GATE PARK

HAIGHT-ASHBURY

625 POSITIVELY HAIGHT STREET, 1996
Private funding
Positively Haight Street,
1157 Masonic at Haight Street
20' x 30', acrylic and spraycan on stucco
Tony and Malia Machado

PRESIDIO

626–632 PRESIDIO OFFICERS' CLUB MURALS: GOING TO
THE FIESTA; THE HAT DANCE; BUILDING THE
PRESIDIO; and THE SURRENDER AT MONTEREY,
1846; all 1952; GUARD AND MOUNT, 1776,
LT. MORAGA, COMMANDANTE; and (DINING
AL FRESCO – two panels), all 1951
Private funding
Bar and Lounge, Presidio Officers' Club, Moraga Street
Seven murals, varying dimensions, oil on plaster or on
canvas
Bill and Edith Runyan

OUTER RICHMOND

476 THE SALINAS VALLEY, 1986
Private funding
Thom's Natural Foods,5843 Geary Blvd. and 23rd
Avenue
10' x 30', Liquitex acrylic on plaster/drywall
Paul Scofield

SUNSET DISTRICT

633 OTHER AVENUES COMMUNITY FOOD STORE
MURAL, 1995
Private funding
Other Avenues Community Food Store,
Judah Street between 44th and 45th Avenue
5' x 45', acrylic on stucco
Suzanne Ritger, Charles Denefield, Anne Marie
Hartgen, and volunteers

SAN FRANCISCO STATE UNIVERSITY

477 CROSS OF QUETZALCOATL, 1991
Precita Eyes Muralists
Basement Cafeteria, SFSU Student Union
8' x 12', acrylic on plywood
Susan Cervantes, Luis Cervantes, Tony Parrinello,
Margo Bors, and others

478 MISSION STREET MANIFESTO, 1990
20th Century Fox for movie, "Class Action"
Basement Cafeteria, SFSU Student Union
16' x 25', acrylic on plywood
Juana Alicia

479 RAICES DE LIBERTAD/ROOTS OF FREEDOM, 1990
League of United Chicano Artists (LUCA),
Taller de Arte Publico
Basement Cafeteria, SFSU Student Union
10' x 16', acrylic on shaped plywood
Miranda Bergman, Raul Valdez, assisted by Ambray
Gonzalez

582 CESAR CHAVEZ, 1994
SFSU Student Union
Cesar Chavez Student Center
7' x 9', Novacolor acrylic on concrete
Carlos Gonzalez

585 *MALCOLM X, 1994
SFSU Student Union
Cesar Chavez Student Center
7' x 9', spray enamel on concrete
Senay

634 OUR OBJECTIVE IS COMPLETE FREEDOM,
JUSTICE AND EQUALITY BY ANY MEANS
NECESSARY, 1995
San Francisco State University Student Center
SFSU Student Union, Malcolm X Plaza
7' x 9', acrylic on concrete
Eric Norberg and Kamau Ayubbi

INGLESIDE

480 THE GREAT CLOUD OF WITNESSES, 1980–85
Private funding
Interior, Ingleside Presbyterian Church and Community
Center,
1345 Ocean Avenue at Granada
2 walls, 15' x 40', 2 walls, 15' x 60', collage on plywood
Reverend Roland Gordon

481 THE GREAT CLOUD OF WITNESSES, 1992
MOCD
Ingleside Presbyterian Church and Community Center
1345 Ocean Ave at Granada
Four walls, each 6' x 60', acrylic on sheetrock
Susan Cervantes with Selma Brown and Ronnie
Goodman

CAYUGA

635 COYOTE GRILL, 1996
Art Department, CCSF
Grill, Balboa High School, 1000 Cayuga Street,
betweeen Onondaga and Seneca
22' x 20', acrylic on concrete
Peter Collins, Gary Graham

636 ALL EYES ON ME, 1996
Art Department, Balboa High School
Balboa High School, 1000 Cayuga Street, between
Onondaga and Seneca
15' x 12', acrylic on plaster
Manuel Valdivia

LAGUNA HONDA

637 A PLACE OF RECOVERY, 1995
MOCD, Youth Guidance Center, Milestones
Back of gym, Youth Guidance Center, 375 Woodside
near Portola
15' x 100', acrylic on concrete
Marta Ayala and Milestones residents

638 ANIMALS AND THE NATURAL ENVIRONMENT, 1997
Creativity Explored, Laguna Honda Hospital
Recreation alcove, 6th floor near east entrance,
Laguna Honda Hospital, 375 Laguna Honda Blvd.
5' x 27', acrylic on panels with cutouts
Jamie Morgan, Chris Clark, Betty Benard, Yolanda
Ramirez, Cam Quach, James Cunningham, Maura
Frias, Bob Neil, and Peggy Huff

UPPER MARKET STREET

482 THE CHANT OF THE EARTH, THE VOICE OF THE
LAND, 1991 (replaces #213)
NBAGCF
Retaining Wall, Market and 19th Street
15'–20' x 254', Novacolor acrylic on concrete
Betsie Miller-Kusz

EUREKA VALLEY-CASTRO DISTRICT

483 TIME AFTER TIME, 1993
Eureka Valley Trails and Art Network,
NBAGCF, CAO's Office
100 Collingwood Street near 19th Street
20' x 60', acrylic on concrete
(also, 8' x 30' satellite mural on nearby steps)
Betsie Miller-Kusz

484 THE TRANSFERENCE, 1987
Recreation and Parks Department
Interior, 100 Collingwood near 19th Street
12' x 20', Politec acrylic on plaster
Betsie Miller-Kusz and 3 apprentices

485 HAHAH, 1990
Private funding
Buffalo Natural Foods, 19th and Castro Streets
8' x 20', acrylic on concrete and plaster
Art Lick Gallery, Luiz daRosa, David Seibold

486 GOOD KARMA, 1977
Private funding
18th Street at Dolores
12' x 10', acrylic on stucco
Apple Floating Cloud Productions

639 ART FROM THE HEART HEALS, 1996
Private funding
Una Mas Restaurant, Castro and 18th Streets
7' x 6', acrylic on stucco
Clif Cox, assisted by Elba Rivers and R. Smith

640 C.H.A.M.P.(Cannabis Helping Alleviate Medical Pain),
1996
C.H.A.M.P., Jerry Garcia Memorial Fund, PEM Urban
Youth Arts
Church and Market Streets
10' x 20', spray enamel on corrugated iron
Estria and Precita Eyes Urban Youth Artists

NOE VALLEY

487 CHURCH STREET RAINFOREST, 1993
Private funding
1079 Church Street, between 22nd and 23rd Streets
Housefront, 20' x 20', acrylic on stucco
Nicolai Larsen

488 RAINFOREST OF THE MIND, 1993
Precita Eyes Muralists
29th Street at Sanchez
8' x 16', acrylic on plywood panels
Henry Sultan

SOUTH OF MARKET

489 *IN PRAISE OF MASS TRANSPORTATION, 1995
SFAI, MRC, Muni-Metro Turnback Mural Project
Steuart and Mission Streets
8' x 120', acrylic on plywood
Jamie Morgan, with Caroline Stern and artists from
Creativity Explored

491 FROM THE MOUNTAINS, IN THE CLOUDS, 1994
MOCD
Woolf House, 801 Howard Street at 4th Street
2 plaques, each 2' x 6', ceramic, photo transfer and
handbuilt
Johanna Poethig and senior residents

492 TO CAUSE TO REMEMBER, 1992
MOCD
Welsh St., off 5th Street near Bryant
40' x 80', acrylic on concrete
Johanna Poethig

493 CONFUSED, FRUSTRATED, VANDALIZED,
MISGUIDED, ACTIVE, POOR, NEED LOVE, GATO,
DESOLATE, 1993
509 Cultural Center, TODCO
Howard Street, near 6th Street
8' x 118', spray enamel on plywood and paper
Brett Cook-Dizney

494 YOUR EYES EMBRACE MY WORLD, 1993
MOCD,NBAGCF
Minna Street at 6th Street
17' x 88', acrylic on cinderblock and artificial stone
Susan Cervantes with community people, assisted by
Precita Eyes Muralists

495 [PLANET EARTH], 1993
Precita Eyes Muralists
Minna Street at 6th Street
5½' x 6', acrylic on wood
Phil Morris

496 FAMILY, 1993
Precita Eyes Muralists
Minna Street at 6th Street
10' x 5', acrylic on plaster
Bob Gayton

497 ENDUP, 1993
Private funding
995 Harrison at 6th Street
Two parts, 15' x 30' and 20' x 45', unknown paint on
wood and stucco
"Brett"

641 VEGAS PREACHER, 1997
Private funding
Harrison and 6th Street
20' x 30', acrylic on wood
Eric Sorenson

498 LOVE WILL COME YOUR WAY, 1992
McLaughlin, Piven & Vogel Securities, Inc., Dept. of
Social Services, New College of California
Children's Protective Services, 1440 Harrison nr.10th
Street
40 square ft, acrylic on wallboard
Susan Cervantes and students of the New College of
California arts and social change mural class.

Diego Rivera. *The Making of a Fresco Showing the Building of a City*, 1931. Detail from a fresco painted in the San Francisco Art Institute. Photograph used by courtesy of the San Francisco Art Institute. (20)

Louie LaBrie. *San Francisco Rising*, 1976. Destroyed. Politec acrylic on concrete. (11)

Fran Valesco and others. (*Fish Swimming*), 1986. North Beach Swimming Pool. Detail. Acrylic on concrete. Photograph by James Prigoff. (31)

Arch Williams and others. *The Right of Education/The Seed of Freedom*, 1987. Francisco Middle School playground wall. Politec acrylic on concrete. Photograph by James Prigoff. (33)

Maxine Albro. *California*, 1934. Coit Tower, Telegraph Hill.
Fresco. Photograph used by courtesy of the San Francisco
Parks and Recreation Department. (46)

James Dong. *Fish Struggling Upstream*, 1983. Ping Yuen Housing Project. Various media
on asphalt playground. Photograph by James Dong. (65)

Victor Fan. (*Chinese-American History*), 1988. YMCA Playground. Acrylic on concrete. Photograph by James Prigoff.
(70)

James Dong and the Kearny Street Workshop. *International
Hotel Mural*, 1975. Destroyed. Acrylic on concrete, brick and
wood. Photograph by Fran Valesco. (73)

Ray Patlan. *Prime Time/No Time*, 1980. New College of
California Law School. One of two interior murals which face
each other. Politec acrylic on plaster. (104)

Keith Sklar. *Learning Wall*, 1988. San Francisco Unified
School District building. Acrylic on stucco. (107)

David Bradford. *WAPAC Mural*, 1975. Destroyed. Unknown
paints on wood. (112)

Peretti and Park. *The People's Game*, 1977. Raphael Weill
Elementary School. Politec acrylic on concrete. (123)

Dewey Crumpler and others. *A Celebration of African and
African-American Artists*, 1984. Western Addition Cultural
Center. Politec acrylic on concrete. (135)

Johanna Poethig. *Harvey Milk Memorial Mural*, 1988. Duboce Park. Acrylic on concrete. Photograph by James Prigoff. (146)

Kevin McCloskey. *Whale*, 1977. San Francisco Fire Department warehouse. Unknown paints on wood. (149)

Clarkston Peadee. (*Street Scene*), 1975. Church's Fried
Chicken. Acrylic on stucco. (150)

Haight-Ashbury Muralists. *Our History is No Mystery*, 1976.
Detail from a destroyed mural. Politec acrylic on concrete.
Educate to Liberate is now painted on this wall. (151)

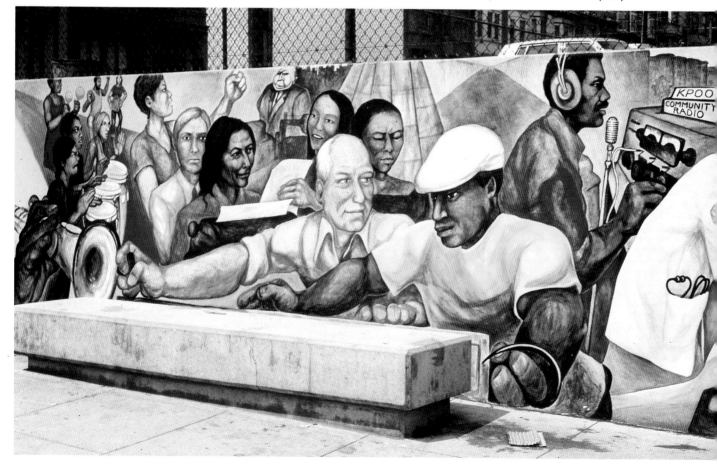

Consuelo Mendez. *Untitled*, 1977. Haight-Ashbury Children's Center. Acrylic on concrete. (153)

Miranda Bergman and others. *Educate to Liberate*, 1988.
Wall at Hayes and Masonic Streets. Detail. Novacolor acrylic
on concrete. Photograph by James Prigoff. (152)

Haight-Ashbury Muralists. *Rainbow People*, 1974. Seeds of
Life Grocery. Politec acrylic on masonite. (156)

Victor Arnautoff. *Life of Washington*, 1935. George Washington High School. Fresco. (176)

Gordon Langdon. *Modern and Ancient Science*, 1936. George Washington High School. Fresco. (179)

Henry Sultan, the Sunset Mural Workshop and others. (*Kites, the Sunset Mandala, and Library Books*), 1982. Ortega branch, San Francisco Public Library. Politec acrylic on stucco. Photograph by James Prigoff. (184)

Ray Patlan and others. *Communiversidad*, 1977. SFSU Student Union basement. Politec acrylic on concrete. Photograph by Ray Patlan. (193)

M.E.T.A.L. *I.L.W.U. Mural-sculpture*, 1986. Side facing
south. Mission and Steuart Streets. Awl Grip polyurethane
epoxy on 3/8" structural steel. (220)

Anton Refregier. *History of San Francisco*, 1948. Rincon
Center. One of twenty-one panels. Casein paint on prepared
wall. (221)

John Wehrle and others. *Reflections*, 1984. Wall facing parking lot at 260 5th Street. Detail. Politec acrylic on concrete aggregate. Photograph by James Prigoff. (234)

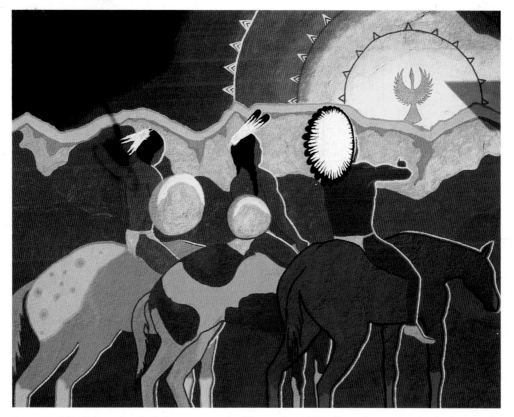

Gary McGill. *When the Buffalo were on the Mountain*, 1976. One of two panels, both now destroyed. Unknown paints on concrete. (250)

Jack Frost. (*Hot Air Balloons over Bryce Canyon*), 1975.
Valencia Gardens. Politec acrylic on concrete. (251)

Chuy Campusano and others. *Lilli Ann*, 1986. 17th Street and Harrison. Oil on concrete. (258)

Juana Alicia, Susan Cervantes and Raul Martinez. *New World Tree*, 1987. Mission Pool. Politec arylic and Novacolor on stucco. Photograph by James Prigoff. (277)

Susan Greene and others. *New Visions by Disabled Artists*,
1986. 20th Street and Folsom. Politec acrylic on plywood.
Photograph by James Prigoff. (281)

Graciela Carrillo. *Untitled*, 1980. Temporary painting for the
Galeria de la Raza billboard.

Derrik O'Keeffe. *Low 'n Slow*, 1975. Destroyed. Temporary
painting for Galeria de la Raza billboard.

Michael Rios. *Salsa Ahora*, 1975. Destroyed. Temporary
painting for Galeria de la Raza billboard.

Juana Alicia. *For the Roses/Pa' las Rosas*, 1985. San Francisco Mime Troupe studio. Politec acrylic, Danacolors and plastic sealer on concrete. Photograph by James Prigoff. (290)

Michael Rios. *MCO*, 1972. Detail from a destroyed mural. Politec acrylic on wood. (305)

Chuy Campusano. *Homage to Siqueiros*, 1974. Bank of
America. Liquitex on Japanese birchwood. (294)

Chuy Campusano and others. *Untitled*, 1973. Jamestown Community Center. Indoor enamel on plaster. (309)

Michael Rios, Anthony Machado, and Richard Montez. *BART*, 1975. BART Station at Mission and 24th Streets. Politec acrylic on concrete. (312)

Mujeres Muralistas. *Para el Mercado,* 1974. Detail from a destroyed mural. Primer, oil enamel and plastic shield on
wood. (313)

Daniel Galvez and others. *Carnaval,* 1983. Apartment above
House of Brakes. Primer, oil enamel and plastic shield on
wood. (314)

Jose Mesa, PLACA. *United in the Struggle*, 1984. West side
of Balmy Alley. Politec acrylic on wood. (322)

Nicole Emanuel. *Indigenous Beauty*, 1984. Destroyed.
Balmy Alley. Politec acrylic on wood. (327)

Irene Perez. *Untitled*, 1973. East side of Balmy Alley. Politec acrylic on wood. (335)

Miranda Bergman and O'Brien Thiele, PLACA. *Culture Contains the Seed of Resistance which Blossoms into the Flower of Liberation*, 1984. East side of Balmy Alley. Politec acrylic on wood. (347)

Domingo Rivera. *Psycho-Cybernetics*, 1975. Destroyed.
Minipark. Acrylic on wood. (364)

Juana Alicia. *The Women Lettuce Workers/Las Lechugueras*, 1985. Franklin market.
Politec acrylic, Danacolors, plastic sealer on stucco and wood. (368)

Michael Rios. *ABC*, 1982. Minipark. Politec acrylic on wood. (365)

Gilberto Ramirez. *LULAC Mural*, 1975. Destroyed. Unknown paints on concrete. (394)

Gilberto Ramirez. *LULAC*, 1975. Destruction of the mural in 1984. Photograph by James Prigoff. (394)

Susan Cervantes, Judy Jamerson and others. *Family Life* and *The Spirit of Mankind*, 1977. Leonard R. Flynn Elementary School. Politec acrylic on stucco. Dedication of the murals. (397)

Mujeres Muralistas. *Latinoamerica*, 1974. Destroyed. Paint on concrete. (402)

Mike Mosher. [*Multicolored Faces*], 1980. Holly Courts. Destroyed. Acrylic on concrete. Photograph by Mike Mosher. (413)

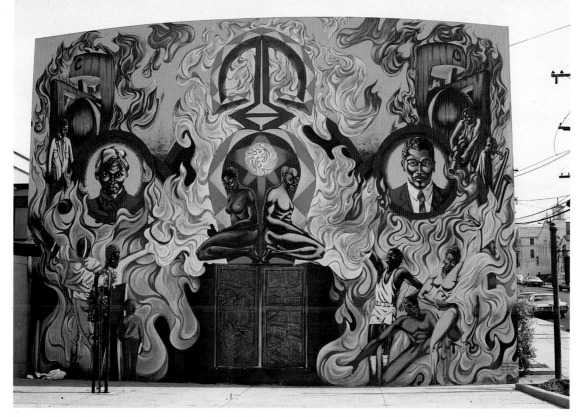

Dewey Crumpler with Tim Drescher. *The Fire Next Time I*, 1977. Joseph P. Lee Recreation Center. Politec acrylic on concrete. (423)

Nicole Emanuel and others. *Reflections of Potrero Hill*, 1987.
1345 17th Street. Politec acrylic on concrete. Photograph by
James Prigoff. (415)

Brooke Fancher. *Tuzuri Watu/We Are a Beautiful People*,
1987. Hunter's Point. Liquitex on stucco. (425)

Johanna Poethig and others. *Lakas Sambayanan/People's
Power*, 1986. Sun Valley Dairy. Acrylic on stucco. Photograph by James Prigoff. (431)

Josh Sarantitis, Emmanuel Montoya, Carlos Loarca. CARNAVAL, 1994. Acrylic on cinderblock. Harrison between 18th and 19th Streets, San Francisco. (707)

Edythe Boone and others. THE ONES WE LOVE, WE REMEMBER, 1997. Acrylic on wood. Balmy Alley, San Francisco. (729)

Jan Cook. UNITED WE STAND, 1996. Acrylic on stucco. Thurgood Marshall School, Conkling Street off Silver, San Francisco. (741)

Aaron Noble. THE EXPULSION OF THE SCABHERD, 1996. Acrylic on wall panels, and Ruby Neri, UNTITLED, 1996. Acrylic and ballpoint pen on wall panels. Labor Temple, San Francisco. (698, 699)

Jose Antonio Burciaga. MYTHOLOGY AND THE HISTORY OF MAIZ, 1986–9. Acrylic on concrete and plaster. Casa Zapata, Stanford University, Stanford. (P47) Detail. Photograph by Moira Harris.

Juana Alicia and others. CALVIN SIMMONS' ANCIENT AND FUTURE HIP-HOP SYMPHONY, 1997. Acrylic on stucco. Calvin Simmons High School, 35th Avenue and Galindo, Oakland. (EB53).

Jeanne LaMarr, with Spencer LaMarr, Ella LaMarr, Kyle Curtis. OHLONE JOURNEY, 1995. Acrylic on concrete. Ohlone Park, Oakland. (EB186).

Nicolai Larsen and others. PROMETHEUS BRINGS FIRE TO MAN, 1996. Acrylic on concrete, US 101 underpass at CalTrain parking lot, South San Francisco. (P1).

Jane Norling, with David Miller, Winfield Coleman, Lou Petrella, Kyle Hurlbut, and Alison Franchina. *PROJECT READ, 1991. Oil on concrete block. Middlefield Road, Redwood City. (P14). Photograph by Moira Harris.

Maxine Albro. MEXICAN POTTERY, 1932. Fresco. Allied Arts guild, 75 Arbor Road, Menlo Park. (P28). Photograph by Grant H. Wilson.

Greg Brown. WOMAN WITH CANARY ON GARDEN HOSE, 1976. Acrylic on stucco. 526 Waverley, Palo Alto. (P60) Photograph by Moira Harris.

Jose Antonio Burciaga, John Sobraske, with Alonso Duenas, Emilio Rodriguez, Martin Bernal, Michael Arguello, and Enrique Lopez. THE SPIRIT OF HOOVER, 1986. Acrylic on concrete blocks. Casa Zapata, Stanford University, Stanford. (P37). Photograph by Moira Harris.

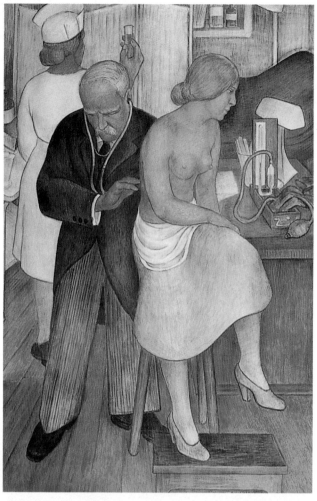

Greg Brown. MAN PUSHING STROLLER, 1976. Bryant at University Avenue, Palo Alto. Acrylic on metal. (P63) Photograph by Moira Harris.

Victor Arnautoff. THE HISTORY OF MEDICINE, 1932. Fresco. (Detail). 300 Homer Avenue, Palo Alto. (P70) Photograph by Fred English.

Jose Meza-Velasquez and others. MURAL DE LA RAZA, 1985. Acrylic on stucco. 2048 Story near Hopkins, San Jose. (P120) Photograph by Moira Harris.

499 [UNTITLED], 1994
Private funding
96 Lafayette Street, off Howard between 11th and 12th
     Streets
12' x 36', spray enamel on concrete and stucco
Benz

642 THE PIED PIPER, 1909
Sheraton-Palace Hotel
Maxwell Room, Sheraton-Palace Hotel,
Market and New Montgomery Streets
6' x 18', oil on canvas
Maxfield Parrish

643 METAMORPHOSIS, 1995
S.F. Redevelopment Agency
Market Street, between 3rd and 4th Streets
16' x 200' acrylic on plywood
Johanna Poethig, assisted by Sophie Siegmann and
     others

644 IN VISION, 1996
S.F. Redevelopment Agency
Williams Building, 3rd and Mission Streets
20' x 100' (wraps around corner), acrylic on plywood
     and concrete
Johanna Poethig, assisted by Sophie Siegmann, Carol
     Murashige, and Innercity Public Art Projects for
     Youth

645 STOP, LOOK, LISTEN, 1995
NBF
6th and Minna Streets
Four panels, 2½' x 2½', ceramic on stucco
Johanna Poethig, Sophie Siegmann, Ericka Clarke
     Shaw, Hua Nguyen (poet)

646 HEALTH, 1996
NBF, MOCD, CAC, Community Arts & Education, SFAC
     Arts and Education Program, Walter and Elise Haas
     Foundation, Hendry Ebert Foundation
SOMA Health Center, Minna and Russ Streets, between
     6th and 7th Streets
Eleven lifesize figures mounted on wall, acrylic on
     ceramic tile mounted on cinderblock and concrete
Johanna Poethig, with Sophie Siegmann, Ericka Clark
     Shaw, Hua Nguyen (poet)

647 FASTPASS, 1997
NBF, SFAC, CAC
Minna and Russ Streets
12' x 45', ceramic on concrete
Johanna Poethig, Sophie Siegmann, Grace Nam,
     Alegria Barkley (poet),and youth from ArtSpan,
     SOMAR, and Innercity Public Art Projects for Youth

648 THE DEFENESTRATION SCULPTURAL
          ORGANIZATION, 1996–7
NEA, Rockefeller Foundation, S.F.Grants for the Arts,
     Hewlett Foundation, New Langton Arts
Howard and 6th Streets
15' x 185', acrylic on plywood
Will Roger with 21 others

649 [ABSTRACT], 1996
Private funding
Yip's Thread Company, 10th and Minna Streets between
     Mission and Howard
5' x 12', acrylic on stucco
Margaret Kilgallen

650 EXTINCT, 1996
Gerbode Foundation Urban Landscape Program, Eyes
     and Ears Foundation
Covered Wagon Hotel/Saloon, Folsom and 5th Streets
40' x 90', acrylic on concrete
Rigo '96, assisted by Kenneth Huerta and Aaron Noble

651 INNERCITY HOME, 1995
Gerbode Foundation and Capp Street Project
New Knox Building, 241 6th Street
37' x 37', acrylic on concrete
Rigo '95 with Charles Linder

652 FRISCO'S WILD SIDE, 1995
NBF, Maltby Electric
Langton Street off Folsom between 7th and 8th Streets
22' x 300', acrylic and spray paint on concrete, with cast
     concrete
Josh Sarantitis, assisted by Claire Bain, Deirdre
     Weinberg, Peter Collins, Chris Kirby; spraycan
     section by Estria and SPIE

653 ONE TREE, 1995
Plough Electric Supply Company, Gerbode Foundation
10th and Bryant Streets
40' x 100', acrylic on corrugated metal with live tree
Rigo '95 and Michael Fox

654 BLOODY THURSDAY, 1995
I.L.W.U. Local 6
Clementina and Minna Streets
10' x 20', mixed media on plywood
Rigo '95, TWIST, Reminisce, Carolyn Castano, L.
     Rodriguez, John Fadeff, Sebastiana Pastor, Chuck
     Sperry. Coordinated by Aaron Noble, Mary Newson,
     and Rigo '95

655 A PLACE TO DREAM, 1996
509 Cultural Center, NBF
Episcopal Sanctuary, 8th and Folsom Streets
Six panels, 10' x 12', acrylic on stucco
Johanna Poethig

656 [UNTITLED], 1995
Private funding
Norfolk Street
12' x 48', spray enamel on concrete
Estria and Raevyn

657 CULTIVATED EARTH, 1996
Private funding
Interior, Rainbow Grocery, 13th and Folsom Streets
10' x 60', acrylic on concrete
Josh Sarantitis and Gabriela Lujan, assisted by Kamau
     Ayubbi and John O'Malley

MISSION

500 EDUTAINMENT, 1991
Precita Eyes Apprentice Mural Program, MOCD, FSSA,
     MRC
Marshall Elementary School, 15th and Capp Streets
12' x 65', acrylic on stucco
Susan Greene, with Meera Desai, Barry Hazzard,
     Gabriela Halsey, and 8 others

501 UNIVERSAL LEARNING, 1992
MOCD, SFPD
Marshall Elementary School, 15th and Capp Streets
12' x 65', acrylic on plywood
Fresco (Ray Patlan and Eduardo Pineda)

502 GRACIAS A LA VIDA, 1992
MOCD
Centro Latino, 1656 15th St. near Mission
5' x 15', acrylic on canvas
Ester Hernandez

503 FRIDA, 1991 (replaces #257)
Private funding
14th St. and Natoma
12' x 18', latex on wood
Bill Wolf

658 WAVES OF WISDOM, 1997
Arriba Juntos, City and County of San Francisco,
California Integrated Management Board
1850 Mission Blvd. at Duboce
30' x 70', acrylic on stucco
Catalina Gonzalez

504 A BOOK IS YOUR KEY TO FREEDOM, 1993
Private funding
Kirkpatrick Bakery, 16th and Folsom
8' x 35', spray enamel on concrete
Dream

505 LA MADRE TONANTSIN, 1992
Private funding
Coro Hispano, Sanchez at 16th Street
7'–8' x 40', acrylic on wooden fence
Colette Crutcher

659 *[UNTITLED], c.1936 (lost after earthquake retrofit
in 1973)
Private funding
Stairwell, Mission High School, 18th Street between
Dolores and Church
12' x 5', oil (?) on canvas
Edith Hamlin

660 MISSION HIGH SCHOOL HEALTH CENTER, 1996
PEM, Mission High School
Interior, Mission High School, 18th Street, between
Dolores and Church
7' x 90', acrylic on stucco
Susan Cervantes, Elba Rivera, Francisco Carrasco,
Cynthia Rojas, Ellen Chestnut (teacher), and
Mission High School students

661 [DIVERSE STUDENTS], 1997
Mission High School
Main hallway, Mission High School, 18th Street between
Dolores and Church Streets
6' x 15', acrylic on plaster
Toby and Garcia

CLARION ALLEY MURAL PROJECT (CAMP)

Starting from Valencia Street, walk east toward Mission Street and
note murals on the left or north side of the alley. Funds are not
dedicated to specific murals, but have come from private donations,
Informal Nation Foundation, NBAGCF, local businesses, landlords,
and The Zellerbach Foundation. Some pairs of murals share a single
space. They are indicated with "above" and "below" notes.

662 *[TWO HORSES], 1994
6' x 8', spray enamel on metal
REM

663 CELIA CRUZ, 1995
7' x 13', acrylic on door
Carolyn Costano

527 *DON'T STOP THE FUNK, 1993
6' x 8', spray enamel on plywood
PEYA (Precita Eyes Youth Arts)

664 FARE EVASION, 1997 (replaces #527 and a later mural
painted in 1995 by the International Studies Youth
Project)
8' x 12', acrylic on plywood
Josh Wallace

526 [UNTITLED], 1994
8' x 25', latex on wooden fence
Chuy Campusano

525 LA LUCHA DEL PUEBLO CHICANO POR SU
AUTODETERMINACION/THE STRUGGLE OF THE
CHICANO PEOPLE FOR SELF-DETERMINATION,
1994
8' x 16', silkscreen, relief, spray enamel on wood
Jesus Angel Perez

665 [BLUE CARTOON FACE OVER CITY], 1995?
12' x 11', acrylic on concrete
Mats Stromberg
NOTE: This location previously had NO MAS DROGAS, 1994,
acrylic on concrete children's project with V.R.L.

666 Below: DRAGONS, 1995
5' x 12', acrylic on brick
Saroun Khan

667 Above: MOURNING, 1996
8' x 8', calligraphy on wood
Khartik Tagarajyan

524 EL MISMISIMO DIABLO, 1994
10' x 24', acrylic on brick
DX

668 *CALIFAZTLAN, 1994
7' x 3', spray enamel on wood
SPIE

669 SUPERHERO WAREHOUSE, 1997
20' x 35', acrylic on stucco
Aaron Noble, Rigo '97

670 CAUTION; EYE IRRITANT, 1997
8' x 50', acrylic on wood
Permi K. Gill

671 Above: FACING WEST: (Cat), 1994
10' x 10', acrylic on cutout plywood
Luno

521 [COLLAGE OF WOMEN IN MEDIA], 1993
7' x 10', photographs on wood
Mari Kono

520 KEEPIN' THE FAITH, 1993
7' x 10', acrylic on wood
Lily Rodriguez

672 TITO PUENTE, 1996
7' x 3', oil enamel on wood
Carolyn Costano

673 Above: [CARTOON HOUSE], 1997
30' x 25', latex housepaint and spray enamel on stucco
Ron Salmeron

674 Below: [UNTITLED], 1996
22' x 22', acrylic on wood
REM

675 Below: [UNTITLED], 1994?
9' x 15', acrylic on stucco
Victor Hugo

676 Above: WHAT WERE YOU THINKING? (MOJO MAN),
1994 (renovated in 1996)
20' x 10', acrylic on stucco
Kenneth Huerta

519 TRIBUTE TO FRANCIS BACON AND INDIGENOUS
MEXICAN THEME
1993 10' x 20', acrylic on plaster and plywood
Michael Roman

Starting from Mission Street, heading west to Valencia Street, murals found on the left or south side of Clarion Alley are, as follows:

677 WHAT I KNOW IS WHAT I OWE, 1997
15' x 40', acrylic on stucco
Brian Tripp

678 DESERT DREAMS, 1996
9' x 18', acrylic on wood
Amy Berk and Carolyn Costano

679 [MEMORIAL TO TRICIA SULLIVAN AND HOMELESS
KIDS], 1997
Faces west on back wall of 30 Sycamore Street
Size unknown, acrylic on wood
Susan Greene

680 OUR HEMISPHERE, 1995
14' x 14', acrylic on wood
Q. R. Hand

518 [ESCALATOR], 1993
12' x 8', acrylic on wood
Julie Murray

681 DEVIL GIRL, 1995?
8' x 8', acrylic on wood
Greta Snider

516 IF I COULD, 1993
acrylic on wood (a poem)
Al Rose

517 PIGEON, 1995 (replaces an untitled work from 1993 by
same artist on same space)
6' x 6', acrylic on wood
Mia Hoalberg

682 Above: TOWER SCULPTURE (black), 1995
6' tall, wood, metal, ceramic, acrylic
Ron Henggeler

683 WHITE ANGEL, 1996
5' x 14', found objects, wood, acrylic
Scott MacLeod

515 [UNTITLED], 1993
7' x 10', acrylic on wood
Mario Joel

684 UFOLOGY, 1996
7' x 12', spray enamel on wood
UFO

514 A HARD GOD(DESS) IS GOOD TO FIND, 1997
(replaces mural of same title painted in 1993–4 by
Fresco (Ray Patlan and Eduardo Pineda)
7' x 21', acrylic on wooden garage doors
Chucho Perez, Maya Hayak, DX, Kenneth Huerta, Rene
Amiri

513 FAUX MISSION MAN, 1994
4' x 12', acrylic on plywood
Keith Knight

512 FEAR AND HOPE, 1994
11' x 22', acrylic on wood
Susan Cervantes, Marta Ayala, Constance Lombardo,
Kate Ruddle, Cynthia Rojas, and others

685 *NINETEENTH STREET TOKENS, 1996
10' x 25', acrylic on wood
V.M.L.

686 JAM, 1995
10' x 20'. acrylic on wood
Vichian Boonmeemak, John Merryfield

511 VOICE OF THE GHETTO, 1994 (renewed in 1995)
10' x 10', spray enamel on steel door
CUBA

510 CHILDREN LEARN TOO, 1993
9' x 12', acrylic on wood
Sebastiana Pastor

509 *OUR HEMISPHERE, 1993
8' x 12', acrylic on wood
Q. R. Hand

687 VUELOS URBANOS, 1996 (replaces #509)
9' x 12', acrylic on wood
Ruben Guzman

508 [UNTITLED], 1993
8' x 12', spray enamel on steel door
TWIST

507 MISSION WILDLIFE HERITAGE, 1993
8' x 12', acrylic on plaster
Scott Williams

506 CAMP, 1993
(informational sign, in several languages)
8' x 12', acrylic on plaster

688 DOES SUGAR COATING MAKE US SWALLOW?, 1996
(above, length of building)
CAMP
5' x 70', acrylic on brick
Alicia McCarthy

522 [DOOR PAINTED BY CHILDREN], 1993
7' x 3', acrylic on wood
The Alexis children

523 [GRAFFITO], 1993
10' x 15', spray enamel on corrugated steel door
Krush

SYCAMORE ALLEY

This is the next alley south of Clarion Alley. Murals are listed reading from Valencia.

689 NUESTRA LUCHA/OUR STRUGGLE, 1997
CAMP
9' x 13', acrylic on plywood
Amilca Fuentes

690 GODDESS OF THE VOLCANO AND THE WATERING
HOLE, 1995
SFAC Literary Arts Commission Pilot Grant, PEM
Sycamore at Valencia near 17th Street
9' x 13', acrylic on plywood
Catalina Gonzalez

691 HOMES NOT JAILS, 1995
CAMP
Sycamore and Valencia near 17th Street
9′ x 13′, acrylic monochrome on plywood
Fiona Glas

692 "WHEN WILL THIS END?" 1994
SFAC Literary Arts Commission Pilot Grant, PEM
Sycamore at Valencia near 17th Street
9′ x 13′, acrylic on plywood
Alvaro Gutierrez, Jaime Wynn

693 EXPORTS, 1995
CAMP
Sycamore at Valencia near 17th Street
9′ x 13′, acrylic on plywood
Diana Cristales, Krush

LABOR TEMPLE, 1996
Creative Work Fund, LEF Foundation Redstone Building, 16th and Capp Streets (The building already contains interior murals. It is an ongoing project, so check for recent additions. Murals are listed as one encounters them).

694 [GENERAL STRIKE MEETING, 1934], 1996
Building lobby
8′ x 21′, acrylic on plaster
Chuck Sperry

695 [SEWER WORKER], 1996
left side of stairway
15′–11′ x 30′, acrylic and gouache on wall panels
John Fadeff

696 [EMPORIUM STRIKE, 1941], 1996
top of stairway
10′ x 14′, acrylic on wall panels
Susan Greene

697 [CHINESE GARMENT WORKERS' STRIKE, 1938], 1996
10′ x 7′, acrylic on wall panels
Sebastiana Pastor

698 THE EXPULSION OF THE SCABHERD, 1996
10′ x 20′, acrylic on wall panels
Aaron Noble

699 [UNTITLED], 1996
10′ x 7′, acrylic and ballpoint pen on wall panels
Ruby Neri

700 APPROXIMATELY 3/4 WATER, 1996
10′ x 20′, acrylic on wall panels
Rigo '96

701 [VIDEO CREW], 1996
10′ x 14′, acrylic on wall panels
Aaron Noble and Matt Day

702 [WOMEN'S BINDERY WORKERS], 1996
surrounding elevator
20′ x 10′, acrylic on wall panels
Isis Rodriguez

703 [UNTITLED], 1996
10′ x 17′, acrylic and oil based varnishes on wall panels
Barry McGee

704 [FILIPINO-AMERICAN CENTER], 1996
10′ x 12′, acrylic on wall panels
Carolyn Castano

705 PORTRAIT OF THE MISSION, 1997
Mission Area Federal Credit Union
3rd floor, Redstone Building, 16th near Mission Street
8′ x 8′, computer-generated image varnished onto
    canvas, steel frame
Josh Sarantitis

(End of Redstone Building murals.)

706 BIRDS AND CARS, 1997
Private fundraising party and landlord's gift
16th and Bryant Streets (behind restaurant)
80′ x 40′, acrylic on wood
Rigo '97, with Juan Jalbuena and Gonzalo Hidalgo

707 CARNAVAL, 1994
PG&E, MECA, NBF, Robert Cloud
Harrison between 18th and 19th Streets
14′ x 300′, acrylic on cinderblock
Josh Sarantitis, Emmanuel Montoya, Carlos Loarca

708 [FENCE AT PROJECT ARTAUD], c. 1992
Project Artaud
499 Alabama between 17th and 18th Streets
7′ x 50′, spray enamel and acrylic on wood
Brett Cook-Dizney, TWIST, and Rigo

709 ART EXPLOSION, 1995
NBF
17th and Hampshire Streets
6′–12′x 120′, acrylic on concrete
Peter Collins, with Catalina Gonzalez, assisted by
    Rachel Chernoff, Ellen Rohne, Alane Faug, Anthony
    May Terri

710 ALL OUR RELATIONS, 1996
Rotational Mural Project
Cell Warehouse, Bryant between 18th and 19th Streets
7′ x 20′ and 7′ x 15′, acrylic on panels
SPIE

711 WHERE LEGENDS MEET, 1996
S.F. Boys and Girls Club Fine Arts Program
Atlas Cafe, 20th and Alabama Avenues
10′ x 30′, acrylic on plywood
Viki Rega, Lisa Prives, Cybele Gerachis, Mission Boys
    and Girls Clubs

712 SALUD, 1996–7
MOCD, Koret Foundation, Zellerbach Family Fund, S.F.
United Methodist Mission, Richard and Lynn Tremelling,
    Sanwa Bank
Bethany Center Senior Housing, 21st Street between
    Mission and Capp Streets
96′ x 48′, acrylic on concrete
Dan Fontes, assisted by Isabelle Graeser

528 MAESTRAPEACE, 1994
Private donations, MOCD, Zellerbach Family Fund,
Astrae Foundation, Inc., Foundation for a
    Compassionate Society
3543 18th Street at Lapidge
65′ x 96′ and 65′ x 96′ (two sides of building), Novacolor
    acrylic on stucco
Juana Alicia, Miranda Bergman, Edythe Boone, Susan
    Kelk Cervantes, Meera Desai, Yvonne Littleton, Irene
    Perez

NOTE: #82 [WOMEN ROLE MODELS] has been moved to this
building from the Downtown YWCA.

586 [WORLD CUP SOCCER], 1994 (replaces #269)
Coca Cola U.S.A.
2300 Mission at 19th St.
10' x 80', acrylic on stucco
Fresco (Ray Patlan and Eduardo Pineda)

529 IS THIS THE END OR THE BEGINNING-THE LEAP,
1992
Precita Eyes Muralists
Las Americas Center, 20th St. at Harrison
8' x 12', acrylic on plywood
Luz Cervantes, Maria Chowentoska, Deirdre Weinberg

530 DEDICATED TO JOSE CORONADO, 1993
MOCD
Jose Coronado Park, Folsom at 21st Street
2½–5' x 250', acrylic on concrete
Fresco (Ray Patlan and Eduardo Pineda)

531 MUSIC AND FLOWERS, 1991
Si Tashjian
21st Street at Mission
11'x 45', acrylic on stucco
Susan Greene and Barry Hazzard, assisted by Meera
Desai

713 DREAM, 1996
NBF and Mission Merchants' Association
Bartlett Street between 21st and 22nd Streets
20' x 20', acrylic on stucco and board
Daniel Galvez

714 [UNTITLED], 1997 (replaces #311)
Funding unknown
24th and Bartlett Streets
12' x 30', acrylic on stucco
Marco Paredes

532 BUTTERFLIES, 1993
NBAGCF
Bartlett St. near 22nd Street
10' x 30', acrylic on stucco
Catalina Gonzalez and Precita Eyes Young Women's
Mural Workshop

533 WHATCHA WANNA DO?, 1994
SFAC Literary Arts Pilot Program
Bartlett Street near 22nd Street
12' x 60', spray enamel on stucco
Francisco Carrasco and PEYA

534 [UNTITLED], 1994
Private funding
Valencia at 22nd Street
6' x 15', acrylic on plywood
P. van Lengen

535 MISSION, 1993
Kiel Company
New Mission Theater, Mission St. near 22nd St.
16' x 28', spray enamel on plywood barricade
Francisco Carrasco assisted by PEYA

536 VIVA LA HUELGA, 1993
NBAGCF, PEYA
Playground, Cesar Chavez Elementary School, Folsom,
between 22nd and 23rd Streets
5½' x 70', spray enamel on concrete
Francisco Carrasco assisted by PEYA

715 I OF MOTION, US OF MOVEMENT 1995
PEM
Folsom at 22nd Street
12' x 20', acrylic on plaster
Catalina Gonzalez, with Alvaro, Alex, Kamau, Nimra,
Jessmmyn, Paul and Anna

716 SI SE PUEDE, 1995
PEM, MOCD, Jose Chapa, SFUSD, Western States Art
Federation, Zellerbach Family Fund, Access Scaffold
Company
Cesar Chavez Elementary School, Folsom between
22nd and 23rd Streets
30' x 210', acrylic on concrete
Susan Cervantes, with Juana Alicia, Margo Consuelo
Bors, Gabriela Lujan, Elba Rivera, Olivia Quevedo,
and others

717 FILIPINO/MEXICAN FARMWORKERS UNITE, 1996
PEM
Cesar Chavez Elementary School, Folsom between
22nd and 23rd Streets
10' x 20', spray enamel on concrete
SPIE and Steele

718 CALIFAZTLAN, 1996
PEM
Cesar Chavez Elementary School, Folsom between
22nd and 23rd Streets
6' x 25', spray enamel on wood
Tase

719 CESAR CHAVEZ, 1996
PEM, Levi Strauss Foundation
Cesar Chavez School, Folsom between 22nd and 23rd
Streets
6' x 85', spray enamel on wood
Francisco Carrasco

720 WITH LOVE, MAGIC, AND ART, WE SHALL
OVERCOME, 1996
Levi Strauss Foundation
Cesar Chavez School, Folsom between 22nd and 23rd
Streets
15' x 104', spray enamel on stucco
Estria and Precita Eyes Urban Youth Arts

583 ROOTS AND FREQUENCIES BASIC TO OUR
EDUCATION, 1994
MRC, NBAGCF
24th Street and Valencia
8' x 20', acrylic on plywood panels
Marta Ayala

537 EL UMBLIGO, 1994
MOCD
Capp Street near 24th St
12' x 125', acrylic on wooden fence
Fresco (Ray Patlan and Eduardo Pineda)

538 FRIENDS DON'T LET FRIENDS DRINK AND DRIVE,
1993
MCC, Kids' Workshop, RAP, MAS School, SFPD
Treat Street at 24th Street
12' x 45', acrylic on stucco
Ernesto Paul

539 MISSION FAMILY CENTER, 1992 (replaces #353)
MOCD
Mission Family Center, 24th Street at Balmy Alley
15' x 80', acrylic on stucco
Fresco (Ray Patlan and Eduardo Pineda)

721 THE MANY CULTURES OF CHILDREN, 1995
Private funding
Interior, Bay View Federal Savings, 2601 Mission at
    22nd Street
3' x 15', airbrush on plaster
Manuel Samaniego

722 SUMMER VOYAGE, 1995
Jamestown Community Center Summer Program
Playground, Edison School, 3531 22nd Street
8' x 16', acrylic on plywood
Cynthia Rojas and youth

723 [UNTITLED-UNITY], 1995
MOCD,
Cypress Alley off 24th Street near Mission
7'–8' x 15', acrylic on wood
Jesus Angel Perez ("Chucho")

724 [MEXICO CITY AND SAN FRANCISCO], 1995
MOCD
Cypress Alley, off 24th Street near Mission
12' x 24', acrylic on wood
Jaime Vargas

725 IMAGENES DE AMERICA, 1995
MOCD
Cypress Alley off 24th Street near Mission
7' x 60', acrylic on wood doors
Jose Meza-Velasquez, with Jesus Perez, Jaime Vargas,
    Juanita P. Meza-Velasquez, America Meza-
    Velasquez, Miguel A. Perez, y amigos del barrio

BALMY ALLEY (WEST SIDE)

Restoration of some Balmy Alley murals has taken place. The
restored murals and the artists involved include:
#347 CULTURE CONTAINS THE SEEDS OF RESISTANCE:
Miranda Bergman and O'Brien Thiele
#352 FIVE SACRED COLORS OF CORN: Mia Gonzalez and
Susan Cervantes, assisted by Juan Lopez, Ramona, In
Lee, Jonathan Huggins, David Gray and Kim Canton
#544 LATINO PRIDE: Francisco Carrasco, assisted by Shariff
Dahlan
#388 NO ONE SHOULD COMPLY WITH AN INMORAL LAW:
Juana Alicia
Replacement murals are noted in the list.

540 *[POEM], 1993
Private funding
Balmy Alley (to the left of #317)
housepaint on wooden fence
Artist unknown

541 PODER ROSA, 1993
Private funding
Balmy Alley (to the right of #318)
housepaint on wooden fence
Artist unknown

542 [UNTITLED], 1989 (replaces #318)
Private funding
Balmy Alley
acrylic on wood
Carlos Gonzalez

543 INSTITUTIONS, 1990 (replaces #326)
Balmy Alley
spraycan on door
Brett Cook-Dizney

544 LATINO PRIDE, 1993 (restored, see above)
PLACA
Balmy Alley (left of #329)
acrylic on wood
Francisco Carrasco and Garfield Park youth

726 THE GOLDEN AGE OF MEXICAN CINEMA, 1996
    (replaces #333)
acrylic on wood
Ray Patlan, Carolyn Castano, Rigo'96

BALMY ALLEY
(east side beginning near 25th Street)

545 HOY (VEY) COMO SIEMPRE, 1993 (replaces #339)
PLACA
Balmy Alley
acrylic on wood door
Eduardo Pineda

546 *COLORS, 1993 (replaces #341)
PLACA, Balmy Alley
spraycan on plywood
Rigo'93

547 CHANGES, 1990 (replaces #342)
PLACA, Balmy Alley
spray enamel on plywood
Francisco Carrasco and others

727 UNTITLED, 1995 (replaces #547)
acrylic on wood
Hector Escarraman

728 LOW RIDING MADNESS, 1996 (replaces #547)
MOCD
spray enamel
Francisco Carrasco, assisted by Shariff Dahlan

729 THE ONES WE LOVE; WE REMEMBER, 1997
    (replaces #548)
acrylic on wood
Edythe Boone, assisted by Elvi Jo Dougherty and Trish
    Tripp; designed by children with H.I.V.

730 TRIBUTO A MUJERES MURALISTAS Y
    GENERACIONES FUTURAS, 1995
    (replaces #345)
acrylic on wood
Precita Eyes Mural Workshop, Elba Rivera, Barbara
    Devane, Laura Smith, David Isaacson, Oscar H.

548 [UNTITLED], 1994 (replaces #343)
Private funding
Balmy Alley
acrylic on wood
P. van Lengen

549 *TOURIST PARODY, 1993
PLACA
Balmy Alley (to the right of #350)
acrylic on wood
High School students at the School of the Arts

(End of Balmy Alley listings.)

550 [AZTEC WARRIOR], 1977
Domiguez Bakery
Alabama at 24th Street
5' x 4', unknown paint on painted brick

551 [AZTEC PRINCE AND MAIDEN], 1985
Dominguez Bakery
Alabama at 24th Street
Two panels, each 6' x 6', unknown paint on painted
    brick
K. Secrist , D. Jackson

552 AZTEC CALENDAR, 1991
Dominguez Bakery
Alabama at 24th Street
4' x 3', acrylic on painted brick
Ernesto Paul, Antonio Vasquez

553 EL INDIO FLECHADOR, 1990
Dominguez Bakery
Alabama at 24th Street
7' x 6', acrylic on stucco
Ernesto Paul, Carlos Gonzalez

554 VIRGEN DE GUADALUPE, 1990
Dominguez Bakery
Alabama at 24th Street
6' x 14', acrylic on stucco
Ernesto Paul

555 500 YEARS OF RESISTANCE, 1992–93
St. Peter's Church
24th Street at Florida Street
11'–25' x 67', acrylic on concrete and plaster
Isaias Mata

556 [UNTITLED], 1990
MOCD
Minipark, 24th and Bryant Streets
8' x 20', 10' x 15' panels, Novacolor acrylic on plywood
Betsie Miller-Kusz

557 HEROES, 1993–94 (replaces #367)
NBAGCF
York St. at 24th St.
12' x 60', acrylic on stucco
Cookie Gonzalez and RAP Youth

558 EVERY CHILD IS A FLOWER, 1989 (replaces #369)
MOCD
Bryant School, 1050 Bryant between 22nd and 23rd
    Streets
12' x 60', acrylic on stucco
Vicki Rega, Susan Cervantes, Margo Bors, assisted by
    Precita Eyes Muralists

731 THE DREAMERS AMONG US STILL LOOK TO THE
    SKY, 1997
SFUSD, MOCD, private funding
Bryant School, Bryant between 23rd and 22nd Streets
32' x 180', acrylic on stucco
Josh Sarantitis, Isaias Mata, Jan Cook

732 MISSING MY BABY; IN MEMORY OF SELENA, 1996
Private funding
25th and Bryant Streets
12' x 36', acrylic on stucco
Ernesto Paul

559 EL ARROYO, 1993
Reynaldo Serrano
Harrison at 23rd Street
15' x 45', acrylic on stucco
Ernesto Paul

560 CELEBRATING SUMMERS OF FUN, c. 1990
San Francisco Boys and Girls' Club
21st Street at Alabama
7' x 45', acrylic on plaster
anonymous, with children

561 OUR MISSION TO AZTLAN, 1993
MCC
York Street at 21st Street
12' x 36', acrylic on stucco
Ernesto Paul

562 OCEAN FRONT, 1992
MOCD, private
Outpatient AIDS Ward 86, SFGH (interior)
7' x 20', Novacolor on oak panels
Arch Williams, Victor Fan, Antony Senna

563 FIESTA DE PAJAROS, 1994
MOCD,UCSF
SF General Hospital Dental School
9' x 20', acrylic on plywood
Carlos Loarca

564 [UNTITLED], 1992
Eikon Studios
7th floor Atrium, SFGH
10' x 15', unknown paint on concrete
Jessie Tapacio

565 PEACE IN THE BARRIOS, 1993
MOCD
Potrero del Sol Park, Potrero at 25th Street
15' x 45', acrylic on concrete
Fresco (Ray Patlan and Eduardo Pineda) and youth

587 VIVA EL SOL, 1991
The Plant, Inc.
Potrero del Sol Park, Potrero at 25th Street
16' x 64', acrylic on concrete
PEYA

566 [UNTITLED], 1994
NBAGCF
Osage Alley at 25th Street
10' x 100', acrylic on concrete
Isaias Mata and students

567 [UNTITLED], 1993
Private funding
25th St. at Mission St.
15'x 35', acrylic on stucco
Ernesto Paul and Cruising Coyote Mural Workshop

568 OUR CULTURE, OUR ART/NUESTRA CULTURA,
    NUESTRA PINTURA, 1993
Private funding
25th St. at Mission St.
15' x 45', acrylic on concrete and plywood
Ernesto Paul, students of M.A.S., and R.A.P.

733 [SEA SHORE], 1996
Funding unknown
Shotwell and 26th Street
10' x 30', acrylic on stucco
Artist unknown

734 [READING CHILD], 1986
Funding unknown
Instituto Familiar, 2826 Mission
6'x 6', acrylic on plaster
Zala Nevel, with Jose Meza-Velasquez and Aaron
    Galvez

735 THE GIFT OF ANCESTORS, 1996
Private funding
Yuet Lee Restaurant, 3601 26th Street at San Jose
12' x 30', acrylic on stucco
Marta Ayala, Patricia Rose, Deirdre Weinberg

736 PRECITA VALLEY VISION, 1997
Creative Work Fund
Precita Valley Community Center, Alabama and Precita
    Avenue
37' x 30', acrylic on stucco, wood, brick
Susan Cervantes, Cynthia Rojas, Elba Rivera

737 STIMULUS MAXIMUS, 1995
Private funding, PEM
Godeous Street off Mission near 30th
10' x 40', acrylic on stucco
Sam McWilliams and Youme Landowne

BERNAL HEIGHTS

569 *[UNTITLED], 1975 (destroyed)
CETA
Housing project, 100 Appleton Street
size unknown, acrylic on concrete
Patricia Rodriguez with high school youth

570 [UNTITLED], 1994
NBAGCF
Bernal Heights Playground, Andover near Cortland
    Street
12' x 75', acrylic on concrete
Lamont Gardner with youth

POTRERO HILL

571 NEW WORLDS, 1994
International Studies Academy
693 Vermont; 19th near Kansas
20' x 100', acrylic on concrete
Rigo'94 and students

572 WORTH SAVING, 1990
S.F. Conservation Corps, California Dept. of
    Conservation: Division of Recycling
Army Street at Indiana
25' x 126', acrylic on stucco
Jo Tucker, Dan Macchiarini and S. F. Conservation
    Corps

HUNTER'S POINT/BAYVIEW/CANDLESTICK

573 ALICE GRIFFITH MURAL, 1990
MOCD
2555 Griffith at Gilman St.
12' x 60', acrylic on plaster
Ray Patlan, Horace Washington

574 *THE HISTORY OF BAYVIEW-HUNTER'S POINT
    MURAL PROJECT, 1994 (painted out, 1996)
Businesses of Hunter's Point Shipyard
3rd Street and Revere Street
8'–30' x 114', acrylic on stucco and concrete
Shipyard Artists: Heidi Hardin, Mary Southall, Peggy
    Huff, Wendy Robushi; and Hunter's Point
    neighborhood artists: Mary LaJackson, Peter Dent,
    Kathy Perry, Keith Lewis, Leboriae P. Smoore, Sister
    Lillian Briggs.

738 SCENES FROM THE BAYVIEW OPERA HOUSE, 1995
NBF
Triangle Building, 3rd Street and Oakdale
10' x 150', acrylic on plywood and wood
Leboriae P. Smoore, Peggy Huff, Wendy Robushi, Mary
    Southall, Keith Lewis, Claudia Quacinella

739 WELCOME TO JOSEPH LEE RECREATION CENTER,
    1996
NBF, PEM
3rd and Oakdale, triangular building across from rec
    center
10' x 180', acrylic on concrete and stucco
Keith Lewis, Wendy Robushi, Mary Southall, Claudia
    Quacinella, Jeanette Osborne, Anthony Ross, Lynn
    Daniels, Hustinove P. Smith and youth

740 FROM FARM TO CITY, 1995
NBF, Bayview Opera House
Dr. George Washington Carver Elementary School, 3rd
    and Palou
8'–12' x 111', acrylic on concrete blocks and wood
    garage doors
Mary LaJackson, Keith Lewis, Mary Southall, Wendy
    Robushi, Leboriae P. Smoore, Peggy Huff, Claudia
    Quacinella, and students

741 UNITED WE STAND, 1996
S.F. Municipal Arts Grant, PEM
Thurgood Marshall School, Conkling Street off Silver
35' x 82', acrylic on stucco
Jan Cook, assisted by Mary Newson, Clara Lusardi,
    students and volunteers

VISITACION VALLEY

575 LIFE UNDER WATER, 1992
MOCD
Coffman Pool, Visitacion and Hahn Streets
8' x 72', acrylic on stucco
Meera Desai, Barry Hazzard, Monica Henderson, Julia
    Baler

UNIVERSITY MOUND

576 THIS IS OUR HOPE, THIS IS OUR FAITH, 1994
S. F. Housing Authority
Alemany Housing Projects, Ellsworth between Crescent
    and Alemany
20' x 25', acrylic on concrete and wood
Josh Sarantitis, assisted by Anthony Greene, David
    Mason, Mico Zanders and members of the Alemany
    Projects community

577 ALEMANY: A PLACE IN THE WORLD, 1995
MOCD
Alemany Housing Projects, Alemany and Ellsworth
    Street
12' x 50', acrylic on concrete
Mary Newson and Keith Lewis

578 SEIZE THE TIME, 1995
MOCD
Alemany Housing Projects, Alemany and Ellsworth
    Streets
12' x 20', spray enamel on stucco
Eric Norberg

742 BANQUET OF LIFE, 1996
     Bernal Heights Housing Development Corp.
     Bayshore Farmers' Market, Bayshore and Alemany
     Three panels: 10′ x 36′, 15′ x 45′, 15′ x 27′, acrylic on
        cinderblock and concrete
     Susan Cervantes and Precita Eyes Community Mural
        Workshop

SUNNYDALE

743 WELCOME TO SUNNYDALE, 1997
     S.L.U.G (SF League of Urban Gardeners)
     Sunnydale Housing Projects
     5′ x 60′, ceramic tile
     Josh Sarantitis, Alexis Fontenot, Julie Barton

EXCELSIOR

579 KEEP OUR ANCIENT ROOTS ALIVE, 1993–1994
     MOCD (first phase); LEF Foundation, McDonald's
        Children's Charities, Zellerbach Fund (second
        phase)
     Cleveland School, Persia and Moscow Streets
     Two panels, 40′ x 28′ each and nine recessed panels,
        3½′ x 41′ each, Novacolor acrylic on stucco
     Susan Kelk Cervantes, Alexandra Fomina, Nicolai
        Bogomolov (Russia), Allen Cowan (London),
        assisted by Precita Eyes Muralists with Jan Cook,
        Elba Rivera, Claire Bain, Toku Ishikawa, Paulette
        Liang, Lissa Dirrim, Constance Lombardo, Olivia
        Quevedo, and others

580 TRUST, 1993
     PEYA, NBAGCF
     Cleveland School bungalow, Persia and Moscow Streets
     20′ x 25′, spray enamel on wood
     Christina Brown and Eduardo Ramos, and PEYA

581 RESPECT, 1993
     PEYA, NBAGCF
     Cleveland School bungalow, Persia and Moscow Streets
     20′ x 25′, spray enamel on wood
     Eric Norberg, assisted by PEYA

744 CHE, VIVA CUBA, 1996
     Private funding
     Mission Street between Russia and Onondaga
     15′ x 60′, spray enamel on wood
     SPIE ONE, Buter, Chief, Rios, Tase, and Rigs

745 EVER UPWARD, 1994
     NBF
     Excelsior Park
     12½′ x 62′, acrylic on concrete
     Jamie Morgan and youth

Some Addditions and Corrections

In a mural book of this complexity, it is inevitable that mistakes have occurred. Following are some corrections to the San Francisco listings and text:

The UNDERWATER SCENE (91) was restored by Lou Silva, Joanne Wittenbrook, and Juan Carlos in 1990.

FOREST SCENE (92) was painted by Lou Silva and the following artists: Joanne Wittenbrook, Mark Clark, Juan Carlos, and Ed Monroe.

THE CITY'S MUSIC (211) had eight shaped panels: four approximately 4' x 4' and four approximately 4' x 16'. Funding was provided by Laguna Hospital Volunteers, Inc.

JAIL/STREET SCENE (241) should include one wall 6' x 10', which was painted in the weight room.

THE MISSION REDS AT WOODWARD'S GARDENS (263) was painted out in February, 1987, seven years after the Holly Courts murals were destroyed.

The correct title of the Holly Courts mural (413) was *UNIFIED DIVERSITY*. It was painted with Politec acrylics on concrete, and the photograph was taken by Claire Josephson. For murals 413 and 414, the correct information is: one wall, 22' x 24', two walls, 8' x 24'; one garbage structure, and two walls, 6' x 8'. The murals were painted out only five months after their creation!

The correct title for the untitled mural (442) is *EL ENCANTIMIENTO DEL TIEMPO*.

The zig-zag mural illustrated in the Portable Murals section was painted for the Chicano Moratorium by Jane Norling, Emmanuel Montoya, Tony Chavez, and Maria Gonzalez.

The Jamestown CYO and its seminal mural were located at 23rd Street and Fairoaks, not Fairview.

The color photograph of Daniel Galvez' *CARNAVAL*, 1983, was taken by James Prigoff and should be so credited. In the same color section, the photograph of *NEW WORLD TREE* was reversed in printing.

In the discussion of the origins of the Mujeres Muralistas, it should be noted that Irene Perez was also one of the key members of the group, that Ester Hernandez did not paint on *LATINOAMERICA*, and that the group did not name itself. When Consuelo Mendez was asked to paint the Mission Model Cities mural *(LATINOAMERICA)* she invited Patricia Rodriguez, Graciela Carrillo, and Irene Perez to join her. Later other women muralists joined the group, but only these four painted *LATINOAMERICA*. They did not have a group name at first, but when Ralph Maradiaga, co-director of the Galeria de la Raza was asked who they were, he responded, "mujeres muralistas," thus giving them their famous title.

List of East Bay Murals

The information for each mural is presented in the following order:

Title [unofficial titles in brackets]. An asterisk indicates that the mural no longer exists.

Date completed

Funding source

Location

Size, medium and wall type [height precedes width. Sizes are often approximations]

Artist(s)

NEWARK

EB1   SAN FRANCISCO BAY WATERSHED 1997
Cargill Salt Company, S.F. Bay Wildlife Society
Environmental Education Pavilion, Don Edwards San Francisco Bay National Wildlife Refuge, Marshlands Road
8′ x 9′, acrylic on stucco
Sean and Patrick Johnson

FREMONT

EB2   [UNTITLED], 1985
Post Office Employees
Fremont Post Office, 37010 Dusterberry Rd. off Thornton
10′ x 25′, acrylic on wallboard
David Gonzales

UNION CITY

EB3   MAYAN MARKETPLACE, 1977
Alameda County Neighborhood Arts Program
Market, Alvarado and Niles Road
9′ x 20′, Politec acrylic on plaster
Enrique Romero and NYC youth

EB4   SI SE PUEDE, 1976
Private funding
Casados Market, 5th and 'E' Streets
15′ x 25′, Politec and sealer on stucco
Rogelio Cardenas, Enrique Romero, and youth

EB5   DECOTO PLAZA MURAL, 1978
ACTEB/ACAP; C.U.R.A., Inc., S.P.E.D.Y.;
Searles School; The City of Union City; Y.C.C.I.P.
Decoto Plaza, 6th and 'E' Streets
5½′ x 60′, acrylic on particle board
Calvin Barajas, Danny Sanchez, Maria De Araujo, Vicente Sanchez, Art Aguilar, Esperanza Lopez, and Gyeong Yoon

EB6   UNTITLED], 1978
Alameda County Neighborhood Arts Program
Our Lady of the Rosary Church,
6th and 'C' Streets
8′ x 18′, acrylic on wood slats
Enrique Romero

EB7   RAZA, EARTH, WIND, AND FIRE, 1976
Alameda County Youth Employment
Tiburcio Vasquez Medical Clinic, 9th Street
12′ x 16′, Politec acrylic on plywood and wood
Rogelio Cardenas, Enrique Romero, and Jose Luis Ramirez

EB8   THE C.U.R.A. MURAL, 1978
ACTEB/ACAP, C.U.R.A., Inc., S.P.E.D.Y.,
Searles School, The City of Union City, Y.C.C.I.P.
33923 10th Street
12′ x 25′, Politec acrylic and latex on redwood
Circulo Anahuac

EB9   [UNTITLED], 1976
The City of Union City
Union City Youth Program, 33623 Mission Boulevard
Panels, 20′ x 20′; one panel, 20′ x 35′,
Politec acrylic on stucco
Zala Nevel and Larry Orozco

EB10   OICW MURAL, 1976
Neighborhood Youth Corps, OICW
Interior, OICW office, Whipple Road
8′ x 20′, Politec acrylic on stucco
Enrique Romero

HAYWARD

EB11   IN RECOGNITION OF 'LA MUJER', WE DEDICATE THIS MURAL TO CELIA DE LA RIVA WHO REPRESENTS THE ENERGY AND THE LOVE FOR OUR RAZA. WE ALSO ACKNOWLEDGE OUR YOUTH—YOU ARE THE FUTURE AND OUR SURVIVAL, 1978
ACNAP, NYC
Market, 'A' Street and Princeton
20′ x 90′. acrylic on stucco
Rogelio Cardenas, Carmen Cesena, and Brocha de Hayward

EB12   RURAL LANDSCAPE, 1938
TRAP
Hayward Post Office, 'C' Street
5′ x 10′, oil on canvas
Tom E. Lewis

EB13 HIJOS DEL SOL, 1981
Hijos del Sol Youth Program
La Familia Counseling Service, Tennyson Center,
Pompano Avenue
1900 square feet, acrylic on stucco
Enrique Romero and local youth

EB14 CENTENNIAL HALL, 1979
NEA, Mervyn's
Centennial Hall, Hayward Civic Center, 22292 Foothill
Road
Three panels, each 8′ x 14′, pencil and acrylic on
stretched canvas
William T. Wiley

EB15 RANCHO SAN LORENZO, 1800, NEAR HAYWARD,
1987
Private funding
Mission and 'D' Streets
8′ x 30′ , acrylic and varnish sealer on stucco
Ricardo

SAN LEANDRO

EB16 *[UNTITLED], 1946
Funding unknown
Auditorium, San Leandro Naval Hospital,
7′ x 120′, unknown paint on plaster
Claire Falkenstein

EB17 WOMEN IN ART MAKE THE DIFFERENCE, 1994
San Francisco Women Artists' Gallery
Warehouse, Harlan Street off San Leandro Boulevard
15′ x 90′, acrylic on stucco
Alice Campbell and 65 other women

EB18 CAMP SWEENY MURAL PROJECT, 1996
Museum of Children's Art, Alameda County Probation
Dept.
Camp Wilmont Sweeny
8′ x 128′, acrylic on plywood
Susan Greene and the young men of Camp Sweeny

EB19 CONSTELLATIONS OF INFORMATION, 1997
Alameda County Arts Commission
Alameda County Sub-Acute Treatment Adolescent
Residential Services, 2050 Fairmont Drive
2′–5′ x 600′, acrylic on concrete
Johanna Poethig

OAKLAND

EB20 DOLLAROCRACY, 1966
I.L.W.U. Local 6
Union Hall, Hegenberger Road and Pardee Drive
8′ x 22′, mosaic tile
Beniamino Bufano

EB21 [UNTITLED], 1994
California Department of Conservation: Division of
Recycling
Oakland Society for the Prevention of Cruelty to
Animals,
8323 Baldwin at Hegenberger Road
13 medallions, each 24′ diameter, acrylic on plywood
Caryl Henry, Colette Crutcher, Debra Disma, Nestor
Gonzalez. and members of Project YES. from
Claremont, Frick, Roosevelt, and Westlake middle
and junior high schools

EB22 ABE SOUZA, 1991/1997
Oakland Coliseum and Oakland Athletics
Oakland Coliseim, interior behind home plate
10′ x 10′, enamel on concrete

EB23 CHARLIE SANTANA, 1992/1997
Oakland Coliseum and Oakland Athletics
Oakland Coliseum, interior behind home plate
10′ x 10′, enamel on concrete
Daniel Galvez, Jos Sances

EB24 SYLVESTER JACKSON, 1993
Oakland Coliseum and Oakland Athletics
Oakland Coliseum, interior, behind home plate
10′ x 10′, enamel on concrete
Daniel Galvez, Jos Sances

EB25–31 ABE SOUZA, CHARLIE SANTANA, SYLVESTER
JACKSON, FRANK VIVALDI, FRANK OGAWA,
WALLY HAAS, JR., BILL GRAHAM, 1997
Oakland Coliseum and Oakland Athletics
Oakland Coliseum, interior, behind home plate
Seven panels, each 8′ x 8′, digitized enamel on vinyl
cloth adhered to plywood
Daniel Galvez and Jos Sances

EB32 THE CASTLEERS, 1989
Jim's Liquors, the Castleers
Jim's Liquors, MacArthur Blvd., and 83rd Street
9′ x 20′, enamel on stucco
Dewey Crumpler

EB33 HARLEM RENAISSANCE, c.1986
Castlemont High School
Castlemont High School, 8601 MacArthur Blvd.
15′ x 45′, acrylic on stucco
Sharon Davis, Frederick Gums, Anthony Wright, Wanda
Scott Alex, supervising teacher

EB34 PRIDE OF THE PAST, FAITH IN THE FUTURE, 1989
Oakland Arts Council, OCD
Castlemont High School, 8601 MacArthur Blvd.
8′ x 40′, Danacolor on stucco
Nzinga Kianga, Joel Freeman, and JPTA students

EB35 [RAINFOREST], 1992
Castlemont High School
Castlemont High School, 8601 MacArthur Blvd.
18′ x 120′, acrylic on stucco
Violet Chew MacLean (teacher) and students

EB36 AS LONG AS THE MIND IS ENSLAVED, THE BODY
WILL NEVER BE FREE, 1993
East Bay Regional Park District's Rev. Martin Luther
King, Jr. Grant Program, Project YES (Youth
Engaged in Service), East Bay Conservation Corps,
California Department of Conservation, Division of
Recycling
Lockwood School, 6701 East 14th Street at 67th
Avenue
10′ x 33′, acrylic on stucco
Caryl Henry

EB37 *[SHADOW MURAL], 1977
California Arts Council Grant
Headstart Building, 65th Avenue, East Oakland
27′ x 20′, Politec acrylic, sealer and varnish on stucco
George Mead and CCAC students

EB38 [UNTITLED], 1994
Project YES (Youth Engaged in Service), East Bay
Conservation Corps, California Department of
Conservation, Division of Recycling
Frick Middle School, 2845 64th Avenue
Three murals, acrylic on concrete
Caryl Henry, Carlos Adriano, Nasri Zacharia

EB39 JOYS AND SORROWS OF MUSIC: LOVE RENEWING
LIFE, THE MORNING STARS, YOUTH AND
INSPIRATION, DESPAIR AND RESIGNATION,
THE IDEA OF DEATH, MEMORY RECALLING
THE DEAD, and THE GOLDEN RIVER, 1924
Mills College
Auditorium, Mills College, 5000 MacArthur Blvd.
6 large, 8 small panels, all fresco except tempera on
canvas on organ screen
Ray Boynton

EB40 [UNTITLED], 1937
Funding unknown
Entrance to Art Department, Mills College, 5000
MacArthur Blvd.
79" x 33 3/8", fresco
Ralph Stackpole, assisted by Joy Bellingley; Jack
Moxon, plasterer

EB41 STUDENT LIFE, 1990
Merritt College Mural Class
Building R, Merritt College, 12500 Campus Drive
8' x 22', Novacolor acrylics on concrete
James Morgan and Merritt College Mural Students

EB42 REDWOODS, 1981
Private funding
Hwy. 13 underpass, Aliso Avenue and Carson Street
21'–24' x 35', Politec acrylic on concrete with graffiti
sealer
Dan Fontes

EB43 MELROSE '79, 1979
Bilingual Arts Residency Program, CAC
Melrose School, 52nd and East 14th Street
15' x 30', Politec acrylic, primer, sealer, and varnish on
wood
Ester Hernandez and students

EB44 WALL OF FRIENDSHIP, 1979
Bilingual Arts Residency Program, CAC
Wall, 53rd and East 14th Street
26' x 20', Politec acrylic primer and sealer on plaster
Ester Hernandez, Pauline Hom, and Maria Pabeyta

EB45 YOUTH ARRESTED, 1986
CCAC
1612 45th Avenue near Bancroft
25' x 60', acrylic on concrete
Malaquias Montoya and CCAC students

EB46 *MURAL DE LA RAZA, 1977
Funding unknown
Building, 43rd and East 14th Street
20' x 40', latex, Politec acrylic and sealer on stucco
Ray Patlan, Zala Nevel, and Xochitl Nevel-Guerrero

EB47 FRUITVALE COMMUNITY CULTURAL HERITAGE
MURAL, 1997
Oakland Mayor's Office of Parks and Recreation,
Fruitvale Community Collaborative, Spanish-Speaking
Unity Council
Fruitvale and 37th Street
15' x 110', acrylic on brick
Steve Bronson, Nestor Gonzalez, Jaime Arabia, Martin
Tatino, Salome Portugal

EB48 [UNTITLED], 1977
Clinica de la Raza
Clinica de la Raza, Fruitvale near East 14th Street
12' x 52', Politec acrylic and sealer on plaster
Xochitl Nevel-Guerrero, Zala Nevel, and Consuelo Nevel

EB49 [UNTITLED], 1993
Private funding
1470 Fruitvale Avenue near East 14th Street
20' x 60', acrylic on stucco
Jose Meza-Velasquez, Xochitl Nevel-Guerrero

EB50 *CENTRO LEGAL, 1975
Alameda County Neighborhood Arts Program
Storefront office, Fruitvale and East 14th Street
8' x 60' , Politec acrylic and primer on plywood panels
Irene Perez

EB51 *[UNTITLED], 1969
Funding unknown
Fruitvale Development Center, Fruitvale and East 14th
Street
3' x 24', liquitex on canvas
Manuel Hernandez

EB52 *[UNTITLED], 1970
Private funding
Emiliano Zapata Street Academy, Fruitvale and East
14th Street
Dimensions and materials unknown
Malaquias Montoya, Sergio Arroyo, Albert Amesquita,
Richard Apodaca, Teresa Mendoza, Frank Garcia,
and CCAC students

EB53 CALVIN SIMMONS' ANCIENT AND FUTURE HIP-HOP
SYMPHONY, 1997
Laney College Institute for Urban Arts
Yard, Calvin Simmons High School, facing 35th Avenue
and Galindo
30' x 150', acrylic on stucco
Juana Alicia, director; designed and painted by Sophie
Hou, Fantumx, Juan Hernandez, Chris Davis, David
Pelles, Lisa von Blanckensee, Chris Durazo,
Madeleine Bair, Brandon Day, Chi Kong, Michelle
Garcia, Aaron Ludwig, Dorian Wells, Shoshana Ben-
Macker, Safahari, Melissa Silver, Mani Simmons,
Yvan Ipurriaga

EB54 NEIGHBORHOOD PRIDE, 1988
CAC, Oakland Cultural Arts Division,
Oakland Graffiti Abatement, OCD, Parks and
Recreation, Spanish Speaking Citizens Foundation
Sanborn Park Clubhouse, Fruitvale and East 16th
Street
10' x 45', acrylic on wood
Xochitl Nevel-Guerrero, Victor Acosta, and Crystal
Nevel-Kaiser

EB55 STRENGTH AND WISDOM, 1978
Oakland Neighborhood Arts Council
Spanish-Speaking Unity Council Building courtyard,
1900 Fruitvale
12' x 40', Politec acrylic, primer, and varnish
Tony Machado and Richard Montez

EB56 NEL, 1993
Public Art Program, Cultural Arts Division,
City of Oakland; Narcotics Education League
Fruitvale Plaza, 35th Avenue and East 14th Street
25' x 62', Novacolor on brick
Fresco (Ray Patlan and Eduardo Pineda)

EB57 HOMAGE TO AMERICA, 1991
Project YES (Youth Engaged in Service), East Bay
Conservation Corps, California Department of
Conservation, Division of Recycling
34th Avenue at Farnam
10' x 60', acrylic on stucco
Jose Meza-Velasquez, numerous foreign artists, and
youth from Carter, Claremont, Frick, Roosevelt, and
Westlake middle and junior high schools

EB58 I HAVE A DREAM, 1993
East Bay Regional Park District's Rev. Martin Luther
King Jr., Grant Program, Project YES (Youth
Engaged in Service), East Bay Conservation Corps,
California Department of Conservation, Division of
Recycling
Warehouse, 2834 Ford Street at 29th Avenue
8' x 50', Novacolor on stucco
Emmanuel Montoya and students

EB59 *[UNTITLED], 1973
Funding unknown
Lazear School, 824 29th Avenue
16' x 80', liquitex acrylic on masonite
Manuel Hernandez

EB60 *[UNTITLED], 1972, 1973
Funding unknown
Lazear School, 824 29th Avenue
8' x 24', liquitex on masonite and concrete
Malaquias Montoya and CCAC students

EB61 OAKLAND IS PROUD, 1989
Private funding
St. Joseph's Professional Care Center,
East 12th and East 27th Avenue
8' x 350', spraycan on brick
Joel (Phresh) Freeman

EB62 *[UNTITLED], 1970
Latin American Library, Oakland Public Library Funds
East Oakland Latin American Library,
Miller and East 14th Street
Five murals in skylight- 4' x 17' (x4 sides), liquitex
acrylic on masonite
Malaquias Montoya, Manuel Hernandez, Andreas
Cisnero, Domingo Rivera, and CCAC students

EB63 DON'T LET OUR PEOPLE GO UP IN SMOKE, 1993
California Department of Health Services, Proposition
99, The Tobacco Tax Initiative, Asian Health
Services, East Bay Asian Youth Center
Roosevelt Junior High School, 19th Avenue at East 20th
Street
12' x 15', acrylic on stucco
Healthy Neighborhood '93 (27 students)

EB64 NO JUSTICE, NO PEACE, 1993
Private funding
Roosevelt Junior High School, 19th Avenue at East 20th
Street
9' x 65', spray enamel on stucco
Artist unknown

EB65 INDIGENOUS ANIMALS OF CALIFORNIA, 1992
Project YES (Youth Engaged in Service), East Bay
Conservation Corps, California Department of
Conservation, Division of Recycling
Bella Vista School, 11th Street between East 24th and
East 28th Streets
16'-4' x 193', Liquitex on concrete
Brett Cook-Dizney, assisted by Emmanuel Montoya and
students

EB66 JURASTIC PARK, 1992
Private funding
East 14th Street at 15th Avenue
12' x 75', spray enamel on concrete cinderblock
Phresh with Krash

EB67 ARE WE QUESTIONING OUR FREEDOM? 1990
Private funding
East 14th Street at 15th Avenue
12' x 18', spray enamel on concrete cinderblock
Phresh

EB68 MYSTICAL, 1992
Private funding
East 14th Street at 15th Avenue
12' x 18', spray enamel on concrete cinderblock
Phresh

EB69 MARILYN, 1990
Private funding
15th Avenue at East 14th Street
12' x 40', spray enamel on concrete cinderblock
Phresh

EB70 MARBEI THE DO NOTHING COMIC, 1993
Private funding
15th Avenue at East 14th Street
15' x 14', spray enamel on concrete cinderblock
Phresh

EB71 HOLLYWOOD MOVIE MONSTERS, 1992
Private funding
15th Avenue at East 14th Street
15' x 40', spray enamel on concrete cinderblock
Krash, Phresh and Poem

EB72 SPIRIT OF CHILDHOOD, 1983
OCD
Franklin Recreation Center, 1010 East 15th Street
10' x 30', acrylic on concrete
Gary Graham and Vista College mural students

EB73 EN EL LIBRO TU LIBERTAD/IN KNOWLEDGE THERE
IS LIBERATION, 1979, 1980
CCAC Mural Class, Oakland Arts Commission, OCD
Clinton Park School, 6th Avenue and 12th Street
13' x 24', latex on wood siding
Malaquias Montoya and CCAC students

EB74 RCA FAMILY, 1989
California Pacific Designs
Whales and Friends Office, 550 2nd Avenue
15' x 50', Novacolor on sheetrock
Dan Fontes

EB75 [ABSTRACT], 1978, restored 1991
Alameda County Neighborhood Arts Program
Entrance, Oakland Public Library, 125 14th Avenue
Two panels, 36' x 14', acrylic on concrete
Ed Cassel

EB76 [UNTITLED], 1976
SFMMA Bicentennial Funds
Centro Infantil, 3rd Avenue and East 11th Street
8' x 15', Politec acrylic paint and sealer on wood panels
Graciela Carrillo and Irene Perez

EB77 NUESTRA HISTORIA, 1983
CCAC Mural Class
Centro Infantil, 3rd Avenue at East 11th Street
13' x 40', latex enamel on wood
Malaquias Montoya and CCAC students

EB78 NO HAY ROSAS SIN ESPINAS, 1985
CCAC Mural Class
Centro Infantil, 3rd Avenue and East 11th Street
13' x 40', latex on wood
Malaquias Montoya and CCAC students

EB79 [UNTITLED], 1986
CCAC Mural Class
Centro Infantil, 3rd Avenue and East 11th Street
10' x 60', latex on concrete
Malaquias Montoya and CCAC students

EB80 [UNTITLED], 1988
CCAC Mural Class
Centro Infantil, 3rd Avenue and East 11th Street
8' x 64', latex on plywood
Malaquias Montoya and CCAC students

EB81 *[UNTITLED], 1975
Laney College
Cafeteria, Laney College, 900 Fallon Street
7' x 15', Politec acrylic on stucco
Lou Silva

EB82 *OPPRESSION VERSUS RESISTANCE, 1976
Laney College
Campus, Laney College, 900 Fallon Street
15' x 45', Politec acrylic and plastic sealer on concrete
Gary Graham, Saul Hopi Means, Terry Phillips, Paula
   Simon, and Third World Artists' Caucus

EB83 EXPLORATION-SETTLING IN CALIFORNIA, 1937
FAP
Lobby, Alameda County Courthouse, 1225 Fallon Street
Two panels, each 15' x 7', marble opus sectile tile
Marion Simpson

EB84 MANY BOOKS, ONE WORLD, 1988
Alameda County Arts Commission
Office building, 12th Street and Madison
25' x 72', Golden colors acrylic on concrete
Brooke Fancher and Kriska

EB85 HOW CHINESE HELPED BUILD CALIFORNIA
   WATERWAYS, 1992
EBMUD
EBMUD Headquarters (interior), 11th Street at Franklin
5' x 32', acrylic on wallboard
Nancy Hom with Selma Brown

EB86 MITZVAH; THE JEWISH CULTURAL EXPERIENCE, 1985
CAC, Hebrew Free Loan Association, Jewish
   Community Relations Council, Koret Foundation, L
   and D Scaffolding, Office of Economic Development
Office building, 1404 Franklin near 14th Street
105' x 100', Danacolor enamel on stucco
Keith Sklar, Brooke Fancher, and Dan Fontes

EB87 [STAINED GLASS MOTIF], 1994
Department of Public Works, Oakland
13th and Clay Streets
8' x 500', acrylic on plywood
Dan Fontes

EB88 PASSAGES, 1992
Public Art Program, Cultural Arts Division, City of
   Oakland
Oakland Convention Center, Broadway at 10th Street
8' x 16', mixed media on wood
Marie Johnson Calloway, April Watkins, Heather
   Watkins

EB89 OAKLAND ARTS EXPLOSION, 1986, 1987, 1988, 1989
Alameda County Arts Commission, Oakland Festival of
   the Arts
Lobby, Hyatt Regency Hotel, 10th Street and Broadway
8' x 48', enamel on canvas
Dan Fontes

EB90 OAKLAND CITY LIFE, 1992
MOCHA, St.Elizabeth Youth Employment
Construction fence, Broadway at 14th Street
8' x 81', acrylic on plywood
Edythe Boone, Susan Greene, and Summer Youth
   Program members

EB91 CHOICES, 1992
Project YES (Youth Engaged in Service), East Bay
   Conservation Corps, California Department of
   Conservation, Division of Recycling
Construction fence, Broadway at 14th Street
8' x 66', acylic on plywood
Brett Cook-Dizney and youths

EB92 THE DOWNTOWN OAKLAND BLACK HISTORY
   MURAL PROJECT, 1992
City of Oakland, Office of Economic Development and
   Employment, Project YES (Youth Engaged in
   Service), East Bay Conservation Corps, California
   Department of Conservation, Division of Recycling
Broadway, Telegraph, and San Pablo at 15th Street
Four large entrances, each approx. 12' x 10', acrylic on
   plywood
Ivan Watkins with Project YES Clubmembers from
   Carter, Claremont, Frick, Roosevelt, and Westlake
   middle and junior high schools

EB93 HEARTS AND HANDS, 1989
City of Oakland Streetworks
Smith Street Building, 15th and Broadway
8' x 12', acrylic on stucco
James Morgan and Edythe Boone

EB94 TWIST OF FATE, 1993
Public Art Program, Cultural Arts Division, City of
   Oakland
Construction fence, City Hall Plaza
8' x 180', acrylic on plywood
Daniel Galvez

EB95 *OAKLAND'S PORTRAIT, 1981
Pro Arts, ACAC, OCD, Liberty House, A Central Place,
   L.J. and Mark Skaggs Foundation
Kahn's Alley, 15th Street between Telegraph and San
   Pablo
23' x 185', enamel on stucco
Daniel Galvez, Keith Sklar, Juan Cannon-Karlos

EB96 *ACORN MURAL, 1976
NEA, National Paint and Coatings Association
Cathedral Building, Broadway and Telegraph Avenue
100' x 30', Danacolor, primer, and sealer on stucco
George Mead, Mike Hardeman, Claire Freitas, and Ivor
   Heskett

EB97 [HOTEL AND RESTAURANT EMPLOYEES AND
   BARTENDERS UNION], 1993
HREBU Local 28
548 20th Street near Telegraph
12' x 24', acrylic on mosaic
Jose Meza-Velasquez, Jose Hernandez Delgadillo

127

EB98   NATURE, 1904; THE ARTS, 1904; RESIGNATION, 1907; CONQUEST, 1907; THE SOIL, 1908; THE GRAIN, 1908; placed in storage in 1974
        Oakland Public Library, Charles Greene branch, 14th Street and Martin Luther King, Jr. Way
        Six murals, each 9'9" x 7'9", oil on canvas
        Arthur Mathews

EB99   POETRY, PROSE, and THE ARTS AND SCIENCES, 1904
        Phoebe Hearst
        Oakland Public Library, Charles Greene branch, Second floor landing, 14th Street and Martin Luther King, Jr. Way
        Three panels, oil on canvas
        Marian Holden Pope

EB100   [UNTITLED], 1994
        Project YES (Youth Engaged in Service), East Bay Conservation Corps, California Department of Conservation, Division of Recycling
        1448 10th Street
        12'–15' x 30', acrylic on wood
        Rigo '94

EB101   PARAMOUNT THEATER, 1929 (restored 1972)
        Miller and Pflueger
        Paramount Theater, 2025 Broadway
        Two panels, each 50' x 15', mosaic
        Gerald Fitzgerald

EB102   OAKLAND ALL NATIONS, 1997
        Private funding
        Castro and 14th Streets
        15' x 45', acrylic on stucco
        A & A Signs and Graphics

EB103   THE LIMITS OF TYRANTS, 1980
        CCAC Mural Class
        Supporting Future Growth Child Development Center, 1825 San Pablo Avenue
        15' x 35', latex enamel and primer on stucco
        Malaquias Montoya and CCAC students

EB104   STREET TATTOO, 1982
        CAC, OCD
        I-580 underpass at San Pablo Avenue and West Grand Street
        15' x 220', oil enamel on concrete
        Daniel Galvez, James Morgan, Dan Fontes, Keith Sklar, O'Brien Thiele, and others

EB105   I HAVE A DREAM, 1993
        East Bay Regional Park District's Rev. Martin Luther King, Jr. Grant Program, Project YES (Youth Engaged in Service), East Bay Conservation Corps, California Department of Conservation, Division of Recycling.
        Martin Luther King, Jr. School, 960 10th Street near Market Street
        12' x 48', acrylic on stucco
        Sana Makhoul

EB106   MARCH OF EXCELLENCE, 1986
        City of Oakland, East Bay Community Foundation
        Peralta Village, Poplar Street between 10th and 12th Streets
        Six walls totalling 8' x 112', acrylic on concrete
        WALLSPEAK!: Dewey Crumpler, Edythe Boone, and Kim Anno

EB107   UNITY, 1989
        City of Oakland, East Bay Community Foundation, Oakland JPTA, Oakland OCD, Private donations, Ruth Mott Fund, World Council of Churches
        Peralta Village, 10th Street between Cypress and Union
        25' x 30', acrylic on concrete
        WALLSPEAK!: Nzinga Kianga, Edythe Boone, Kim Anno, Karen Bennett, Miranda Bergman, and local youth

EB108   KNOWLEDGE, 1988
        City of Oakland, East Bay Community Foundation, Oakland JPTA, Oakland OCD, Private Donations, Ruth Mott Fund, World Council of Churches
        Peralta Village, 10th Street between Cypress and Union
        25' x 30', acrylic on concrete
        WALLSPEAK!: Dewey Crumpler

EB109   AND STILL WE SPEAK OF PEACE, FREEDOM, AND DIGNITY, 1988
        City of Oakland, East Bay Community Foundation, Oakland JPTA, Oakland OCD, Private Donations, Ruth Mott Fund, World Council of Churches
        Peralta Village, 12th Street at Kirkham
        25' x 30', Novacolor acylic on concrete
        WALLSPEAK!: Jimi Evins

EB110   BLACK AMERICAN, 1988
        City of Oakland, East Bay Community Foundation, Oakland JPTA, Oakland OCD, Private Donations, Ruth Mott Fund, World Council of Churches
        Peralta Village, 12th Street at Kirkham
        25' x 30', spraycan on concrete
        WALLSPEAK!: Joel (Phresh) Freeman

EB111   [UNTITLED], 1987
        Thomas A. Short Company
        Billboard near Wood and 34th Street, visible from eastbound I-580
        Mr. Frazier

EB112   POOL, 1993
        Public Arts Program, Cultural Arts Division, City of Oakland
        de Fremery Park Swimming Pool, Poplar and 18th Street
        Two panels, each approx. 20' x 4½', photographs computer-digitalized on ceramic tile
        Mike Mandel and Larry Sultan

EB113   KNOWLEDGE IS POWER, 1993
        CAC, MOCHA
        Ralph Bunche School, 18th Street and Poplar
        16' x 36', Novacolor acrylic on plywood
        Susan Greene and students

EB114   CULTURE AND COMMUNITY, 1995
        Oakland Neighborhood Revitalization Program
        San Pablo and 63rd Street
        8' x 300', acrylic on wood
        Keith Williams, with Dan Fontes and others

EB115   DO THE SLOW DOWN IN OAKTOWN and IT'S TIME 2 WAKE UP AND LOVE OUR YOUTH, 1996
        MOCHA (The Museum of Children's Art)
        Chestnut off West Grand Street
        Two panels, each 7' x 20', acrylic on stucco
        Keith Williams and youth

EB116 WE NEED SOME 'ONE LOVE' EVERYTIME, 1996
MOCHA (The Museum of Children's Art)
Linden and West Grand
Two panels, each 7' x 22', acrylic on stucco
Keith Williams and youth

EB117 THE NINETIES MURAL, 1990
Private funding
West Street and San Pablo Avenue
15' x 45', airbrush exterior housepaint with verathane
    coating on brick
Darien Hamilton

EB118 NO SMOKE SCREENS/NO COLOR LINES, 1993
Lowell Street Mural Project, Summer Youth Training
    Program, City of Oakland Office of Housing and
    Neighborhood Development, East Bay Community
    Foundation, LEF Foundation
Golden Gate Recreation Center, 1075 62nd Street at
    Herzog
15' x 45', Novacolor on concrete
Rigo '93 and 9 youths

EB119 ROOTS OF THE COMMUNITY, 1995
Lowell Street Mural Project
5625 Lowell Street, off Stanford
19' x 150', acrylic on concrete
Jimi Evins, Candi Farlice, Jamie Morgan, Patricia
    Montgomery

EB120 WALK IN THE RAINBOW SPIRIT, 1995
Southwest Neighborhood Watch
San Pablo at Haskell
9' x 30', acrylic on stucco
Selma Brown

EB121 FREEDOM IS NEVER VOLUNTARILY GIVEN BY THE
    OPPRESSOR. IT MUST BE DEMANDED BY THE
    OPPRESSED, 1993
East Bay Regional Park District's Rev. Martin Luther
    King, Jr. Grant Program, Project YES (Youth
    Engaged in Service), East Bay Conservation Corps,
    California Department of Conservation, Division of
    Recycling
Marcus Book Store, 3900 Martin Luther King, Jr. Way at
    39th Street
10' x 12', acrylic on plywood
Jimi Evins

EB122 ANIMURALS, 1985
Oakland OCD
I-580 underpass at Broadway
Six zebras: 16' x 18' to 12' x 6', oil on concrete
Dan Fontes

EB123 GIRAPHICS, 1984
Oakland OCD
I-580 underpass at Harrison Street
Seven giraffes: 32' x 6' to 16' x 5', oil on concrete
Dan Fontes

EB124 GIRAFFICS PARK, 1994
Caltrans
I-580 underpass at Harrison Street
32'–35' high pillars, Danacolor on steel
Dan Fontes

EB125 LAKE MERRITT MURAL PROJECT, 1988
Alameda County Arts Commission, Oakland
    Redevelopment Agency, Supervisors' Fund
Auto dealership, 27th Street and Broadway
28'–21' x 89', oil on concrete
Dan Fontes

EB126 PAY EQUITY, 1991
Service Employees International Union
SEIU local 790 (interior), 522 Grand Avenue at Perkins
8' x 16', Novacolor on masonite
Fresco (Ray Patlan and Eduardo Pineda),

EB127 GRAND PERFORMANCE, 1984
CAC, East Bay Community Foundation, Zellerbach
    Family Fund, Kaiser Cement
I-580 underpass at Grand Street
23' x 145', oil enamel on concrete
Keith Sklar, Daniel Galvez, Brooke Fancher, Dan
    Fontes, and Karen Sjoholm

EB128 TO IGNORE EVIL IS TO BECOME AN ACCOMPLICE
    TO IT, 1993
Project YES (Youth Engaged in Service), East Bay
    Conservation Corps, California Department of
    Conservation, Division of Recycling, East Bay
    Regional Park District's Rev. Martin Luther King, Jr.
    Grant
I-580 underpass, at Lake Park and Lake Shore Avenues
13' x 30', Novacolor on concrete
Susan Greene and Meera Desai

EB129 INVISIBLE COLORS, 1992
Public Art Program, Cultural Arts Division, City of
    Oakland
I-580 underpass at Park Blvd.
8' x 150', outdoor white paint with glass "highway"
    beads
Seyed Alavi and 16 high school students

EB130 INFORM(N)ATION, 1992
Public Art Program, Cultural Arts Division, City of
    Oakland
I-580 underpass at Fruitvale Avenue
8' x 160', outdoor white paint with glass "highway"
    beads
Seyed Alavi and 16 high school students

EB131 eRACISM, 1992
Public Art Program, Cultural Arts Division, City of
    Oakland
I-580 underpass at High Street
8' x 80', outdoor white paint with glass "highway" beads
Seyed Alavi and 16 high school students

EB132 [UNTITLED], 1978
Oakland Neighborhood Arts Program
I-580 underpass, MacArthur Blvd. and High Street
20' x 170', Politec acrylic, sealer, and varnish on
    concrete
Tony Machado and Richard Montez

EB133 D IFFERENCE, 1992
Public Art Program, Cultural Arts Division, City of
    Oakland
I-580 underpass at Buell Street
15' x 140', outdoor white paint with glass "highway"
    beads
Seyed Alavi and 16 high school students

EB134 CHILDREN'S MURAL OF THE NORTH OAKLAND
    WELFARE DEPARTMENT OFFICE, 1975
North Oakland Welfare Department, 4501 Broadway
10' x 29', acrylic on masonite panels
Osha Neumann and Janet Kranzberg

EB135 *STAR WARS MURAL, 1978
CAC, Oakland Housing Authority
449 49th Street
12' x 16', Politec acrylic and varnish
George Mead and area children

EB136 CALIFORNIA HISTORY, 1927
Graduating classes
Oakland Technical High School, Auditorium, 4351
Broadway at 42nd Street
30' x 68', above proscenium in theater (believed
destroyed but may be in storage)
Maynard Dixon

EB137 [AGAINST IMPERIALISM], 1979
Private funding
Oakland Technical High School, 4351 Broadway at 42nd
Street
8' x 24', acrylic on masonite panels
Brigada Orlando Letelier

EB138 *CCAC MURAL, 1981
CCAC Mural Class
California College of Arts and Crafts, Broadway at
College Avenue
25' x 16', latex enamel and oil primer on plywood
Malaquias Montoya and CCAC Mural Class students

EB139 *[WOMEN'S LIBERATION], 1984
CCAC Mural Class
California College of Arts and Crafts, Broadway at
College Avenue
25' x 16', latex on plywood
Malaquias Montoya and CCAC Mural Class students

EB140 *[UNTITLED], 1988
CCAC Mural Class
California College of Arts and Crafts, Broadway at
College Avenue
25' x 16', latex on plywood
Malaquias Montoya and CCAC Mural Class students

EB141 *CENTRAL AMERICA, 1988
CCAC Mural Class
California College of Arts and Crafts, Broadway at
College Avenue
25' x 16', latex on plywood
Malaquias Montoya and CCAC Mural Class students

EB142 THE OTHER SIDE OF CENSORSHIP IS
SELF-DETERMINATION, 1989
CCAC Mural Class
California College of Arts and Crafts, Broadway at
College Avenue
25' x 16', latex on plywood
Malaquias Montoya and CCAC Mural Class students

EB143 ONE BLIND MOUSE, 1992
CCAC
California College of Arts and Crafts, Broadway at
College Avenue
25' x 16', acrylic on plywood
Juana Alicia and CCAC students

EB144 FREE WINDS BLOW, 1966
Funding unknown
Lake Temescal Park underpass, south end off Broadway
Terrace
Two panels, 5' x 60', unknown paint on concrete
Anthony, OP, and Timothy, OP

EB145 FRONTIERS OF SPACE, 1980
Caltrans, OCD
Rockridge BART station, College Avenue and Grove-
Shafter Freeway
20' x 120', acrylic on concrete
Gary Graham, Charles Lobdell, Jack Greene, and Vista
College Mural Class students

EB146 FIRESTORM COMMUNITY MURAL PROJECT, 1994
Office of the Mayor and Community Arts Division, City
of Oakland; Oakland Community Fund; BART, Pro
Arts; volunteers
Rockridge BART station, College Avenue at Keith
8' x 150', more than 2,000 ceramic tiles
Hundreds of people affected by the Oakland fire of 1993

EB147 HISTORY OF COFFEE, 1993
Private funding
Interior, 6021 College Avenue at Claremont
10' x 30', acrylic on sheetrock
Josh Sarantitis with Roberto Guerrero

EB148 *LAKE TEMESCAL, 1978
Private funding
L.J. Kruse Plumbing and Heating Company, 6247
College Avenue
9' x 12', acrylic and latex paint and varnish on stucco
Stefen

EB149 BUTLER'S FARM, 1978
Private funding
Butler's Natural Foods (interior), 2944 College Avenue
2,000 square feet, acrylic and varnish
Stefen and Anodea Judith

EB150 *BEGGAR'S BANQUET, 1977
Berkeley Art Services, CETA
University Lutheran Chapel, Emergency Food Project,
2425 College at Haste
8' x 50', Politec primer, acrylics, and sealer on
plasterboard
Osha Neumann and O'Brien Thiele with others

EB151 OCEANUS, 1978
Caltrans, Laney College, Vista College
Hwy. 24 underpass at Claremont Blvd.
20' x 150', Politec acrylic and plastic sealer on concrete
Gary Graham, Lou Silva, Ed Monroe, and mural
workshop participants

EB152 NDEBELE ARTISTS, 1987
Private funding
The Urban Village, 4401 Telegraph Avenue at 44th
Street
6' x 25', Danacolors on masonite
Nzinga Kianga

EB153 PROJECT YES, 1990-1992
Project YES (Youth Engaged in Service), East Bay
Conservation Corps, California Department of
Conservation, Division of Recycling
Hwy. 24 underpass, Telegraph Avenue near Aileen
10' x 60', acrylic on concrete
Artist unknown

EB154 GEOMETRIC SPIRAL, 1979
OCD
Hwy. 24 ramp, Telegraph Avenue and 51st Street
20' x 25', acrylic on concrete
Lois Mann Fischer and Vista College Mural Class
students

EB155 OUT OF MANY ONE, 1991
Private funding
4927 Shattuck Avenue at 51st Street
15' x 45', acrylic on stucco
J.J. Jackson

EB156 HOPE IS ALIVE, 1994
Private funding, The Center
Shattuck Avenue at 59th Street
18′ x 47′, acrylic on stucco
O'Brien Thiele, Sharon Siskin, and people living with
HIV and their friends, including Kerrie L. Campbell,
John Nielson, Marlon Kera, Ron Coleman, Ed
Seidel, Richard "RC" Comstock, Lowell Brook, and
others

EB157 [UNTITLED], 1975
Recycling Center Summer Program
Recycling Center, Telegraph Avenue and 54th Street
15′ x 30′, Politec acrylic on wood
Osha Neumann

EB158 JUNGLE MURAL, 1989
Private funding
Campanile Veterinary Clinic, 5666 Telegraph Avenue
20′ x 18′, acrylic on stucco
Ray Regan

EB159 *SELF-DETERMINATION, 1983
CCAC Mural Class
Magnetic Imaging affiliate of the Alta Breast Center,
5730 Telegraph Avenue at 58th Street
25′ x 100′, latex on stucco
Malaquias Montoya and CCAC Mural Class students

EB160 [UNTITLED], 1985
Funding unknown
Magnetic Imaging affiliate of the Alta Breast Center,
5730 Telegraph Avenue at 58th Street
20′ x 100′, unknown paint on stucco
Gary Graham, Charles Lobdell, Matt Courtway, and Ed
Monroe

EB161 SURREAL BEACH, AND DECO FOUNTAIN AND
MOON, 1989
Private funding
Apartment house, 5915 Telegraph Avenue near 59th
Street
One panel 20′ x 12′, two panels 20′ x 10′, acrylic on
stucco
Ray Regan

PIEDMONT

EB162 POPPIES, 1934
FAP
Piedmont High School (interior), 800 Magnolia Street
6′8″ x 14′2″, fresco
Claire Falkenstein

EB163 SCHOOL LIFE, 1937/1973 (copy)
Piedmont High School
Piedmont High School (interior), 800 Magnolia Street
6′ x 6′, fresco
Hideo Noda

EB164 EDUCATION: ANCIENT AND MODERN, 1937
FAP
Piedmont High School (interior), 800 Magnolia Street
Two panels, 12′ x 8′ each, mosaic
Edgar Taylor

EB165 JUNIPERO SERRA, 1937
PWAP
Piedmont High School (interior), 800 Magnolia Street
12′ x 8′, tempera
Joseph Sheridan

EB166 THE MONTCLAIR DUCK POND MURAL, 1994
Department of Public Works, Oakland
Montclair Recreation Center, Moraga Avenue at Hwy.13
10′ x 27′, acrylic on cinderblock
Dan Fontes

BERKELEY

EB167 [UNTITLED], 1987
CCAC Mural Class
Willard Junior High School, 2425 Stuart at Telegraph
Avenue
8′–15′ x 135′, latex enamel on concrete
Malaquias Montoya, CCAC students and students from
Willard Junior High School

EB168 *INTERSECTIONS, 1980, mostly destroyed; repainted
with changes,1997
CAC
Gymnasium, Willard Junior High School, Telegraph
Avenue at Ward
45′ x 67′, acrylic on stucco
Osha Neumann and Daniel Galvez; repainted by
O'Brien Thiele and Osha Neumann

EB169 *TAKE CONTROL, 1978
Berkeley Women's Health Collective Raffle
Berkeley Women's Health Collective, 2942 Ellsworth
near Howe
8′ x 16′, Politec acrylic and varnish on plywood
Deborah Greene and Ariella Seidenberg

EB170 BLOOMING, 1974
Private funding
Center for Independent Living, 2539 Telegraph Avenue
12′ x 80′, acrylic on stucco
Gary Graham and Joan Briscoe

EB171 [UNTITLED], 1977
Center for Independent Living; Laney College
Center for Independent Living, 2539 Telegraph Avenue
8′ x 75′, paints and primer on concrete
Gary Graham

EB172 *PEOPLE'S HISTORY OF TELEGRAPH AVENUE, 1976
At least two other murals were painted on this wall, one
c.1969 and the other in the early 1970s. This mural
was destroyed in 1997.
Private donations
Wall, Telegraph Avenue and Haste Street
20′ x 88′, Politec acrylic, oil primer, and epoxy varnish
on stucco
Osha Neumann, Daniel Galvez, Janet Kranzberg, and
O'Brien Thiele

EB173 PEOPLE'S PARK MURAL, 1996
Chaplaincy to the Homeless, Margaret and Moshe Alafi,
First Congregational Church of Berkeley, Northern
California Grantmakers
Wall, Telegraph Avenue and Haste Street
8′ x 72′, acrylic on plywood
Edythe Boone, assisted by Elvi Jo Dougherty and Trish
Tripp

EB174 [PEOPLE'S PARK BATHROOM MURALS], 1989–1994
Private funding
Bathroom, People's Park, Haste Street east of
Telegraph Avenue
8′ x 80′, acrylic and spray enamel on cinderblock
Artists unknown

EB175 *SERVE THE PEOPLE, 1976
Chicano Studies Department
Villa Hermosa restaurant (interior), Telegraph Avenue
  and Haste Street
12' x 30', latex and Politec acrylics and sealer on plaster
Ray Patlan and Patricia Rodriguez

EB176 *STORY OF THE RAINBOW, 1978
Private funding
Sunset Gold Store, 2911 Telegraph Avenue
6,000 square feet (interior walls and ceiling), Gibson
  latex on plaster
Anodea Judith, Roxanne Hanna, and Stefen

EB177 *RAINBOW BRIDGE, 1978
Private funding
Rasputin's Records (north interior wall), 2379 Telegraph
  Avenue
12' x 50', Politec acrylic, liquitex, and Gibson paints
Stefen and Anodea Judith

EB178 LARRY BLAKE'S RATHSKELLER-RESTAURANT, 1974
Private funding
Larry Blake's Rathskeller-Restaurant, 2367 Telegraph
  Avenue
Two walls, 8' x 9' each, and the ceiling, oil base primer,
  latex and acrylic on plywood
Stefen

EB179 STILL LIFE AND BLOSSOMING ALMOND TREES,
  1931
Sigmund Stern Family
Stern Hall (foyer), University of California campus,
  Gayley Road near Hearst Avenue
5' x 8½', fresco
Diego Rivera

EB180 [UNTITLED], 1977
Chicano Studies Mural Class
Wurster Hall (5th floor), University of California
10' x 20', Politec acrylic on concrete and wood
Ray Patlan and Patricia Rodriguez

EB181 [UNTITLED], 1936-7
WPA
Campus Office Supplies Building (formerly Old
  Powerhouse), a brick building just east of Sather
  Gate along Strawberry Creek, University of
  California
Two panels, 18' x 10', mosaic tile
Helen Bruton

EB182 BEAR MURAL, 1993
University of California
Edwards Stadium (south wall), Bancroft and Oxford
  Streets
7' x 14', acrylic on concrete
Dale Bogaski

EB183 [UNTITLED], 1979
Lucas Bookstore
University Press Bookstore, 2430 Bancroft Way
18'–28' x 128', latex primer, Politec and latex paints on
  stucco
Lou Silva

EB184 [UNTITLED], 1978
Private funding
YWCA Daycare Center, Allston Street at Oxford
6' x 80', Politec gesso on plaster and brick
Ariella, Bonita, Buffy, Burl, Carolyn, Deborah Greene,
  Osha Neumann, and Victor

EB185 INCIDENTS IN CALIFORNIA HISTORY, 1937
TRAP
Berkeley Main Post Office, Milvia and Allston Streets
8' x 16', tempera and oil on canvas
Suzanne Scheuer

EB186 OHLONE JOURNEY, 1995
LEF Foundation, City of Berkeley, La Pena Cultural
  Center
Ohlone Park, Milvia and Hearst Streets
Two walls, 10'3"–12' x 20', two walls, 10'3" x 29', acrylic
  on concrete
Jeanne LaMarr, with Spencer LaMarr, Ella LaMarr, Kyle
  Curtis

EB187 [UNTITLED], 1976
Berkeley Art Services
Berkeley High School, 2246 Milvia
Three panels, 7' x 15', Politec acrylic, gesso and sealer
  on concrete
Waldo Nilo and Irene Perez

EB188 *YMCA ENTRANCE, 1975
Berkeley Art Services, CETA
Berkeley YMCA, 2001 Allston
Two panels, 11' x 11' and 8' x 4'. Politec primer and
  acrylic on concrete
Irene Perez

EB189 *UNTITLED, 1975, destroyed 1990
Berkeley High School
Berkeley Community Theater, Allston near Martin Luther
  King, Jr. Way
6'–15' x 100', acrylic on concrete
Victor Ichioka, Barbara Scales, and students

EB190 BERKELEY, THE CITY, AND ITS PEOPLE, 1973
City of Berkeley, NEA, Civic Arts Commission,
  Zellerbach Family Fund
Berkeley Unified School District Building, Council Room
  (2nd floor)
11' x 15½', mixed media on panels
Romare Bearden

EB191 [BERKWOOD-HEDGE MURALS], 1980
  (partially destroyed 1989)
Private funding
Berkwood-Hedge School, 1809 Bancroft Way at
  McKinley
Three panels, 10' x 60' total, but only one remains,
  acrylic on stucco and cinderblock
Brigada Orlando Letelier and students

EB192 LEARNING TO FLY, 1993
Private funding
Berkwood-Hedge School, 1809 Bancroft Way at
  McKinley
12' x 16', Novacolor acrylic on painted concrete brick
Jane Norling, Tim Drescher

EB193 MANY ROADS TO HEALTH, 1977
Berkeley Arts Services, CETA, Herrick Hospital
Herrick Hospital Emergency Room, 2001 Dwight Way
  near Milvia Street
10' x 12', Politec acrylic, primer, and sealer on framed
  masonite panels
Osha Neumann and O'Brien Thiele

EB194 [UNTITLED], 1981
Herrick Hospital Mural Fund and private donations
Herrick Hospital, 2001 Dwight Way near Milvia Street
8' x 20', acrylic on plaster
Margo Bors

EB195 RECYCLING CENTER, 1978
Private funding
Recycling Center, Dwight and Martin Luther King, Jr.
Way
6' x 25', Politec primer and sealer, wax sealer on
plywood
Osha Neumann

EB196 WALL FOR PEACE, 1989
Alameda County (John George), Women for Peace,
Clinton A. White, City of Berkeley, private funding
Rev. Martin Luther King, Jr. Park, Martin Luther King, Jr.
Way at Allston
Ten panels, 21" x 111"; ten panels, 33" x 111"; two
panels, 39" x 111", fired ceramic tiles
Carolyn Marks and "5000 people who painted tiles-
including Archbishop Desmond Tutu, the Reverend
Jesse Jackson, Congressman Ronald V. Dellums."

EB197 MALCOLM X SCHOOL, 1976
Berkeley Arts Services
Malcolm X School, Ellis and Ashby Streets
20' x 70', Politec acrylic, gesso, and varnish on concrete
Waldo Nilo and Irene Perez

EB198 STARRY PLOUGH, 1979
Private funding, Vista College
Starry Plough Pub, 3101 Shattuck and Prince Streets
13' x 10', Politec primer and acrylic on stucco
Osha Neumann and the Vista College Mural Workshop

EB199 SONG OF UNITY, 1978; repainted 1986
Commonarts, private funding, BCD, ACAC
La Pena Cultura Center, 3105 Shattuck Avenue
75' x 40', Politec sealer and acrylic on papier-mache
and masonite
Commonarts: Ray Patlan, Osha Neumann, O'Brien
Thiele, and Anna de Leon

EB200 *ALCATRAZ LIQUORS, 1977, 1978
Private funding, Commonarts
Alcatraz Liquors, Alcatraz and Sacramento Streets
4' x 30', latex and Politec acrylic on aluminum
Commonarts: Ray Patlan and O'Brien Thiele

EB201 *GROVE STREET MURALS: BLACK, LATINO,
PUERTO RICAN STRUGGLES, 1969
Private funding
Grove Street College, Martin Luther King, Jr. Way and
58th Street
Three panels, approx. 10' x 50' each, oil on wood
Wilma Bonnett, Joan X, Shirley Triest, David Bradford,
Manuel Hernandez, Malaquias Montoya, and David
Salgado

EB202 *[UNTITLED], 1978
Alameda County NAP, CETA, private donors
Warehouse, 61st-62nd Street and Doyle, Emeryville
30' x 110', latex and primer on wood, metal and
concrete
Anna Horvath and Foad (Floyd) Satterfield

EB203 VIVA LA RAZA, 1977
CETA
Goodwill, 1512 Adeline Street
15' x 70', masonry primer/sealer, latex primer, enamel,
oil, varnish on brick
Daniel Galvez, Osha Neumann, O'Brien Thiele, and
Stephanie Barrett

EB204 *SOME OF OUR BEST FRIENDS, 1978, 1979
Private funding
Berkeley Humane Society Adoption Center, Eighth
Street and Carlton
12' x 30', Politec, MPC base and sealer on stucco
Ariella Seidenberg and Deborah Greene

EB205 THE FIFTH STAR, 1987
Private funding
Outback, 2517 Sacramento Street at Blake
20' x 100', latex ultracolor on brick
Rick Molina

EB206 *[UNTITLED], 1979
CETA, Commonarts
East Bay Skills Center, San Pablo and 67th Avenue
10' x 15', Politec on interior wallboard and plaster
Commonarts: Osha Neumann, Ray Patlan, and O'Brien
Thiele

EB207 [ABSTRACT], 1990
Private funding
Berkeley Potter's Studio, San Pablo and Channing
20' x 60', enamel on stucco
Kai

EB208 [UNTITLED], 1978
Private funding
Berkeley Youth Organization, Allston and Bonar
5' x 30', acrylic on stucco
Ray Patlan and the Berkeley Youth Organization

EB209 THE TREE OF LIFE, 1981
Berkeley Parks Design Department
Columbus School, Allston Way at 7th Street
25' x 20', acrylic on concrete
Eduardo Pineda and Linda Wolfe

EB210 BASKET FULL OF FUN, 1987
Berkeley Arts Fund Special Projects
Columbus School, Allston Way at 7th Street
8' x 28', acrylic on concrete
Eduardo Pineda and Linda Wolfe

EB211 *ADELANTE, 1979
California Arts Council
Adelante, Inc., Allston Way and 6th Street
14' x 25', Politec acrylic, sealer,
and latex primer on stucco
Ray Patlan

EB212 *LA FAMILIA, DENTAL ENTRANCE, SANDPAINTING,
AFRICAN, 1976
Berkeley Arts Services
Berkeley Health Clinic, 7th and University
Four panels: 6' x 12', 4' x 6', 3' x 6', 2' x 15', Politec
acrylic, gesso, and varnish on concrete
Irene Perez

EB213 BERKELEY READS, 1988
Berkeley Reads (Literacy Program)
West Berkeley Library, 1125 University Avenue
Two panels, 12' x 14' and 13' x 9', acrylic on stucco
Ray Patlan, Eduardo Pineda, and Jim Valdez

EB214 WINDS OF CHANGE, 1977 (partially obscured)
Co-Op Credit Union
Andronico's Park and Shop, University Avenue
16' x 135', Politec primer and acrylic on stucco
Commonarts: Osha Neumann, O'Brien Thiele, Daniel
Galvez

EB215 *THE SAN FRANCISCO BAY AS SEEN FROM
       BERKELEY (THE DUTCH BOY MURAL), 1974,
       destroyed 1977
       Dutch Boy Paints and Stefen
       James' Painting and Decorating Company, 2000
       University
       25' x 100', latex acrylic on stucco
       Stefen, with Gary Graham

EB216 [UNTITLED], 1986
       CCAC Mural Class
       Assemblyman Tom Bates' office,
       Berkeley-Richmond Jewish Community Center, 1414
       Walnut
       8' x 24', latex on plaster
       Malaquias Montoya and CCAC Mural Class students

EB217 GARDEN OF HOPE, 1990
       Berkeley Unified School District, Zellerbach Foundation
       Berkeley Adult High School, University Avenue at Curtis
       8' x 44', Novacolor acrylic on plywood
       Susan Greene and members of the Creative Living
       Center

EB218 BY THE BAY, 1992
       East Bay Conservation Corps, California Department of
       Conservation: Division of Recycling, Bank of
       America, Stuttgart Foundation
       Ecology Center, 2530 San Pablo Avenue at Parker
       15' x 50', Novacolor on concrete
       Jo Tucker with Dan Macchiarini, Terry Rayburn,
       Stephanie Fiske

EB219 PINBALL FLOOR MURAL, 1992
       For Private Amusement Only
       1010 Grayson Avenue off 7th Street
       17' x 17', enamel on hardwood floor
       Dan Fontes

EB220 *AN CISCO, 1979
       Brothers' Bagel Factory, private donations
       Toot-Sweets Bakery, 1277 Gilman
       13' x 62', acrylic primer, oil paints and varnish on stucco
       John Wehrle

EB221 [UNTITLED], 1994 (replaces #220)
       Private funding
       Toot-Sweets Bakery, 1277 Gilman
       13' x 62', Keim silicate on stucco
       John Wehrle

EB222 WHO HOLDS THE MIRROR? WOMEN'S LIVES,
       BREAST CANCER AND THE ENVIRONMENT, 1997
       Breast Cancer Oral History Action Project
       Portable mural
       8½' x 10½', acrylic on canvas, banner design
       Miranda Bergman

EL CERRITO

EB223 [AZTEC MOTHER], 1989
       CAC; Richmond Arts Center
       El Cerrito High School, Ashbury and Central Avenues
       10' x 20', acrylics on fibreboard
       Johanna Poethig and Latino Student Union

EB224 REFLECTIONS, 1990
       CAC, Richmond Arts Center
       El Cerrito High School, Ashbury and Central Avenues
       10' x 40', acrylics on fibreboard
       Johanna Poethig and Black Student Union

EB225 TRANSPORTATION AND THE CONTRIBUTIONS OF
       DIFFERENT RACIAL AND ETHNIC GROUPS, 1975
       DMV
       Calif. DMV, Kearney & Manila Streets, near San Pablo
       10' x 30', acrylic on concrete
       Dorothy Kalaveras

EB226 DR. FOUR PAWS PET HOSPITAL, 1994
       Private funding
       8' x 78', acrylic (?) on stucco
       Stefen

RICHMOND

EB227 REVISIONIST HISTORY OF SAN PABLO AVENUE,
       1993–6
       City of Richmond Arts and Culture Commission
       I-80 underpass at San Pablo Avenue
       21' x 265', Keimsilicate on concrete
       John Wehrle and Daniel Galvez

EB228 PAST PERFECT, 1990
       Richmond Arts and Culture Commission
       I-80 underpass at Macdonald Avenue
       16½' x 150', unknown paints on concrete
       John Wehrle

EB229 FAMILIAS UNIDAS, 1987
       Funding unknown
       Clinic, 205 39th Street
       Dimensions unknown, Roy Anderson paints and Politec
       acrylic on stucco
       Eduardo Pineda, Laurali Patneaud, Dina Moreno,
       Andrea Davis, Dedtra Williams, Marcell Arcea,
       Michelle Nath, Bakeeba Waters, and Eric Whittington

EB230 LIBERTY SHIP, 1989
       City of Richmond Arts and Culture Commission
       BART underpass, Barrett and Marina Way
       4'–20' x 200', Bott's Dots Highway Markers on concrete
       Rigo '89 assisted by Dina Diniz

EB231 MURAL CITY (unfinished), 1986
       Contra Costa College Mural Class
       Storefront, 141 Harbour Way near Chancellor
       15' x 35', acrylic on concrete
       Eduardo Pineda and CCC students

EB232 GETAWAY, 1986
       Contra Costa College Mural Class
       St. Mark's Church, 131 Harbour Way near Chancellor
       12' x 35', acrylic on stucco
       Eduardo Pineda and CCC students

EB233 LA CULTURA NOS CURA, 1995
       Familias Unidas, Richmond Art Center, Private Industry
       Council, San Francisco Foundation, Richmond
       Rotary
       BART underpass, 37th Street near Chancellor
       6' x 45', acrylic on concrete
       Emmanuel Montoya and youth

EB234 LA SIDA NO DESCRIMINA, 1994
       Richmond Art Center, Familias Unidas, Walter and Elise
       Haas Fund, San Francisco Foundation
       BART underpass, 37th Street near Chancellor
       12' x 48', acrylic on concrete
       Emmanuel Montoya, with Alicia Fernandez and local
       youth

EB235 STAND TOGETHER, 1986
Private funding
St. Mark's Church, 131 Harbour Way near Chancellor
40' x 12', Politec acrylic on concrete
Eduardo Pineda and CCC students

EB236 CITY OF RICHMOND, 1949
City of Richmond
City Hall, Supervisors' Chambers, City Hall Plaza, 2600
   Barrett Avenue
7' x 12', enamel on shaped metal relief panel
Sargent Johnson

EB237 RICHMOND TEEN MURAL PROJECT, 1993
Richmond Art Center, National Institute of Art and
   Disabilities, Richmond Senior Center
Harbour Way and Macdonald Avenue
Eight panels, 8' x 8' each, Novacolor on plywood
Fresco (Ray Patlan and Eduardo Pineda), Herschel
   West, Elizabeth Medrano, and students

EB238 THE IRON TRIANGLE COMMUNITY GARDEN, 1997
Richmond Redevelopment
Harbour Way and Macdonald Avenue
Two panels, 16' x 24'; three panels, 16' x 30', acrylic on
   plywood
(l. to r.): Richmond Seniors, Richmond Art Center Teen
   Mural Project, Peres Elementary School, NIAD,
   Lincoln Elementary School (Jamie Morgan and Jimi
   Evins)

EB239 [UNTITLED], date unknown
Memorial Youth Center, City of Richmond, United Way,
   Walter and Elise Haas Fund, Familias Unidas
33rd Avenue off Macdonald Avenue
15' x 60'-hemisphere, acrylic on stucco
Jaime Vargas

EB240 SAY NO TO DOPE, 1990
Neighborhood House of North Richmond
305 Chelsey at Third Street
10' x 60', Novacolor on cinderblock
Fresco (Ray Patlan and Eduardo Pineda)

List of Peninsula Murals

The information for each mural is presented in the following order:

Title [unofficial titles in brackets]. An asterisk indicates that the mural no longer exists.

Date completed

Funding source

Location

Size, medium and wall type [height precedes width. Sizes are often approximations]

Artist(s)

SOUTH SAN FRANCISCO

P1   PROMETHEUS BRINGS FIRE TO MAN, 1996
City of South San Francisco and
South San Francisco Art Commission
US 101 underpass at CalTrain SSF parking lot, Grand
and Dubuque Streets
20′ x 60′, acrylic on concrete
Nicolai Larsen, designer; assisted by Catalina
Gonzalez, Ron Loria, Kai Larsen, Rene Bastian,
Kelly McCormick

P2   SOUTH SAN FRANCISCO IN PAST AND PRESENT,
1942
Section
Lobby, USPS, Linden branch, 322 Linden Avenue
Three panels: 4′–8′ x 11′, oil on canvas
Victor Arnautoff

P3   HISTORY OF SOUTH SAN FRANCISCO, 1995
Private funding
Hotel Metropolitan, Grand and Linden Streets
Four panels: 10′ x 20′, 10′ x 26′, 26′ x 20′, and 15′ x 20′,
acrylic on brick
Carlota Espinoza

SAN BRUNO

P4   [ETHNIC ART ON WORLD MAP], 1960, relocated 1973
Pacific and Orient Steamship Company
San Francisco International Airport - in storage
16′ x 35′, acrylic and gold leaf on vinyl
Edith Hamlin

P5   SANCTUARY, 1998
San Francisco Art Commission
International Terminal, San Francisco International
Airport
23′ x 35′, fresco and bas relief carved basswood
Juana Alicia and Emmanuel Montoya

P6   EARTH BOOK, 1987
Skyline College
Alcove at entrance of Building 2, Skyline College, 3300
College Drive
10′ x 12′, acrylic on concrete
Juana Alicia, assisted by Barry McGee and Sia Yang

SAN MATEO

P7   HISTORY OF THE BANK OF AMERICA, 1960–1
Bank of America
A.P. Giannini branch, Bank of America, 300 El Camino
at 3rd Avenue
Five panels, 25′ x 75′, glass mosaic
Louis Macouillard, designer

P8   LIFE IN EARLY CALIFORNIA, 1937
TRAP
USPS, St. Matthew Station, 210 S. Ellsworth at 4th
Street
Three panels, total 6′ x 39′, egg tempera
Thomas Laman

P9   LIBRARY HALL LANE, 1990
City of San Mateo
B Street between 2nd and 3rd Streets
30′–36′ x 120′, acrylic on stucco
Norine Nicolson, designer; assisted by C. Campanile,
Scott Branham, Tony Parrinello, Selma Brown

P10 TE GRACIA A LISTO, 1993
Private funding
Tres Amigos Restaurant, 2243 B St. between 2nd and
3rd Sts.
15′ x 30′, acrylic on plaster
Alvaro Gutierrez

P11 *[UNTITLED], 1990; bldg. demolished 1996
Private funding
Whole Earth Access at Fashion Island Shopping Center
Dimensions unknown, acrylic on concrete
Dan Fontes

SAN CARLOS

P12 [PEOPLE AT CAFE TABLE], 1985
Private funding
Paul Joe's Restaurant, 1768 El Camino, near Eaton
15′ x 20′, acrylic on concrete
Chris Seybold

REDWOOD CITY

P13 BURGLAR, c.1980
Private funding
Gelb Music, 2726 El Camino near Oakwood Drive
15′ x 20′, acrylic on concrete blocks
Charles Leno

P14 *PROJECT READ, 1991, building demolished 1995
Project Read and Community Impact
Redwood City Hall, Middlefield Road
30′ x 20′, oil on concrete block
Jane Norling with David Miller, Winfield Coleman, Lou
    Petrella, Kyle Hurlbut, Alison Franchina

P15 *DANZAS MEXICANAS, 1978, painted over 1987
CAC, San Mateo Foundation, Canada College
Great Western Savings & Loan, 2400 Broadway
22′ x 147′, acrylic on concrete
Gilberto Romero Rodriguez and Jose Antonio Burciaga

P16 FLOWER FARMING AND VEGETABLE RAISING, 1937
TRAP
USPS, Downtown branch, 855 Jefferson at Broadway
4′ x 11′, oil on canvas
Jose Moya del Pino

P17 *HOUR FOR SENIOR POWER, 1977
CETA
Fair Oaks Community Center, 2555 Middlefield Road
8′ x 12′, acrylic on birch panels
Artist unknown

P18 *[UNTITLED], 1978
CETA
Fair Oaks Community Center, 2555 Middlefield Road
Dimensions unknown, acrylic on handball courts
Emmanuel Montoya

P19 *MAINSTREAM, 1980
Funding unknown
Fair Oaks Senior Citizens Drop-In Center, 2555
    Middlefield Road
20′ x 60′, acrylic on concrete
Jose Antonio Burciaga, Cañada College students

P20 [UNTITLED], 1977
Multicultural Arts Council
Fair Oaks Community Center, 2600 Middlefield Road at
    Douglas
10′ x 18′, acrylic on concrete block
Terry Yee

P21 BILLIARD-PLAYING DOGS, and
POKER-PLAYING DOGS, c. 1992
Private funding
Atherton Club San Luis, Middlefield and Eighth Street
Two panels, 6′ x 8′ and 7′ x 7′, acrylic on glass
Flavio

P22 [UNTITLED], 1977
Multicultural Arts Council
Garfield School, 2600 Middlefield Road
10′ x 20′, acrylic on stucco
Jose Antonio Burciaga and 400 students

WOODSIDE

P23 MUCKROSS ABBEY AND THE LAKES OF
    KILLARNEY, 1925
Mr. and Mrs. William Bowers Bourn II
Ballroom, Filoli, Canada Road
Seven panels, dimensions unknown, oil on canvas
Ernest Peixotto

MENLO PARK

P24 TUBAL CAIN THE FIRST ARTIFICER, 1932
Mr. and Mrs. Garfield Merner
Exterior wall, Allied Arts Guild, 75 Arbor Road at
    Cambridge
112″ x 88″, fresco
Maxine Albro

P25 CALIFORNIA, LAND OF ABUNDANCE, 1932
Mr. and Mrs. Garfield Merner
Courtyard of Abundance, Allied Arts Guild, 75 Arbor
    Road at Cambridge
54″ x 47″, fresco
Maxine Albro

P26 JUAN RODRIGUEZ CABRILLO DISCOVERS
    CALIFORNIA, 1542, 1932
Mr. and Mrs. Garfield Merner
Courtyard of Abundance, Allied Arts Guild, 75 Arbor
    Road at Cambridge
45″ x 36″, carved concrete and tile
Margaret de Lemos

P27 GASPAR DE PORTOLA AND THE INDIANS AT THE
    PALO ALTO BIG TREE, NOV. 6, 1769, 1932
Mr. and Mrs. Garfield Merner
Courtyard of Abundance, Allied Arts Guild, 75 Arbor
    Road at Cambridge
45″ x 36″, carved concrete and tile
Esther de Lemos

P28 [NATIVE AMERICAN POTTERS, HANDS OF THE
    POTTER, MEXICAN POTTERS], 1932
Mr. and Mrs. Garfield Merner
Maxine Albro Alcove, Allied Arts Guild, 75 Arbor Road
    at Cambridge
Three panels, each 5′ x 6′, fresco
Maxine Albro

P29 CERVANTES IN HIS LAST DAYS WRITES A
    DEDICATION TO THE CONDE DE LEMOS, 1932
Mr. and Mrs. Garfield Merner
Court of Cervantes, Allied Arts Guild, 75 Arbor Road at
    Cambridge
54″ x 67″, carved concrete with tile shards
Pedro de Lemos

P30 [HISTORY OF CALIFORNIA], 1973
Private funding
Barbecue Patio, *Sunset Magazine* Headquarters, 80
    Willow Road at Middlefield Road
5′ x 13′, 65 handpainted ceramic tiles
Millard Sheets

P31 MURAL PROGRAM, 1992 to present
School district and local businesses
Hillview Middle School, Santa Cruz Avenue at Hillview
Varying dimensions throughout school, acrylic on
    stucco
Terry McMahon, teacher, Hillview students

STANFORD UNIVERSITY

P32 FOUNDING OF AZTLAN, 1992–3
Stanford University
Entrance to Casa Zapata, Lucie Stern Hall, Alvarado
    and Campus Drive
10′ x 10′, acrylic on concrete
Jose Antonio Burciaga, M. Huidor, Martin Martin

P33 TRIPTYCH; GUERRILLAS, DANCER, WOMAN WITH
        FLOWERS, 1990
    Stanford University
    Exterior wall, entrance, Casa Zapata, Lucie Stern Hall,
        Alvarado and Campus Drive
    Three panels, 10′ x 15, 10′ x 15′, 10′ x 6′, all acrylic on
        concrete
    Ray Patlan, Eduardo Pineda and members of SWOPSI
        (Stanford Workshops on Political and Social Issues)
        mural class: Karenina Legg, Catalina Albanil,
        Stephen Dorow, Martin '90, Marlene Holguin, Jose
        Cordova, Mark Aragon, and Bruce Arthur

P34 MUJERES DE FUEGO, 1987
    Stanford University
    Entrance, Casa Zapata, Lucie Stern Hall, Alvarado and
        Campus Drive
    10′ x 10′, acrylic on concrete
    Juana Alicia and students: Valentin Aguirre, George
        Cuevas, Karen Davalos, Maria de la Rosa, Mo Eich,
        Daniel Luna, Andrea Ramirez, Jose Torres

P35 HECHO A MANO "88 y QUE?", 1988
    Stanford University
    Courtyard, Casa Zapata, Lucie Stern Hall, Alvarado and
        Campus Drive
    15′ x 30′, acrylic on concrete
    Ray Patlan, with Xavier, Anita DeLucio, Daniel Luna
        Garcia, Jamar Stewart, Jose Antonio Burciaga

P36 [MEXICAN DANCERS], date unknown
    Stanford University
    Basement dance studio, Casa Zapata, Lucie Stern Hall,
        Alvarado and Campus Drive
    5′ x 7′, oil on concrete
    Artist unknown

P37 THE SPIRIT OF HOOVER, 1986
    Stanford University
    3rd floor lounge, Casa Zapata, Lucie Stern Hall,
        Alvarado and Campus Drive
    7′ x 16′, acrylic on concrete blocks
    Jose Antonio Burciaga and John Sobraske, with Alonso
        Duenas, Emilio Rodriguez, Martin Bernal, Michael
        Arguello, Enrique Lopez

P38 [CHE ON MEXICAN FLAG], 1970–90
    Stanford University
    3rd floor lounge, Casa Zapata, Lucie Stern Hall,
        Alvarado and Campus Drive
    8′ x 16′, acrylic on canvas
    Zarco Guerrero

P39 HUELGA,1974
    Stanford University
    Stairwell, Casa Zapata, Lucie Stern Hall, Alvarado and
        Campus Drive
    7′ x 10′, acrylic on concrete
    Zarco Guerrero

P40 WAIT! WAIT! LISTEN! WE DON'T ALL HAVE TO BE
        SHEEP, YOU KNOW!, 1983
    Stanford University
    Stairwell,Casa Zapata, Lucie Stern Hall, Alvarado and
        Campus Drive
    7′ x 14′, acrylic (?) on concrete
    Gary Larson

P41 [PRE-COLUMBIAN GODDESS], 1978–9
    Stanford University
    Stairwell, Casa Zapata, Lucie Stern Hall, Alvarado and
        Campus Drive
    8′ x 5′, acrylic on concrete
    Linda Santamaria

P42 [PEASANT WOMAN, POLICEMAN, CARICATURES],
        1970–90
    Stanford University
    Stairwell, Casa Zapata, Lucie Stern Hall, Alvarado and
        Campus Drive
    7′ x 20′, acrylic on concrete
    Zarco Guerrero

P43 [PRE-COLUMBIAN FIGURE], 1970–90
    Stanford University
    Stairwell, Casa Zapata, Lucie Stern Hall, Alvarado and
        Campus Drive
    5′ x 3′, acrylic on concrete
    Zarco Guerrero

P44 REVOLUCION MEXICANA, 1974
    Stanford University
    Stairwell between 2nd and 3rd floors, Casa Zapata,
        Lucie Stern Hall, Alvarado and Campus Drive
    Dimensions unknown, acrylic on concrete
    Zarco Guerrero, Francisco Camplis, Jose Picabilla,
        Linda Santamaria

P45 [UNTITLED MEChA SYMBOL], 1970–90
    Stanford University
    3rd floor stairwell, Casa Zapata, Lucie Stern Hall,
        Alvarado and Campus Drive
    3′ x 5′, acrylic on concrete
    Zarco Guerrero

P46 A REACTION TO VIOLENCE AND INSTITUTIONAL
        RACISM IN THE MEDIA, c.1986
    Stanford University
    Entrance to Dining Hall, Casa Zapata, Lucie Stern Hall,
        Alvarado and Campus Drive
    6′ x 24′, acrylic on plywood
    Zarco Guerrero

P47 MYTHOLOGY AND HISTORY OF MAIZ, 1986–9
    Stanford University
    Dining Hall, Casa Zapata, Lucie Stern Hall, Alvarado
        and Campus Drive
    14′ x 67′, acrylic on concrete and plaster
    Jose Antonio Burciaga

P48 [UNTITLED], c. 1982
    El Centro Chicano
    Stanford University, Chicano Student Center
    4′ x 51′, acrylic on masonite panels
    Malaquias Montoya and students

P49 SOLO UNA MIRADA, 1984
    El Centro Chicano
    Stanford University, Chicano Student Center
    7′ x 21′, acrylic on concrete
    Juana Alicia and students

P50 [UNTITLED], 1988
    El Centro Chicano
    Stanford University, Chicano Student Center
    10′ x 17′, acrylic on slip plastered sheetrock
    Pablo Soto

P51 [CHICANO SYMBOLS], 1994
El Centro Chicano
Stanford University, Chicano Student Center
8' x 20', acrylic on plaster
Martin

PALO ALTO

P52 RUE DU CHAT QUI PÊCHE, 1989
Stanford Shopping Center
Street Market, Stanford Shopping Center, 180 El
Camino Real
8' x 180', acrylic on stucco
John Pugh

P53 *BURT AND THE ALIEN, 1976, bldg. destroyed 1985
CETA and Public Art Commission
Norm's Starlite Super, 361 Lytton Avenue
4' x 6', acrylic on stucco
Greg Brown

P54 THE ALIEN'S RETURN, 1992
Private funding
University National Bank, 250 Lytton Avenue at
Emerson
6' x 6', acrylic on stucco
Greg Brown

P55 *WOMAN WALKING PELICAN, 1976; building
demolished 1995
CETA and Public Art Commission
487 University at Cowper
6' x 6', acrylic on stucco
Greg Brown

P56 PELICAN WITH MONEY IN ITS BEAK, 1996
Private funding
Cupertino National Bank and Trust, Emerson Street at
Lytton
Second floor window, 4' x 3', acrylic on stucco
Greg Brown

P57 *TRENCHCOAT MAN, 1976, repainted 1992; building
demolished 1995
CETA and Public Art Commission
Wiedeman's Clothing Store, 281 University
6' x 4', acrylic latex with lacquer varnish
Greg Brown

P58 TRENCHCOAT MAN, 1996
Private funding
Cupertino National Bank and Trust, Lytton and Emerson
6' x 4', acrylic on stucco
Greg Brown

P59 NUN FLYING PAPER AIRPLANE, 1976, repainted 1992
CETA and Public Art Commission
436 University Avenue at Kipling
6' x 3', acrylic on stucco
Greg Brown

P60 WOMAN WITH CANARY ON GARDEN HOSE, 1976,
repainted 1992
CETA and Public Art Commission
Palo Alto Sport Shop, 526 Waverly near University
6' x 3', acrylic on stucco
Greg Brown

P61 *CAT BURGLARS OR ROOFHOPPERS, 1976; building
demolished 1995
CETA and Public Art Commission
Wiedeman's Clothing Store, 281 University
22' x 6', acrylic on stucco
Greg Brown

P62 CAT BURGLARS OR ROOFHOPPERS, 1996
Private funding
Great Western Bank, 300 Hamilton Avenue at Bryant
22' x 6', acrylic on stucco
Greg Brown

P63 MAN PUSHING STROLLER, 1976, repainted 1986
CETA and Public Art Commission
Bryant and University Avenues
6' x 6', acrylic on metal doors
Greg Brown

P64 CAÑON DE LOS SUEÑOS, 1979
Alan Morris and Steve Monday
Schmidt Building, Emerson near University
20' x 80', acrylic on stucco
James Sibbet and Thom Hawken

P65 *EGRETS, 1979, building demolished 1992
Public Art Commission
201 University at High Street
12' x 30', acrylic on concrete blcok
Noel Consigny

P66 GARBAGE MAN, 1976, repainted 1992
CETA and Public Art Commission
Hamilton Avenue and High Street
7' x 4', acrylic on stucco
Greg Brown

P67 THE PALO ALTO, 1974
Alexander Kulakoff
Exterior, Casa Olga, 180 Hamilton at Emerson
60' x 20', Byzantine mosaic
Alfonso Pardinas

P68 SHARK, 1974
Private funding
Interior, Casa Olga, 180 Hamilton at Emerson
9' x 25', Byzantine mosaic
Alfonso Pardinas

P69 BOY FISHING, 1976, repainted 1992
CETA and Public Art Commission
USPS, Palo Alto main branch, Hamilton and Gilman
Streets
12' x 12', acrylic on stucco
Greg Brown

P70 THE HISTORY OF MEDICINE, 1932, restored 1980
Palo Alto Clinic
Entrance, Roth Building, 300 Homer Avenue at Bryant
4 panels in color, 7 panels in grisaille, 4 sepia roundel
portraits, all fresco
Victor Arnautoff
NOTE: Portions of these Roth Building murals may be reproduced
in medallion form for the new Palo Alto Medical Foundation complex on El Camino Real.

P71 LIGHT, 1995
Palo Alto Utilities Dept., Public Art Commission
Alma between Homer and Channing
8' x 150', acrylic on wood cutouts on wood fence
Marta Thoma

P72 MAYFIELD TRAIN STATION, 1980
Private funding and donations from friends
Printers' Inc. Bookstore, 310 California Avenue at Birch
    Street
25' x 90', acrylic on stucco
Noel Consigny

P73 HOTEL CALIFORNIA, 1983
Private funding
2400 Ash at California
Lifesize figures on second story, acrylic on stucco
Jan Meyer and Carolyn Paterson

P74 VICTORIAN HOUSE, 1996
Private funding
410 California at Waverly
10' x 12', acrylic on concrete
Patricia Musgrave

P75 [UNDERWATER SCENE], 1997
California Avenue Area Development Association, City
    of Palo Alto
Pedestrian tunnel, California Avenue near CalTrain
    station
8' x 60', acrylic on concrete block
Oscar Castillo and students

P76 MARSH LANDINGS, c.1990
Public Art Commission
Animal Services, 3281 E. Bayshore Road between San
    Antonio and Embarcadero
12' x 20', acrylic on plaster
Noel Consigny

EAST PALO ALTO

P77 *EMPOWERMENT THROUGH EDUCATION, 1989–90;
    building demolished 1997
Catholic Charities
Families in Transition, 2066 Capitol Avenue
8' x 50', acrylic on stucco
Christa

MOUNTAIN VIEW

P78 888 VILLA, 1986
Omar Lee and MVP Center
888 Villa at Castro Street
67' x 90', acrylic on concrete and cinder block building
John Wullbrandt and Steve Schuck

P79 [SHOPPERS], 1988
Private funding
New York Fabrics and Crafts, San Antonio Shopping
    Center, 2435 California at Pachetti
11' x 60', acrylic on concrete
John Wullbrandt

P80 [HISTORY OF CALIFORNIA], 1977
Private funding
Home Savings of America, 749 El Camino at Castro
5' x 25', mosaic
Millard Sheets

P81 MILK PAIL MARKET, 1991
Private funding
2585 California
12' x 44', acrylic on cinderblock and wood
Joyce Oroz

P82 OLD MOUNTAIN VIEW, 1987
Mountain View Art Council
384 Castro at California
18' x 75', acrylic on concrete
Pat Nyland and CSMA Art Kids Workshop

P83 MOUNTAIN VIEW TODAY/TOMORROW CIRCUIT, 1994
City of Mountain View
384 Castro at California
Four panels set within previous mural, each 1½' x 5',
    acrylic on concrete
Adhoc Mural Team

LOS ALTOS

P84 A dozen commercial trompe l'oeil murals painted in the
    late 1980s and early 1990s throughout the Main Street
    shopping area by Painted Illusions (Carolyn Paterson
    and Jan Meyer).

P85 AUBERGE DU POULET, 1985
Kentucky Fried Chicken
Main and First Streets
15' x 50', acrylic on stucco
Painted Illusions (Carolyn Paterson and Jan Meyer).

P86 BLACH GALLERY, 1972–to date
School district and area businesses
G.P. Blach Middle School, 1120 Covington
65 murals, latex enamel on plywood
Russell Hoffman, director; student muralists

P87 COVINGTON MUSEE, 1988–to date
School district, area businesses
Covington School, 201 Covington
12 murals, various dimensions, latex enamel on
    plywood
Chris Halmo and Clay Cahoon, students

ALVISO

P88 OHLONE VILLAGE, c. 1770, 1981
U. S. Department of Fish and Wildlife
Bayside Canning Company, Hope and Elizabeth
20' x 30', acrylic on concrete and plywood
Hollis H. Kreb

P89 HISTORY OF ALVISO, 1982
U. S. Department of Fish and Wildlife
Bayside Canning Company, Hope and Elizabeth
20' x 130', acrylic on concrete and plywood
Dawna

P90 FAMILY HEALTH, 1995
Family Health Center
Ernie's Fiesta en America, Gold and North Taylor
    Streets
12' x 25', acrylic on stucco
Hector Mendoza and Family Health Center kids

P91 HISTORY OF ALVISO, 1977
Alviso Rotary Club
Exterior, George Mayne School, 5030 First Street
12' x 105', acrylic on stucco
Rogelio Duarte

CUPERTINO

P92 THE CUPERTINO MURAL, 1995
City of Cupertino
Lobby, City Hall, Torre Avenue
Two panels, 7' x 13' each, acrylic on canvas
T. Scott Sayre

P93 SPRING IN CUPERTINO, 1995
City of Cupertino
Lobby, City Hall, Torre Avenue
Two panels, 8′ x 8′, watercolor on paper
Zhan Wang Zhao

SAN JOSE

P94 [UNTITLED], c.1994
Beautification & Barbecue Corps of Central San Jose
Pedestrian tunnel, The Alameda at Hester Street
7′ x 80′, acrylic on concrete
Mike Ellner, director; Lincoln High School students

P95 [JUNGLE ANIMALS], 1996
Private funding
Andy's Pet Shop, The Alameda near Julian
9′ x 25′, acrylic on concrete
Diane Gatto

P96 [EARLY SETTLERS], 1935, restored 1994
Southern Pacific Railroad
CalTrain and Amtrak Station, 654 Cahill at San
    Fernando near Montgomery
12′ x 8′, oil on canvas (?)
John McQuarrie

P97 OPEN ARMS, 1995
New Children's Shelter Fund and SJAC
4525 Union Avenue near Hwy. 85
12′ x 50′, ceramic tile
Johanna Poethig

P98 TRANSPORTATION, 1996–7
City Year Silicon Valley, SVTA, private businesses
CalTrain Tamien Station, Alma and Lick Avenues
20′ x 100′, acrylic on sound barrier
Rick Salas and Lukas Allenbaugh

P99 IN MEMORY OF JOSHUA HERNANDEZ, 1995
Beautification and Barbecue Corps of Central San Jose
South 8th and East William Streets
12′ x 36′, acrylic on plaster
Mark Fitzgerald Rogers

P100 MARDI GRAS, 1994
Louisiana Territory Restaurant
Pavilion Shops, N. First Street and Paseo de San
    Antonio
Inner stairwell, acrylic on plaster
Taylor John Blackwell

P101 JAZZ IN NEW ORLEANS, 1993
Louisiana Territory Restaurant
Garage, Pavilion Shops, N. 1st St. and Paseo de San
    Antonio
8′ x 12′, acrylic on concrete block
Taylor John Blackwell

P102 [CALIFORNIA], 1989
City of San Jose
Above entrance, McEnery Convention Center, 150 W.
    San Carlos
58′ x 125′, handpainted ceramic tiles
Lin Utzon

P103 *[HOTEL EMPLOYEES], painted over 1996
Fairmont Hotel
Garage entrance, N. First Street and Paseo de San
    Antonio
25′ x 15′, acrylic on concrete
Jamie Cabrera and David Thomas

P104 IN MEMORY OF REV. SABORI, before 1991
Private funding
Ryland Park, San Pedro at Fox Street
Underpass wall, acrylic on concrete
Andrew Sabori

P105 *MURAL REFLEJANDO LA ORGANIZACION DE
        OBREROS, 1990
Service Employees International Union, local 1877
SEIU union building, 186 East Gish at 4th Street
Dimensions and media unknown
Gustavo Bernal

P106 A THOUSAND YEARS OF VALLEY HISTORY, 1977
San Jose Mercury News
Terminal C, San Jose Airport
20′ x 30′, acrylic on canvas
Millard Sheets

P107 LOS VIAJEROS VIENEN A SAN JOSE, 1990
Funding unknown
Terminal A, San Jose Airport
6′ x 15′, ceramic tile
Maria Alquilar

P108 BIBLIOTECA LATINOAMERICANA, 1980
Biblioteca Latinoamericana
Biblioteca Latinoamericana, 690 Locust at Grant
6′ x 32′, acrylic on plywood
Jaime Valadez, Daniel De Los Reyes, Phmoc Ngo,
    Ernie Balderas, Eva Ugarte, Jesse Barrjas, Alberto
    Amezquita

P109 [MEXICAN SCENES], 1986
Private funding
Restaurant, East Taylor and Fourth Streets
12′ x 24′, acrylic on concrete block
Alfonso Enrique Salazar

P110 PILIPINAS, 1993
Filipino Youth Coalition, Filipino Community Center of
    Santa Clara County
635 N. 6th Street, near Jackson
10′ x 60′, acrylic on cinderblock
Randolf Dimalanta, Niel Salinas, Julius Willis III

P111 [MEXICAN HERITAGE], 1986
Private funding
Empire and N. 10th Streets
5′ x 25′, acrylic on stucco
Edward Earl Tarver III

P112 MEMORIAL TO JULIE LAMB, 1979
Private funding
Chevron station, Santa Clara at 4th Street
35′ x 30′, acrylic on brick
Alfredo Flores and Saeed Mahboub

P113 [CHICANO HERITAGE], 1974
Private funding
El Chaparral market, East Santa Clara and 21st Street
20′ x 90′, acrylic on concrete
Rogelio Duarte

P114 [ETHNIC SYMBOLS], 1994
Brookwood Terrace/Beautification and Barbecue Corps
    of Central San Jose
Market, S. 22nd Street and E. San Antonio Road
9′ x 45′, acrylic on plaster
Brigitte Curt, designer, volunteers and students

P115 COMMUNITY BROTHERHOOD, date unknown
School District
San Antonio School,1855 E. San Antonio Road at King
15' x 30', mosaic, broken tile
Artist unknown

P116 LA MEDICINA Y LA COMUNIDAD, 1990
Gardner Health Clinic
195 E. Virginia at 5th Street
6' x 50', acrylic on stucco
Gustavo Bernal

P117 LA EDUCACION, 1990
Funding unknown
Miller Elementary School, 1250 S. King Road at Marsh
Mural covers three buildings, 8½'–12' x 50', acrylic on
    stucco
Gustavo Bernal

P118 CHICANO HISTORY, 1988
Private funding
2148 Story Road near Hopkins
10' x 40', spray enamel on stucco
Estria, TWS, Raevyn, Style

P119 [UNTITLED], date unknown
Private funding
2140 Story near Hopkins
10' x 40', spray enamel on stucco
Artist unknown

P120 MURAL DE LA RAZA, 1985
East San Jose Council, East Side Youth Center
2048 Story near Hopkins
12' x 75', acrylic on stucco
Jose Meza–Velasquez, Summer Youth Project

P121 NUESTRA CASA YOUTH LEADERSHIP PROJECT,
    1993
Nuestra Casa
Nuestra Casa, 1998 Alum Rock at Sunset Avenue
15' x 90', acrylic on concrete
Ramon Cervantes

P122 [CALIFORNIA TREES], 1997
San Jose Beautiful
Restrooms, Overfelt Botanical Gardens, McKee Road
    and Educational Park Drive
10' x 44', acrylic on concrete block
Katie Bosak, David Sokh, and Girl Scout troop

P123 [UNKNOWN], 1993
Evergreen Valley College
Learning Center, Evergreen Valley College, 3095 Yerba
    Buena Road
8' x 40', acrylic (?) on wallboard
Jesus Rodriguez, Byron Sanchez, Jim Tsukuda

Index of Artists, Groups and Murals

Index and Abbreviations Used

156

157

Selected Bibliography

Cave Paintings:

Leroi Gourhan, Andre. *The Dawn of European Art: An Introduction to Paleolithic Cave Painting.* Cambridge and other cities: Cambridge University Press, 1982. An excellent introduction to cave painting.

Raphael, Max. *Prehistoric Cave Paintings.* Washington, D.C.: The Bollingen Series IV, Pantheon Books, 1945. Extremely difficult to find, but a brilliant essay.

Sieveking, Ann. *The Cave Artists.* London: Thames and Hudson, 1979. An excellent introduction to Paleolithic cave art.

Mexican Murals:

Hurlburt, Laurance P *The Mexican Muralists in the Unite States.* Albuquerque: The University of New Mexico Press, 1989. An excellent book covering all the work of Los Tres Grandes in the United States.

Orozco, Jose Clemente. *Jose Clemente Orozco, An Autobiography.* Austin: The University of Texas Press, 1962. A basic work on Orozco, but one wishes for a modern edition with better color.

Rochfort, Desmond. *Mexican Muralists: Orozco, Rivera, Siqueiros.* New York: Universe, 1993. Rochfort, a muralist himself, has produced the best introductory text on these important artists. His analysis of individual murals is especially good.

Siqueiros, David Alfaro. *Art and Revolution.* London: Lawrence and Wishart, 1975. A selection of writings from the most theoretical and polemical of the Tres Grandes.

Wolfe, Bertram D. *The Fabulous Life of Diego Rivera.* New York: Stein and Day, 1963. The standard biography of a fascinating life.

___. *Diego Rivera: A Retrospective.* New York and London: Founders Society of the Detroit Institute of Art in association with W. W. Norton & Company, 1986. A fundamental work, with fourteen essays, a list of Rivera's work, bibliography, and excellent color plates. An exhibition catalogue.

New Deal Murals:

Jewett, Masha Zakheim. *Coit Tower: Its History and Art.* San Francisco: Volcano Press, 1983. A gem of a book with full discussion of the famous Coit Tower murals written by the daughter of one of the artists, and excellent, complete, color photographs.

McKinzie, Richard D. *The New Deal for Artists.* Princeton: Princeton University Press, 1973. A thorough survey of the whole spectrum of New Deal programs.

Marling, Karal Ann. *Wall-to-Wall America: A Cultural History of Post-Office Murals in the Great Depression.* Minneapolis: University of Minnesota Press, 1982. Well illustrated and anecdote-filled account of the New Deal post office murals.

Melosh, Barbara. *Engendering Culture. Manhood and Womanhood in New Deal Public Art and Theater.* Washington, D.C.and London: Smithsonian Institution Press, 1991. A different approach to New Deal art with a complete listing of murals.

O'Connor, Francis V. *Art for the Millions.* Boston: New York Graphic Society, 1973. Essays about the WPA written by artists and administrators of the program.

Park, Marlene and Markowitz, Gerald. *Democratic Vistas: Post Office and Public Art in the New Deal.* Philadelphia: Temple University Press, 1984. Another well-illustrated and excellent survey of New Deal murals.

Contemporary Community Murals:

Barnett, Alan. *Community Murals: The People's Art.* Philadelphia: The Art Alliance Press, and New York and London: Cornwall Press, 1984. A large book, with much information and many photographs.

Cockcroft, Eva, John Pitman Weber, and James Cockcroft. *Toward A People's Art. The Contemporary Mural Movement.* New York: E.P. Dutton & Co., Inc, 1977. An excellent book on the contemporary mural movement in the U. S. written by muralists. Unavailable for years, a new edition of this book will be published in late 1998 by the University of New Mexico Press. It will contain a new forword by Lucy Lippard, an essay on historical context by Ben Keppel, and an update by Timothy W. Drescher sketching developments in the two decades since the original publication.

Cockcroft, Eva Sperling and Holly Barnett-Sanchez, editors. *Signs From the Heart: California Chicano Murals.* Venice, California: Social and Public Art Resource Center, 1990. Two of the five essays relate directly to San Francisco's Chicano murals.

Dunitz, Robin J. *Street Gallery: Guide to L. A.'s Murals.* Los Angeles: RJD Enterprises, 1993. Accurate information, detailed maps, descriptions of a thousand Los Angeles murals, along with thorough indexes and small but useful photographs.

Juarez, Miguel. *Colors on Desert Walls: The Murals of El Paso.* Photograhs by Cynthia Weber Farah. El Paso: Texas Western Press, 1997. In English and Spanish, this guide to the city's 200 murals gives a complete list with accurate documentaton, color photographs, and interviews with major local muralists.

Kunzle, David. *The Murals of Revolutionary Nicaragua, 1979-1992.* Berkeley, Los Angeles, London: The University of California Press, 1995. The definitive compendium of these spectacular murals, with superb documentation, color and black and white photos supplementing an excellent text which sets the necessary historical and social contexts.

Rogovin, Mark, Marie Burton and Holly Highfill. *Mural Manual: How to Paint Murals for the Classroom, Community Center and Street Corner.* Boston: Beacon Press, 1975. The only how-to book about painting Community murals, with complete information and numerous illustrations. Out-of-print.

Rolston, Bill. *Politics and Painting: Murals and Conflicts in Northern Ireland.* London and Toronto: Associated University Presses, 1991. This is an excellent (albeit somewhat scholarly) discussion of the often confusing politics of Northern Ireland and the role of murals in that conflict. Rolston's more accessible volume, *Drawing Support: Murals in the North of Ireland*, was published by Beyond the Pale Publications in 1992.

___. *Community Murals Magazine, 1978-1987.* Back sets/copies are available in some libraries. Contains articles and photographs of murals throughout the world.

_____. *Public Art Review.* A quarterly publication from St. Paul, Minnesota, which carries articles and notes about new murals as well as other forms of public art.

Spraycan Art:

A number of books, magazines, videos, and even Websites deal with spraycan art, both worldwide and in California. The most important books are:

Castleman, Craig. *Getting Up: Subway Graffiti in New York.* Cambridge: M.I.T. Press, 1982.

Chalfant, Henry and James Prigoff. *Spraycan Art.* London: Thames and Hudson, 1987. A superb photographic survey of the most sophisticated spraycan work from the United States and Europe.

Cooper, Martha and Henry Chalfant. *Subway Art.* New York: Holt, Rinehart and Winston, 1984. The standard text on New York's subway graffiti, with an astonishing collection of beautifully photographed trains in full color.

Cooper, Martha and Joseph Sciorra. *R.I.P.: Memorial Wall Art.* New York: Henry Holt and Company, an Owl Book, 1994. Color photographs, an introduction and explanations of individual memorial walls in New York.